D1368538

# Christian Nation?

# Christian Nation?

The United States in Popular
Perception and Historical Reality

T. ADAMS UPCHURCH

PRAEGER

AN IMPRINT OF ABC-CLIO, LLC
Santa Barbara, California • Denver, Colorado • Oxford, England

**Library of Congress Cataloging-in-Publication Data**

Upchurch, Thomas Adams.
    Christian nation? : the United States in popular perception and historical
reality / T. Adams Upchurch.
       p. cm.
    Includes bibliographical references and index.
    ISBN 978-0-313-38642-8 (hard copy : alk. paper) — ISBN 978-0-313-38643-5 (ebook)
       1. United States—History—Religious aspects—Christianity. 2. United States—Religion.
3. Christianity—United States—History. 4. Church and state—United States—History.
5. Christianity and politics—United States—History. 6. National characteristics, American.
7. United States—Historiography. I. Title.
    E179.U63   2010
    322′.10973—dc22        2010001090

ISBN: 978-0-313-38642-8
EISBN: 978-0-313-38643-5

14   13   12   11   10      1   2   3   4   5

This book is also available on the World Wide Web as an eBook.
Visit www.abc-clio.com for details.

Praeger
An Imprint of ABC-CLIO, LLC

ABC-CLIO, LLC
130 Cremona Drive, P.O. Box 1911
Santa Barbara, California 93116-1911

This book is printed on acid-free paper ∞

Manufactured in the United States of America

To Betty LeGrand, Abby Tideman, and Mary McAlpin—
each an angel in disguise

# Contents

# Preface

## PURPOSE, METHODS, AND LIMITATIONS

Barely two months after Barack Obama took the oath of office as president of the United States in 2009, he made an overseas diplomatic tour that included a stop in Turkey, a nation with a Christian heritage but which in recent centuries has been controlled by Muslims. There, in a press conference, the new president made a statement that immediately flashed across the airwaves and into the blogosphere with lightning speed for its controversial, provocative flavor. Of the United States and its people, he said, "we do not consider ourselves a Christian nation or a Jewish nation or a Muslim nation. We consider ourselves a nation of citizens who are bound by ideals and a set of values." Although he went on to explain that the United States is a "predominantly Christian nation," just as Turkey is a "predominantly Muslim nation," this second comment largely went unnoticed in the media. The first comment so tantalized Americans that it seemed not to matter what he said in clarification thereafter. The brouhaha that resulted lasted only briefly, soon to be eclipsed by more pressing concerns of economics, health care, war, and such. Even though the furor died down for the moment, the controversy over whether the United States is, was, or was ever supposed to be a "Christian nation" will never go away. How do we know? Because 2009 was not the first time a U.S. government official proclaimed to the Muslim world that America is not a "Christian nation." That sentiment was, in fact, first expressed in 1797 in the Treaty of Tripoli, a product of the John Adams administration, which was ratified by the U.S. Senate. History thus shows that the issue has been with us from the beginning and has surfaced and receded over the years with the regularity of the tides—partly (and unfortunately) because too many Americans do not know their own history.

Since the founding of the United States more than 230 years ago, Americans have argued almost incessantly amongst themselves over the proper relationship between God and government in their nation. The separation of church and state is a complex issue to be sure, polarizing people based on their religious beliefs or lack thereof, as well as on their political opinions. In the ongoing ideological war between the forces of secularism and Christian fundamentalism, rarely has common ground been found or amicable compromise been reached. The war has spawned dozens of legal battles, in which the courts have periodically redrawn the lines in favor of one side or the other. In the first decade of the 21st century, both the legal battles and the larger war of ideology itself seem to be more intense than ever. This study is a product of that intensification of interest in the separation of church and state in America.

This book seeks to answer the question that lies at the root of the ongoing church-state debate: "Is the United States now, has it ever been, or was it ever supposed to be, a Christian nation?" Everyone who has ever argued one side or the other has always had a question like this in mind, even if they have not articulated it in these precise words. The question assumes that, at the time of nation-building from roughly 1775 to 1815, the builders (called the "Founders" throughout),[1] representing the will of their respective state legislatures and the people of the United States in general, had a uniform intention. Many scholars have spent their careers trying to ascertain the Founders' "original intent," in the hope that such a discovery would bridge the chasm between the opposing sides, not only on the church-state issue but other divisive political issues as well. Original intent, however, has proven just as difficult for scholars to agree upon as the controversies that lead them to seek it in the first place. One facet of this study is the exploration of the issue of who the Founders were, what they believed, how they behaved politically and religiously, and what their original intent(s) were or might have been regarding the separation of church and state.

This study makes no pretense of being the final authority or the last word on the subject at hand. Even the most honest and reasonable of people have come to different conclusions about this most complex issue, both historically and contemporaneously, and it would require supreme arrogance to assume that a single treatise could suddenly change that. Anyone who would dare claim to have found the one-size-fits-all "truth" about this topic should be met with skepticism. The modest aims herein, therefore, are merely to: 1. introduce questions for contemplation and topics for discussion among the general public, college students, and nonspecialists in this field, and 2. discover a few grains of truth and facts of history that will lead to a more enlightened understanding of the subject among those who seek it, whomever they may be.[2] It will seek to accomplish these aims mainly by surveying the literature. Since it deals largely with public perceptions of "truth" and interpretations of "facts," what people have written about this topic is the focal point herein. For that reason, this is not a monograph in which heretofore unpublished information is brought to light. The sources cited are, therefore, mostly secondary.

There are several reasons why even the most honest and reasonable people disagree about whether America was, is, or should be a "Christian nation." One is the problem of objectivity. It is impossible for anyone to be 100 percent objective, because his/her own religious beliefs or lack of them will color his/her perception.[3] As self-described "Catholic historian" Leslie Woodcock Tentler put it, "there can be no doubt that such convictions, no matter how ostensibly 'private,' do in fact affect a believer's reconstruction of the past." Yet, after a thorough self-examination of her work as a historian, she added, "I can see no obvious ways in which my written work betrays a Christian author—though it probably betrays an author who regularly votes Democratic."[4] An author's religious background bleeding through in his/her writings, however, is quite different from an author approaching the topic with an agenda. Those who study church-state relations can, of course, spot agenda-driven works easily and immediately. For the rest of the reading public, some help may be necessary to see the difference. In part for that reason, a section on the historiography of the church-state issue is included in the first chapter. It should be noted from the outset that this study is not agenda-driven; its purpose is not to prove one side or the other right or wrong. It criticizes each side with equal dispassion when factually wrong, and acknowledges each side's accuracies when they seem incontrovertible. With that said, while absolute objectivity has been the goal of this study, it would again be supremely arrogant to assume that perfection has been achieved.

Concerning objectivity, in any study of church-state relations, the author must decide whether or how much discussion of theology is pertinent. Depending upon the focus and scope of a particular study, in some cases very little is necessary. In others, such as this one, which are broad, general surveys of the subject, more theological inquiry may be required. Some secularists may take exception to the speculation upon the existence of God that appears herein, in the presumption that such an idea should be automatically dismissed as a fable. To those who would say such speculation is an abdication of scholarly responsibility (since historians should deal with physical evidence, not metaphysical myths), the reply proffered is that *not* to consider the possibility of the existence of God is a disservice to the millions of people who, rightly or wrongly, believe in such an entity. That by no means implies that this book is a study of theology. It is not. It does not make value judgments about doctrines, dogma, or anyone's beliefs, no matter how silly or superstitious those beliefs may seem to others. It does not, for instance, take a stand on whether God is a "he" as tradition would have it, or a "she," an "it," or a "they," as some modern interpretations would have it. It does, however, contain some discussion of issues pertaining to the nature of the entity commonly known as God, because they are unavoidable. For example, if there is a God, whomever or whatever God is, this being must be so much greater, larger, more profound, and unearthly than anything mere mortals can fathom that human terms cannot adequately describe the entity.

Some theologians may likewise take exception with the decision herein to label as "Christians" not only those who believe in the divinity of Jesus and worship him accordingly but also those who do not believe in his divinity yet follow his teachings as their primary, if not exclusive, moral compass. When using the term *Christian* this way, it becomes merely a descriptor of the type of belief system that a person mainly possesses, which may leave room for the incorporation of other religious teachings into their Christian beliefs as well, rather than a statement of religious exclusivity. By setting the parameters for what is Christian this way, it becomes possible for a person to be a *professing* Christian and a *professing* something else, such as a Unitarian or Deist, at the same time. This is quite important in determining whether the Founders were, or should be today, considered "Christians."

Another problem inherent in this kind of study, which causes even the most honest and reasonable people to disagree, is that of historical relativism, which may take several forms. One is the temptation to read current American political-religious values on church-state issues into the past. Making judgments about people and events of the past based upon current values is a dangerous game that often results in the writing of inaccurate history. The historian's job is to recognize the ambiguities in people—in their personal behavior, in their relationships with other people, and in the interactions with institutions such as churches and governments.[5] The so-called good guys and bad guys in history are rarely (with notable exceptions) so clearly identified as such. All people are complex, we are often irrational, sometimes hypocritical, and our thinking and behavior evolve over the course of our lives. Historical figures did not have the benefit of the knowledge that later generations have possessed on a wide range of topics—science, technology, medicine, economics, government, and human rights, for example. Historians should therefore not take sides in the disputes of the past. Taking sides on the Protestant Reformation, for instance, because of one's own personal Catholicism or Protestantism today is ludicrous, because both Protestants and Catholics of the 16th century might very well unite in condemning all professing Christians in the 21st century if they saw how people live today. Both sides would possibly declare even their own modern followers reprobates! Why then should an observer of history today see a Martin Luther or an Ignatius Loyola, for instance, as either hero or villain? Bringing this point to bear on early United States history, taking sides between Federalists and Anti-Federalists or between Jeffersonians and Hamiltonians seems equally foolish. We do not generally view either side as heroic or villainous, even if we have a personal preference for one or the other of their respective ideologies. If that is the case, why then should we take sides between the people of that generation who favored church disestablishment over those who did not, or vice versa?

All historians of course sometimes feel that when the egregiousness of a certain historical figure's actions warrant it, as in the case of an Adolf Hitler or Joseph Stalin—both of whom were indisputable mass murderers—they simply *must* state an opinion. In such cases, objectivity is not necessarily lost just because neutrality is abandoned.[6] When a Hitler or a Stalin is weighed in the balances of history, it is clear that their "bad" or "wrong" far exceeded any good thing they may have done in their lives. Historian Marvin Perry explains that such characters actually tried to overturn the "essential values of western civilization."[7] Although he does not specify what those essential values are, it is axiomatic that democide—whether in the form of genocide, politicide, religicide, or other—which both Hitler and Stalin tried to perpetrate, are as diametrically opposed to those values as can be imagined.[8] Therefore, to state the obvious, Hitler and Stalin were evil, and for a historian not to say so would be an abdication of scholarly responsibility. As one has put it, "The historian, although acutely aware of his own and his colleagues' changing perceptions, must not equate 'historical relativism' with 'ethical relativism.' Some articles of faith, some moral convictions, must remain unchanged and absolute. . . ."[9] By this logic, it is simply unacceptable to argue for the rightness of a clearly evil cause (Nazism, for example) or person (Hitler) because an ethical principle is at stake: How can mass murder ever be justified? If the answer is never, then it must be concluded that all such acts, regardless of who ordered or committed them, should be equally condemned. Notable examples that are pertinent to the church-state issue include the Catholic Church's Inquisition and the Puritans' Salem Witch Trials, but dozens of others could also be cited.

Yet historical relativism allows for fudging the facts of history on less clearly defined causes or people (such as those involved in the American church-state debate), in which assigning labels of "good guys" and "bad guys" is not so easy. Since the founding of the United States, neither the state nor any recognized church has openly murdered anyone else exclusively for their religious beliefs. Although cases of murder involving, for instance, Mormons (such as what happened in Missouri in 1838) look primarily like state-sponsored religious persecution, the states in each case can claim that their actions were aimed at enforcing the law (in this case against polygamy), not at interfering in someone's private religious practices.[10] This is a dicey area where historical relativism becomes quite obvious—one in which the truth seems to be in the eye of the beholder, and thus one that defies consensus. Similar instances involving persecution and/or cold-blooded murder of American Indians (such as happened at Wounded Knee in 1890) fall into this same category. What is indubitable is that both the state and the churches have been guilty of the lesser crime of discrimination against minority groups at times, which may take many forms—racial, religious, political, and so forth.

When it comes to making judgments about the church-state issue in American history, easy ways of identifying the "bad" or "wrong" people and ideas are almost nonexistent. This fact brings up the third problem causing even the most honest and reasonable people to disagree—the problem of terminology and definitions. Take for instance the following. Three major groups existed at the time of the founding of the United States: orthodox Christians, religious dissenters, and secularists. Each has engaged in a struggle against the others that has lasted to the present, with every succeeding generation producing a new set of disciples for each group. The orthodox Christians include not only mainstream church members but also all those who identify their beliefs with a particular mainstream denomination. Religious dissenters include those who are not committed to a particular denomination, religion, or secular ideology, as well as those who profess an affiliation with a particular group but are mainly concerned with opposing the orthodox churches, generally because they feel persecuted by them, unwelcome in them, or uncomfortable around them. Secularists include not only atheists, agnostics, and skeptics, but also those believers in religion who take a radical stance in favor of divorcing all aspects of religion—even their own—from the government; they are thus "separationists." The composition of each group has changed over time, but essentially these same three groups have existed all along in American history. All Americans today fall into one or the other of these very broad categories (within which there are multiple subcategories). The natural tendency is to try to identify those people in history, particularly the Founders, who fit most neatly into one's own current category, and then make a judgment about the religious nature of the whole nation based upon that group. Therein lies the aforementioned "dangerous game" that objective historians must avoid playing. If the objective historian has any association with such a game at all, it must be merely to serve as a referee for those who are, rightly or wrongly, playing it.

The idea of historical relativism also has another possible application in church-state studies of this kind. It can be invoked to justify the perpetuation of patriotic myths about America and Americans that might be judged by some as innocuous because they are designed to instill love of country and produce good citizenship. As such, it constitutes yet another problem that causes even the most honest and reasonable people to disagree. Consider the difference between "facts" of history and "perceptions" of history as they pertain to the question, "Is the United States now, has it ever been, or was it supposed to be, a Christian nation?" Some scholars have decided the answer *should be* "yes," and in so doing have deemed it better to let that perception stand than to tear it down, because they believe it does no harm to anyone and in fact serves to bolster the collective morality of the nation. Historical facts in such cases have thus been tampered with for the sake of something considered more important—having a positive moral impact on the American people. "A fact may be an emotion, a sentiment, or an ideal . . . so long as it is generally accepted. . . ."[11] Implied in this statement is that "facts" do not have to be even pieces of information much less *true* pieces of information, just some "thing" that is widely believed, felt, or shared. A myth may thus be substituted for truth, and once enough people believe it, it can *become* truth.[12] Myth "structures and intensifies feelings, unifies people, elicits total commitment, and incites heroic action."[13]

According to this view, the question for the historian to ask is whether, for instance, iconography—turning the nation's Founders into demigods for American children to look up to—does more harm or more good to the nation's general welfare. If the latter, then according to historical relativists, the legend or popular view should be left to stand, despite its historical inaccuracy.[14] For example, evident from history is the idea that some American political leaders, including the Founders, have tried to create what this study will call a "civic religion" out of patriotic legends and myths. This civic religion has been defined in various ways, but perhaps the most accurate definition is "Progressive Patriotic Protestantism." By that definition, the United States is equally committed to promoting the progressive principles of scientific, intellectual, and academic advancement; a variation of Protestant Calvinistic Christianity that embraces capitalism, representative government, individualism, property rights, and diversity; and love of the constitutional, republican system that offers all good things to its people.[15] If this civic religion was indeed created deliberately by some politicians of the past, then it is artificial. The question then becomes, *should* such an artificial identity have been created for the United States?

To answer this question, consider the purpose of the civic religion: originally it was to create a distinct nationality out of the variegated population and states that might not otherwise unite. In effect, the purpose was to make the dream of *E Pluribus Unum* (out of many, one) a reality. Its purpose since the Founding generation has been to keep American nationalism alive and well, thus perpetuating the United States. How would this be accomplished? First, by making "Americans" out of immigrant children by imprinting upon the *tabula rasa* (blank slate) of their impressionable minds the "American way" (the precepts of the Progressive Patriotic Protestant civic religion) beginning in elementary school, and then, by continuing the Americanization of succeeding generations through inculcation of the American way. If indeed people from all nations, races, backgrounds, and creeds could be brought together in America like one large family, it logically follows that the same might be replicated worldwide, one country at a time. This is the idea of the *Novus Ordo Seclorum* (a new order for a new age). The American civic religion and the American way are basically the same concept with different names—the former for religiously minded people who do not find such a concept offensive, and the latter for secularists who obviously do not appreciate the idea of a national religion. Consider national holidays such as Thanksgiving and Christmas. Religiously minded Americans may see both as Christian holy days, whereas secularists may see them simply as festivals or times of rest and recreation. Both are equally appropriate in the United States.[16] This kind of duality of mind in America will be a major topic of exploration in this study.

Back to historical relativism, political scientist and historian Clinton Rossiter, in pondering the question of whether making relativistic historical judgments is ever appropriate, came to the following conclusion: "I confess a reluctance to take a firm stand about the role of religion" in creating a unified United States in the years of the Early Republic, for the "question is one about which I am far too uncertain . . . [but] it is almost certainly better for a man, both as a private person and as citizen, to worship some version of divine providence rather than his nation or race, an ideology or charismatic leader, history or science."[17] In other words, he contends that it was a good thing for the Founders to have been religious, or better yet, for the masses to perceive that they were, as opposed to their being considered followers of other modes of thought that have since proved disastrous for the nations that embraced them; most notably atheism as exhibited in Nazi Germany and the Communist Soviet Union. Such an observation seems to advocate a conspiracy among historians to keep the masses ignorant for their own good. (The thought thus goes, "Christianity breeds morality, which in turn breeds law-abiding citizens and good neighbors, and we all want good neighbors, so let's promote the Christian nation thesis regardless of what the truth may be.") This type of historical relativism disguised as scholarship is only one step better than the pro-Christian nation propaganda that is pushed by evangelical Christian writers, which is another topic of this study.

Such historical relativism, however, works both ways. Those writers pushing a secularist agenda often sacrifice the "facts" to create a new or modern perception that Christianity had little importance to the Founders or the first generation of Americans. They believe the world (and hence the United States) would be a better place if all people could just see the light of secular humanism and abandon religious superstitions and outdated belief systems. If they can make the Founders look too enlightened to have taken religion seriously by fudging the facts a little, then they can change the national perception in the current and future generations. This too will be a topic of this study. This book tries to avoid such historical relativism, and by so doing, hopes to project objectivity and factual accuracy to the greatest degree humanly possible. Only if it succeeds in this aim will the interpretation and conclusion reached prove valuable.

## ACKNOWLEDGMENTS

Many good friends, esteemed colleagues, and accomplished scholars read the entire manuscript, or select parts of it, and each made thoughtful and insightful suggestions to improve it. Among them were historians representing several different specialties, a political scientist, an English professor and literary critic, theologians and pastors representing a variety of denominations, two avowed atheists, and a couple of agnostics. Some corrected my factual mistakes, some critiqued my writing, and some pointed out that what I thought was common knowledge was not common knowledge at all, except for people from certain religious backgrounds. All of their criticisms were constructive, and I took almost every suggestion and revised the manuscript accordingly. Without such generous help, this book would suffer an embarrassing number of defects, if it made it to print at all. I am therefore deeply indebted to these proofreaders, fact checkers, and friends: Steve Belko, John Bressler, Tom Caiazzo, Reid Derr, Stanly Godbold, Jeff Howell, Rhett Kelly, Bob Marsh, Dee McKinney, and Thomas Thibeault. (Y'all have my never-ending gratitude!) Now, any and all errors that remain within these pages are solely my own fault. Likewise, the opinions and historical interpretations expressed herein are mine alone.

# Introduction

## *The Church-State Issue as Historical Entertainment*

### PERCEPTIONS

Americans have a fascination with the issue of separation of church and state. For generations, scholars and laymen alike have been interested in this complex and controversial topic. In recent years, the fascination has reached a crescendo, growing to the point that one wonders what could possibly remain to be said about church-state relations that has not already been said. Pick up a newspaper at random in Anytown, USA, and chances are that a church-state issue will appear periodically as a local concern. Watch television news talk shows or listen to radio talk shows, and odds are the result will be the same. Go to any large library or bookstore, and the shelves will likely be stocked with church-state books. A simple Internet search for "separation of church and state" will currently yield more than 2 million hits. Then there are publishing houses that are devoted to printing nothing but church-state literature. There is even a scholarly journal published under the auspices of a major university that is devoted to nothing but this one issue.[1] Few other historical topics can boast of so much ongoing attention.

The driving force behind all this attention, more often than not, is the religious right (orthodox Christian organizations that oppose the complete divorce of church and state) and/or individual Christians who feel it necessary to share their faith and therefore their political views publicly and regularly. Columnist Stanley Fish complained about this evangelical outspokenness, expressing incredulity that Christian writers Tim LaHaye and Jerry Jenkins's *Left Behind* series has become a "publishing phenomenon," that Mel Gibson's controversial movie *The Passion of the Christ* was a box-office smash in 2004, that so many professional athletes take the opportunity during post-game interviews to give thanks "to Jesus Christ" for their physical skills, and that "Every speech given by every politician ends with 'God Bless America.'" He asked with seeming incredulity, "What's going on here?"[2] Millions of Americans share his sentiment, worrying about the growing influence of evangelicalism all around them, fearing that Pastor Rick Warren's *The Purpose Driven Life* might drive the nation's politics too far to the right.[3] Indeed many questioned the wisdom of presidential candidates Barack Obama and John McCain and their parties agreeing to hold a nationally televised political forum at Warren's Saddleback Baptist Church in California in 2008. For them, organizations such as the Freedom From Religion Foundation (FFRF) in Wisconsin, whose political agenda is evident from its name, is the first line of defense against radical evangelicals. The FFRF prints books, pamphlets, brochures, and a newspaper, as well as engages in other activities, all devoted to achieving the complete secularization of the United States. It publishes such works as *Just Pretend: A Freethought Book for Children*, which teaches impressionable young minds that God is no more real than Santa Claus or the Easter Bunny, and *The World Famous Atheist Cookbook* "for those who prefer to do their frying in the here and now."[4]

For every person, however, who fears a hostile takeover of America by evangelical Christians, there is an evangelical who laments what he or she perceives to be the judicial, educational, and entertainment takeover of the nation by secularists that has been in progress for a half-century already. One need only consider the recent brouhaha over Dan Brown's *The Da Vinci Code* (both the book and the movie) to see how reactionary some Christians can be when they feel their beliefs are under attack.[5] While their lamentations are most often voiced in sermons and Sunday school lessons, there is a growing body of literature, some of a scholarly nature and some of the popular variety, that voices them as well. There are many publishing houses, some large and some small, devoted to this type of literature, such as Wallbuilder Press in Texas. A quick glance at its reading list immediately indicates that it is devoted to advocating the pro-Christian nation message.[6]

Such private organizations as these mentioned, on both sides of the political/religious spectrum, have a constitutional right to publish what they do, of course, but their books, pamphlets, videos, and other media generally present a one-sided interpretation of American history that flirts with the ethical boundary where honesty meets half-truth. Debunking the exaggerations, distortions, and half-truths of each side is one of the primary goals of this study.

For an illustration of how this emotionally charged church-state issue is routinely hashed out at the local level, consider a debate that went on for several editions in the Georgia Southern University student newspaper, the *George-Anne*, in 2004. Located in the rural town of Statesboro, a municipality of about 25,000, the university has a student body of about 18,000. The student body, the townspeople, and the local governing officials are predominantly political and religious conservatives, while the faculty and the student newspaper editors and columnists are mainly political and social liberals. The discussion was initiated by a columnist who took a strong stance on the moral and constitutional right of homosexuals to marry, pointing out that the only ones who seem to object to "gay marriage" in America are fundamentalist Christians, and adding that the nation's Founders, if alive today, certainly would agree with the liberals on this issue. A local reader wrote a letter to the editor in response, vigorously arguing the contrary, saying that the Founders were God-fearing Christians of one stripe or another who most certainly would not have approved of homosexual marriage. Another reader responded to this letter in mocking derision, complaining that whether the Founders were "Christians" in modern fundamentalist terms or not is beside the point; they were all scientifically inquisitive men who, if alive today, would consult the American Psychological Association for information on whether homosexuals were "normal" and should thus be granted constitutional protections and civil rights equal to heterosexuals, or whether they should be branded as deviants and misfits and thus treated as inferiors, just like they treated their wives and their slaves![7] Similar ideological exchanges have taken place in small towns all over America in this first decade of the 21st century.

Why all the animus over this issue? It all stems from differing perceptions of whether the United States was, is, or should be a "Christian nation." Perceptions can be powerful things. They can substitute for facts in people's minds. They can shape our collective thinking and ultimately influence what becomes reality. In that sense, the old adage "perception is reality" is not far from being an absolute truth. Fitting perfectly in the mold of the Hegelian Dialectic, there are three perceptions about whether the United States is a "Christian nation," and everyone holds one of them: (1) Yes, it is a Christian nation; (2) No, it is not a Christian nation; and (3) It depends on the definition of "Christian nation," and when defined properly, it is a synthesis of both.[8] Following is a brief look at each.

When people perceive that the United States is a Christian nation, they do so based on several factors. First, a majority of Americans identify themselves as Christians today, far more than all other religions combined. Not only that, but there is a multiplicity of churches in every city and town—dozens of them for every one synagogue, mosque, or other place of worship, such that one can hardly drive through Anytown, USA, without being constantly reminded of how Christianity pervades the landscape. Second, the origin of the United States as a set of English colonies populated mainly by Protestants of various types is common knowledge, as are the stories of Pilgrims, Puritans, and other sects coming to America in search of religious freedom.

Third, from there, it is easy to make the leap to the United States being founded as a Christian nation, especially when considering that the Declaration of Independence contains some very religious-sounding language, and

that several of the original thirteen states had constitutions sanctioning a particular Christian denomination over others, including requiring that those
states' political leaders be professing Christians. Fourth, this perception is but-
tressed by the fact that the First Amendment to the United States Constitution
did not, and actually could not, force the disestablishment of these state
churches. The states voluntarily chose to abolish their established churches in
their own ways and in their own times. Such facts suggest that the United
States was always Christian through and through—in practically every way
except "officially" via legal codification.[9] Thus pro-Christian nation proponents (generally called fundamentalists and/or evangelicals in both popular
usage and in this book) believe they have both the high moral ground and the
historical tradition of the nation on their side.[10]

When others perceive that the United States is not a Christian nation, they
do so based on a conflicting and seemingly contradictory set of facts. First,
the United States Constitution is the fundamental law of the nation, not the
Declaration of Independence and not the state constitutions. It contains no religious-sounding language of any kind, much less a uniquely Christian kind
(which is not to say it does not address religion; it does in Article 6). Moreover, the First Amendment protects the right of Americans to be free *from* religion as well as *to* believe or practice a religion. Second, the leading
Founders of the United States were mostly not orthodox Christians but were
instead Deists, Unitarians, and Freethinkers of sundry types who stood firmly
against the idea of having established churches in their day. Add to that the
fact that men such as George Washington, Thomas Jefferson, James Madison,
and Benjamin Franklin—the main architects of the American system of
government—went out of their way to prevent the intermingling of orthodox
Christianity and temporal power in their new nation. Third, all of the concessions that they and their progeny have made to the Christian religion are
strictly nonsectarian in nature. For example, "In God We Trust" and "one
nation, under God" and other similar religious messages that have found their
way into the national polity do not promote Christianity specifically over any
other religion. Fourth, only a fraction of the American people was registered
as church members at the time of the nation's founding. How could anyone
call a nation with less than 20 percent church members a "Christian nation?"
Fifth, the current movement to de-Christianize the public sphere through the
removal of the Ten Commandments from government buildings, prayer and
Bible-reading from schools, and Nativity scenes from public property, has
been upheld in the Supreme Court and other federal courts more often than
not for more than a half-century.[11] Thus, the anti-Christian nation contingent
(generally called secularists and/or separationists in both popular usage and in
this book) believe they hold the correct interpretation of the Constitution and
are consequently closer to the original intent of the Founders.[12]

The people in the third category, the "it depends" group, generally lace the
best elements of both arguments together and come up with a composite.

They believe the United States is a Christian nation in the sense that Christianity is, and always has been, the predominant religion in the country and, as such, has influenced the nation's culture more than any other social force. They also understand that it is not a Christian nation in the sense that the nation has nothing in its Constitution that even *allows* it to be classified legally as a "Christian" nation much less *requires* it. To them, the United States is Christian mainly but not exclusively; it is Christian socially and culturally but not politically or legally; and it is Christian traditionally and historically but not automatically or necessarily. The growing trend within this category of writing has been to stress what could be called the "duality thesis" of American history, which holds that the United States is both a "Christian nation" and a "secular nation" simultaneously. Cut either aspect of the nation's history out of the equation, say these "dualists" (as they shall be called in this book), and it becomes impossible to get an accurate portrayal of the American past.[13]

All three perceptions are valid to some extent, but critical observations can be made about each. The fundamentalist-evangelical group, which is far and away the largest, is prone to rely too much on emotion, to take too much on faith, and to tune out those with opposing views. The main proponents are pastors, evangelists, and priests who weave certain aspects of American history and current events into their sermons and written documents. They expect their audience to accept at face value their interpretation of the Constitution, their understanding of the Founders' original intent, their reading of American history, their criticism of contemporary secularists and secularism, and their jeremiads against the United States if and when it ever gets too far away from its Christian roots. They largely have their expectations of not being challenged on their "facts" met by their congregations and followers. Why? In many churches, lack of education partly accounts for the blind acceptance of their leaders' political teachings. But in most churches, regardless of their education level, there is a "need" to believe that their nation is just a larger, collective version of their own community and their own kind of people—or at least that it should be.

Peer pressure plays a role as well. Those in the congregation who would dare question their leaders risk ostracism. After all, these same people show up at worship services every weekend to listen to and accept on faith the religious nostrums their leaders prescribe to help them find eternal salvation and to navigate their way through personal struggles in a troubled world. Why then would these devotees question their leaders on issues of lesser importance such as the history of their country or interpretations of its founding documents? They would not, of course. They are thus not easily dissuaded from their perception.

Preaching is by definition essentially propaganda. Calling it "propaganda" does not imply that it is false. It merely means that it is one-sided. Neither the devil, atheists, nor other religions are given equal time for rebuttal in a church sermon. While this one-sidedness works well in proclaiming religious doctrines, it produces a semi-ignorance of American history. Many church-goers never hear, read, or otherwise encounter arguments contrary to what their leaders preach on the subject.[14] What they do encounter often goes something like the following shards of information taken from a fundamentalist-evangelical Web site: (1) "There is no such thing as a pluralistic society. There will always be one dominant view. . . . Our U.S. Constitution was founded on Biblical principles and it was the intention of the authors for this to be a Christian nation"; (2) 52 of the 55 delegates to the Constitutional Convention of 1787 were "evangelical Christians," nine of whom were students of the Princeton professor and Presbyterian preacher Jonathan Witherspoon; (3) 94 percent of all quotes that the founders repeated in the public writings from 1760 to 1805 came from the Bible.[15]

The secularist-separationist camp, a smaller group that wields influence out of all proportion to its size in the national polity, suffers from equally egregious although totally different shortcomings. This group believes their own perception of the issue with just as much zeal, fervor, and conviction as the evangelicals they chide. They tend to think a strong dose of legalisms and rationalism is the best remedy for the religious crowd's ignorance. Their political and historical "facts" are meant to counteract their undereducated opponents' religious and emotionally based "truth." The problem is, their facts are just as one-sided as those they criticize, making them purveyors of a sort of counter propaganda. Consequently, they seem to be "preachers" of the philosophy of secularism, which many observers would consider a religion in its own right (the oxymoron of a "secular religion" notwithstanding). As psychiatrist Scott Peck has put it, "Anyone who has known a died-in-the-wool atheist will know that such an individual can be as dogmatic about unbelief as any believer can be about belief. . . . Science itself . . . is a religion. The neophyte scientist, recently come or converted to the world view of science, can be every bit as fanatical as a Christian crusader or a soldier of Allah."[16] Such defenders of secularism make an argument that is not so much wrong as simply incomplete. They fail to tell the whole story of American history. They de-emphasize the role of religion in the founding and development of the United States until it emasculates what really happened. Historian Walter Burns made the case this way: "If the Founders had intended to establish a Christian commonwealth . . . it was remiss of them—indeed, sinful of them—not to have said so. . . . But the Constitution was ordained and established to secure liberty and its blessings, not to promote faith in God."[17]

Moreover, the secularist-separationists seem to have an agenda to educate or reeducate their opponents that often makes them appear hostile to Christianity and Christians, if not to religion in general. They are often in influential positions in academia and the media, which gives them the ability to wage their campaign of reeducation. A tone of condescension shows through in their writing and public pronouncements that, whether intentional or not, comes across as offensive to the church crowd. Human nature is such that most people resist efforts by their well-meaning and noble-intentioned ideological adversaries to reeducate them on any issue in which religion and emotion are involved. In decades and centuries past, the fundamentalist-evangelicals tried to shove their religion down the throats of the nonreligious and agnostics, which merely drove most of them further away.[18] In recent years, the roles have been reversed to a great extent. The fundamentalist-evangelicals are now averse to the notion of being "enlightened" by those they politely perceive as secularists, or not-so-politely perceive as anti-Christ. The problem is only exacerbated when the reeducators seem obnoxiously condescending toward their potential student/convert base. Then it becomes almost certain that no potential proselyte will begin to "see the light" of the anti-Christian nation thesis. Add sarcasm, satire, or mockery of Christianity (in the name of comedy and free speech) to this already volatile mix, however, and the fundamentalist-evangelicals hunker down in their trenches for a war of attrition.[19]

The secularist-separationist group was in ascendancy from the 1920s to the 1980s with practically no opposition in high places of academia or publishing outside of private religious schools and presses. It is still in ascendancy today, although the higher it rises in influence in education or politics, the more it produces a backlash among the religious right.[20] This ongoing change toward the secularization of America could rightly be considered just part of the liberal intellectual movement of modern times, created as a by-product of ever-increasing scientific knowledge. Unlike the Founders and their 19th-century progeny, who thought it possible to be both enlightened rationalists and religiously oriented thinkers simultaneously, 20th-century intellectuals have, for the most part, found it impossible to reconcile religion with secular knowledge. For the past seventy-five years or so, most American academics and other thought-shapers have been suspicious of "religion for both personal and intellectual reasons." Moreover, "some openly dislike it . . . religion is often identified with repressive upbringings and closed-minded attitudes that are hostile to the life of the mind. . . . In this view, religion is something that might best disappear from American life. . . ."[21]

Turning now to the dualists, the only criticisms worth mentioning of them are that they are a much smaller group than the other two and, as such, are frequently overshadowed in the public perception by the large, noisy extremists, and that their composite position excites nobody to action. The issue of whether the United States was, is, or should be a Christian nation is emotionally charged. Saying the United States is "sort of" a Christian nation just does not have the same appeal as a resounding "yes, it is!" or "no, it isn't!" In the opinion of people on the opposite extremes of the debate, the dualist position amounts to little more than fence-sitting. Neither extreme has much respect for this group they perceive to be noncommittal or vacillating. This is understandable when viewed in light of the fact that, while the issue of where to draw the line separating church and state is debatable at the philosophical level, it is only solvable at the judicial level, unless and until the Constitution is amended. Even if it were settled by such a legislative procedure, it would likely end up in court soon thereafter anyway, putting it more within the domain of lawyers than either preachers, professors, politicians, or philosophers.[22] Thus, both sides feel that they have much at stake and much to lose (their whole worldview and way of life) if they concede even an inch to the other, and they will unfortunately but undoubtedly go on relentlessly waging their sociopolitical tug-of-war.

The fundamentalist-evangelicals are likely to pull out a Bible verse such as Joshua 24:18 to quote to the fence-sitters, "And if it seem evil unto you to serve the Lord, choose you this day whom ye will serve . . . but as for me and my house, we will serve the Lord" (KJV). The secularists are just as likely to accuse the noncommitted of being scared to stand up to the "religious right," or maybe of actually being one of the religious right themselves, although perhaps in denial . . . or disguise! Mostly, however, extremists on both sides merely ignore those in the middle. This is unfortunate, because the middle is where the common ground is on this issue as on most other issues involving a diversity of opinions. Unless one extreme or the other can be shown to have a monopoly on the facts—and that is largely what this book seeks to determine—extremists would do well to inch toward that ideological midpoint.[23]

Assuming, for the sake of argument, that the middle way turns out to be the most factually accurate, why should it be so difficult for a majority of Americans to find, appreciate, or stay there ideologically on the question of whether the United States is a Christian nation or not? Perhaps it is because this issue, more than any other, weds the two most divisive features of this country, politics and religion. It thus draws attention from two different constituencies that probably would otherwise have infrequent contact. Like a massive celestial body, the church-state issue has gravity. As illustrated in the opening paragraphs of this study, it attracts a wide range of controversial sub-issues, such as abortion, homosexuality, creationism versus evolution, American imperialism abroad, and race and gender relations at home, just to name a few. In fact, practically every social issue that crops up in American politics derives in one way or another from divergent opinions on the relationship between God and government. Ultimately, it forces us to grapple with the most rudimentary question that can be asked: What is the basis upon which American civilization was founded and has been perpetuated? Democracy? Freedom? Humanitarianism? Tolerance? Diversity? Social mobility? Capitalism? Or some combination of these and/or other things?[24] Such a question strikes at the very root of our being as a nation and a people. Discovering an answer that does not fit the preconception of people on either extreme, therefore, threatens to destroy their personal, family, community, and/or regional identity. Few are eager to sign up for such an identity change.

These strange bedfellows, politics and religion, are indeed married, in the church-state issue, in an unevenly yoked union of holy and profane. The marriage is awkward and complex—so complex in fact that above-average knowledge of history is required even to begin to understand it. Yet even among professional historians (who of all people should be able to understand it) there is no consensus about whether the United States was, is, or should be a Christian nation. This is because most of them spend their workweek in secular ivory towers, but many of them also go to weekend worship services in the church of their choice. The scholarly discipline called "history" is, not surprisingly, fraught with all kinds of interpretive discrepancies on a host of different topics. Frequently, there are opposing historiographical camps that compete for ideological adherents and converts, which raises the all-important question: If the scholars—the historical experts—cannot agree on the truth of history, what hope is there that the American people in general can ever arrive at a consensus on this most troublesome question? Indeed, after the question is filtered through the sieve of politics, religion, and history, it comes out (to use a metaphor) full of unwanted debris on one side of the sieve and is watered down to nothingness or meaninglessness on the other side. To explain: The sieve catches the lumps of inconsistency and irrationality in the arguments of the extremists while letting the purity of the dualists pass through. As previously mentioned, rather than the two extremes being willing to see any possible errors in their views caught up in the filter, they merely unite in accusing the middle-of-the-road dualists of having a meaningless argument that serves neither side. Where does that leave the open-minded inquirer then? Where does it leave the reader who has not already made up his or her mind? Answer: Having gone around in a big circle and arriving back at the starting point. If such is the case, is it merely an exercise in futility to try to find the "truth" or the "facts?" Perhaps. But this study has optimism about the endeavor, for maybe it will bring some illumination to the subject and make a difference for some, if not all, readers.

This study explores these three perceptions of whether the United States was, is, or should be, a Christian nation. It tests each of them against the best historical evidence available. It offers insights that will help each reader make up his or her own mind. It is intended to supply information in as objective a way as humanly possible on this issue that is so often the subject of bitter controversy and so frequently skewed by propaganda. It will help demystify and demythologize this most important topic—a topic that is relevant to all time periods of American history, including the present, and will likely continue to be well into the future, probably as long as there shall be a United States of America. As an additional disclaimer, this book is not intended as an inquiry into the contemporary church-state issue but as an historical study that will help illuminate the present debate. Nor is it an exhaustive documentation of every instance when the issue has been raised or disputed in American history. It is focused mainly on the Founding generation, the time from the American Revolution through the War of 1812. Those were the formative years of the United States, an era that gave us our most treasured national icons—the Declaration of Independence and Constitution, and the men who wrote them. To put the Founders and their accomplishments in perspective, however, and to make their work meaningful and applicable to the country today requires broadening the scope a little beyond that one generation in both chronological directions. Context is important. The extremists on both sides today are notorious for taking the words of the Founders out of it, just like the partisans comprising the first two political parties in America spun their words to suit their own views in the 1790s.[25] The study at hand takes great care to avoid one-sided interpretations.

Although a 200-page treatise providing evidence that supports this third perception is not likely to change the minds of extremists on either side, it will serve as a witness against both and as ammunition for neither. The extremists cherry-pick the historical documents that justify their positions and weave their interpretations from them, and to neither side "is history really important."[26] Even the most objective historians suffer from human limitations. They throw words and explanations "like fishermen's nets into the unfathomable depths of the past," as Thomas Haskell has put it, adding, "No doubt much eludes us, for beneath its tranquil surface the past contains things stranger than any surface dweller can readily imagine. But any scheme is better than none at all. Without a net we would catch nothing at all."[27] Likewise, Joseph Ellis, in explaining how he approached his seminal study of the Founders, said he wanted "to write a modest-sized account of a massive historical subject," and to do so, "rowed out over the great ocean of material generated in the founding era of American nationhood, lowered my little bucket as far down as my rope could reach, then made sense out of the characteristic specimens I hoisted up. . . ."[28]

## HISTORIOGRAPHY

Historiography is generally defined as the study of the writing of history or the study of differing interpretations in the discipline of history. It might better be defined as "the study of the *study* of history," or the "study of the *history* of history."[29] One main reason to include this section on historiography is that sometimes making a study of the *history* of a field of "history" sheds much light by which the historian can see to do his or her work. The problem with the historiography of church-state studies is that it is so vast that keeping track of it poses a challenge even to specialists.

Consider, for example, the papers of the most prominent Founders, Benjamin Franklin, George Washington, John Adams, Thomas Jefferson, James Madison, and Alexander Hamilton. Each has been published in multivolume 500–600-page encyclopedic reference books, and except for Hamilton's papers, which run to 26 volumes, none of the others is complete. (Hamilton's is complete only because he died young!) The editorial work of preparing those primary documents (largely comprised of barely legible handwritten letters) for publication, despite continuing for decades and being handled by teams of some of the best professional archivists and historians in the world, is excruciatingly slow. Perhaps within another decade, the task will be finished for some collections. So far, however, Franklin's papers run to 36 volumes and Adams's 13. Jefferson's and Madison's papers, 32 and 12 volumes, respectively, so far, have been divided into two parts, and will probably be three eventually (pre-presidential, presidential, and eventually post-presidential). So voluminous are Washington's papers that they are divided into five parts (Colonial, Revolutionary, Confederation, Presidential, and Retirement) and run to an amazing 47 volumes . . . and are still not complete![30] Such publications are a mixed blessing. On the one hand, they mean that "every man who reads, carefully and critically, can dare to be his own historian,"[31] but on the other hand, even the most careful and critical professionals can get lost in, bogged down for years in, overwhelmed by, and even disillusioned by their research.

Moreover, church-state literature diverges from, or converges with, many other fields—intellectual history, religious history, constitutional and legal history, philosophy, sociology, political science, anthropology, and theological studies, just to name some of the most obvious. Each of these fields contains a vast body of literature in its own right, and some are comprised of multiple subfields. Take, for instance, the subfield of Puritan studies in the larger field of Colonial American history. Edmund S. Morgan protested about it as early as 1966 that "we already know more about the Puritans than sane men should want to know," and that "we ought therefore to declare a moratorium on further investigation and turn our attention to less familiar fields."[32] More than three decades later, David Harlan added to this sentiment, complaining of an "alarming, cancer-like thickening of the literature. . . . Every subfield within the discipline . . . has been covered with a crust of interpretations so thick as to be virtually impenetrable. And they keep coming almost daily."[33]

Why do new interpretations keep coming? Perhaps because scholars believe, as Morgan opined, that "the law of diminishing returns does not always operate in scholarship; the rewards often increase instead of diminishing as investigation spreads and deepens."[34] The never-ending quest to reinterpret the past, however, leads to the publication of only a few seminal books in any given genre and dozens, if not hundreds, of also-rans. Historiography is a complex subject because it studies many thousands of historians who wrote many more thousands of books spanning multiple centuries. But it seeks to boil them all down into a handful of categories of writing/schools of thought. It is at best an inexact art.[35] For the purpose of the study at hand, which is merely to set the table for discussing the church-state issue in American history, it must be simplified to the most elementary level, as per the following discussion.

American historical writings fall into three basic chronological/methodological categories: Puritan, Patrician, and Professional. The first two categories are fairly monolithic, while the latter is multifaceted. The Puritan historians wrote from their own religious point of view during the Colonial era. They mainly described what they experienced, witnessed, or heard from other Puritans in the New England colonies, but they often wrote not of how life really was but how they wished it to be. They were the first proponents of the "chosen people" or "chosen nation" ideology, meaning they believed God had sent them to America to settle the wilderness and create a distinctly Christian civilization. Their work is today used mainly for primary source material by researchers rather than cited as reliable history, except among evangelical propagandists, who use it as ammunition.[36]

The Patrician historians began writing shortly after the founding of the United States. The most prominent of them was George Bancroft, whose "Christian sentimentalism blurred the line between religious and political ideas" and who "wrote the history of the United States as if it were the Kingdom of God."[37] Bancroft "set out to explain how in only two centuries the happiest and most enlightened civilization in history had arisen from the wilderness to become a model for the rest of the world" and concluded what seemed obvious to him, that the United States was merely fulfilling its God-given "mission."[38] These Patricians wrote one-sided histories, partly pro-Christian in nature but mainly just pro-American. They too believed in the "chosen nation" ideology, but they wove new strands into the old Puritan fabric. They believed God had ordained the United States to be a white, Anglo-Saxon, and Protestant (WASP) nation. They were thus driven as much by the forces of nationalism, imperialism, and racism, which pervaded virtually all of Western civilization in the 19th century, as by Christianity.[39] They glorified the Founders as men who could practically do no wrong.[40] They presented the American Revolution "as the next most important event to the birth of Christ."[41] They lived in a time when Christianity reached the high tide of its influence in American politics and culture, they basically assumed their readership was Christian, and they wrote accordingly. Historian Adolf Koch has complained that the result of this Christians-writing-for-Christians approach dragged the writing of American history into its "dark ages."[42]

Before automatically condemning the Patricians as the worst kind of propagandists, however, we should consider the possibility that they were merely reflecting the 19th-century zeitgeist. That zeitgeist, or "spirit of the times," was one of a stuffy, intense, prudish morality, usually associated with the "Victorian age"—a term deriving from and technically applied to Great Britain, but which had its American semiequivalent in the Gilded Age. It crossed the Atlantic ocean and united Americans with their mother country under the WASP banner and showed that in many ways the Americans and the British were just one people despite being two nations.[43] This zeitgeist phenomenon can be likened to a "shared conceptual framework," "conventional wisdom," or the "paradigm" of that generation.[44] All generations, including today's, have one. In current parlance it is most often called "political correctness," and it simply means the view on any given topic that is the most dominant, widely held one within scholarly, academic, and media circles. Such views are legitimized by the elites (professors, publishers, editors, journalists, entertainers, and preachers) and then fed to the masses as truth.[45]

Moving toward the end of the 19th century and into the early 20th century, a new class of historians emerged who were trained in universities—in Ph.D. programs—to be critical researchers and scrutinizers of sources. They were the "Professional" historians. Although a few of them came on the scene during the Gilded Age in the 1870s–1880s, the first large class of them came along during, and/or helped give rise to, the Progressive era of U.S. history, from the 1900s through the 1920s. This first class of Professional historians is thus called the Progressives. The name most synonymous with this category is Charles Beard, who, by emphasizing the financial motivations that led individual Founders to want a new Constitution, brought these demigods "down to earth and made them walk and act like men."[46] This school was determined to pull American historical writing out of its so-called dark ages and into the light of progressivism and secularism. They were so good at critiquing and scrutinizing sources that they completely revised the work of their forebears, becoming largely antithetical to everything the religious historians had believed in and stood for. They were thus mostly secularist-separationist in orientation, at least in the sense that they rejected the traditional fundamentalist conception of history. They were more interested in First Amendment free speech and free press issues that would allow them to discuss openly controversial political views, such as Marxism/Socialism/Communism, than in religious issues. But the effect of their collective work—which was bolstered in the post–World War I years by a group of secular-minded poets, novelists, literary critics, and journalists known as the "Lost Generation"—was to turn the tide of intellectualism toward secularist-separationist sentiment.[47]

The Progressive school of historians actually outlived the Progressive era of American history. From the 1930s to the present, scholars in this school have generally been called "Liberals," although "Modernists" and "Humanists" are terms that have been used to describe them as well. Those who have come along since the 1960s have typically been called the "New Left" historians. No matter what they were called or when they came on the scene, they essentially embraced and helped disseminate the German philosopher Frederick Nietzsche's "God is dead (so man must make his own salvation)" worldview, although most did so (or continue to do so) innocuously rather than recklessly. To fundamentalist-evangelicals, these early Liberals were the ones who began to plunge America into its "dark ages," not the other way around. The two world wars should have been enough, the fundamentalist-evangelicals have countered, to show the absurdity of trying to organize a civilized world without God. In other words, the Kaiser's, and later Hitler's, Germany are prime examples of what happens to Christian nations that no longer find a place for God or try to substitute someone or something else for God. But instead, the Liberal historians largely supported the secularist American Civil Liberties

Union after World War I and the iconoclastic People United for the Separation of Church and State in the midst of World War II, not to mention helping
foster the atheistic Humanist Manifesto between the wars. So this group of
historians was the first to stir the pot of church-state controversy in a major
way, and the question then became in the minds of the old-fashioned fundamentalist-evangelicals whether or not America could survive this so-called
"Death of God."[48]

Not until the mid-20th century did a new breed of professional historian
begin to arise that could be considered genuinely objective and dispassionate
about the role of religion in American history. They have generally been
described as Post-Modernists. Among those who stand out as founders of this
Post-Modernist school are William W. Sweet and Perry Miller. They and their
school of thought essentially believed and still believe that it is impossible to
understand aspects of American history such as politics, economics, society,
or diplomacy without viewing them alongside religion. Religion, they say, is
at least equal in importance to these other pieces of the American mosaic and
thus equally worthy of study. Who would be foolish enough, they ask, to try
to understand the history of Europe without giving a great amount of attention
to the impact of the Catholic Church and the Protestant Reformation upon it?
No one, of course. Why then should American historians try to understand this
nation's history from a strictly secular point of view? Yet that is precisely
what secularists have done and continue to do. Because of their own lack of
religion, they refuse to take religious studies seriously as an academic discipline worthy of being taught in public schools and colleges.[49] Post-Modernists
have set out to reform that opinion. One way to do it, they believe, is to study
the *followers* of religion rather than the *leaders*. This is admittedly difficult to
do, since the writings of preachers comprise the largest single source of firsthand information we have about colonial America. But studying the people
rather than their leaders has been a worthy goal, and one that makes use of
the skills of social scientists, such as sociologists, anthropologists, and cliome-
tricians, in gathering and analyzing data and forming conclusions based upon
it. Post-Modernists understand that they do not have to agree with Christianity
or believe in it or any God to study the impact that religion has had on the
United States. Some of these Post-Modernists actually admit to being agnostics and atheists while making their livelihoods as specialists in American
Christian studies. They see no contradiction, and rightly so. Religious disbelief
and religious scholarship need not be mutually exclusive.[50]

Some of them, however, have seen a contradiction in how the field of
American religious studies within the national polity is framed as "church-
state" studies. They have thought it wise to do away with the terminology of
"church and state" as used in the context of American history because it is
antiquated and only marginally accurate. It really applies to European history
from the Middle Ages through the Reformation. The United States never had
a government sanctioned church and neither "church" nor "state" appears in

the First Amendment. As Sydney Mead put it, the term has "resulted in more confusion than enlightenment" because it starts discussion of the relationship between religion and politics in America from the wrong frame of reference.[51] With this complaint duly noted, the American public at large, including most scholars and specialists in the field, have not taken this idea to heart, nor will this study, because the terminology serves the purpose for which it is routinely employed. Besides, it is easier to keep it like a comfortable old hat than replace it with something new. It is not such a poor choice of words anyway. It indicates with perfect accuracy that the dynamic tension between politics and religion in the United States has always focused on Christianity, not some other religion. After all, the term is *church* and state, not *synagogue* and state, not *mosque* and state, and not *temple of reason* and state.

## Chapter 1

# The American "Way"

*Fabricating a New Creed for a Nascent Nation*

## THE NATIONAL PARADOX

The United States is a nation of paradoxes. It may seem trite to have to point that out, but it is necessary for establishing a context for the coming discussion. Consider some of the following examples. The United States is a country in which about 90 percent of the people believe in God, about 80 percent claim to believe in some version of Christianity, and perhaps 50 percent are actively involved in their churches and/or other religious activities, whether regularly or sporadically. It is also a country in which pornography, gambling, and brewing/distilling are all legal, multimillion dollar businesses. It is a country whose national capital, Washington, D.C., has no less than seventeen different references to the Judeo-Christian God on its federal government buildings and monuments, from the Capitol dome, rotunda, and both chambers of Congress, to the Library of Congress, the Dirksen Congressional Office Building, the Supreme Court, the Washington Monument, the Jefferson Memorial, and the Lincoln Memorial. It is also a country where billboards and neon signs advertise sex shows, and where movies glorify violence and bloodshed. Consider a billboard on I-85 in South Carolina, for example, that blares, "Fireworks . . . Adult Novelties . . . Bibles, Wholesale." It is a country whose national anthem, "The Star Spangled Banner," contains the words, "Blest with victory and peace, may the heaven-rescued land Praise the Power that hath made and preserved us a nation. Then conquer we must, when our cause it is just, and this be our motto: 'In God is our trust';" and whose other greatest songs of national pride, "America the Beautiful," "My Country 'Tis of Thee," and the "Battle Hymn of the Republic" all contain references of thanksgiving to the Christian God. It is also a country in which millions embrace a secular "sex, drugs, and rock-and-roll" lifestyle. It is a country whose currency proclaims our collective trust in God. It is also a country where everyone is free to spend that money on sin and vice of all kinds. It is a country full of Christian churches. And it is a country that legally allows the Church of Satan to exist, and on the same tax-exempt basis as any other church or religious body.[1]

In the United States people are tugged from one side by those trying to convince everyone that this is a Christian nation. They say, "No Western nation is as religion-soaked as ours. . . . America is a religion-mad country . . . a nation obsessed with religion." And "The essence of the American is the belief that God loves her or him, a conviction shared by nearly nine out of ten of us. . . ."[2] They contend that "Nearly every American who has ever acclaimed the greatness of his country or announced his belief in its glorious destiny has grounded his enthusiasm to some extent upon devotion to religion. He has assumed that the republic was founded for religious purposes and that divine favor has been its guide and companion ever since. Not only does he regard America as a Christian nation but he thinks of it as more Christian than any other."[3] Such a statement, however, even if true at some time in the distant past, has been obviously false for at least forty years now. Hundreds, indeed thousands, of celebrities of various kinds—from movie stars to rock stars to porn stars, from irreverent satirists to iconoclastic comedians, from eccentric millionaire capitalists to militant atheists—have all proclaimed the greatness of America not for religious reasons but because of the freedom to live as they please here.[4] If their country is "religion-soaked," it has never seemed to get them wet.

When given a choice between following an orthodox religion that emphasizes morality, ethics, spirituality, and preparation for the afterlife on the one hand, or following a hedonistic lifestyle or bacchanalian philosophy on the other, the people of America have always split down the middle. On Sundays in America the churches are filled by only those people who really want or need to be there; meanwhile ball fields and stadiums are full of those who would rather be there; the roads and the shopping malls are occupied by those who prefer driving and shopping; the parks and recreation areas are dotted with individuals, couples, families, and groups enjoying leisure time; restaurants are open in preparation of one of the busiest days of the week; and a large segment of the workforce is on the job just the same as any other day. There is obviously no one single America, but two—one religious, one secular. Within the two are many subsets. The United States, it has been said, "as a whole is not easily comprehended, so many-faced and many-voiced are its people and so varied their ways of life."[5]

These diverse elements all have one thing in common, one thing that ties them together and makes them compatible: love of freedom—freedom to worship an invisible, eternal Sovereign; and freedom to "worship" Dionysus, follow Epicurus, or simply to *carpe diem*. This fact has led some observers to conclude that freedom, not Christianity is "America's real religion." If so, the Founders must have been the original "Apostles" of this new religion, because the religious/secular paradox has been a part of the United States from its inception.[6]

## THE FOUNDERS AND WHAT THEY FOUNDED

When answering the question of whether this country was meant to be a Christian nation or not, the Founders' original intent must first be discovered. Unfortunately, original intent is a topic that provokes as much controversy as any other aspect of the church-state issue. The root of the controversy lies in the nebulous usage of the term *Founders* and its antiquated masculine synonym *Founding Fathers*.[7] It is often confused with or overlaps the *Signers* and *Framers*. Before proceeding to their original intent, some clear definitions and parameters for the discussion must be defined. Technically, the Founders should refer only to those people engaged in helping build the nation before the drafting of the Constitution, which includes the Signers of the Declaration of Independence, but not them exclusively; and technically the Framers should refer only to those engaged in the process of writing and ratifying the Constitution. These are big *shoulds*, however, which are not always followed in scholarly studies, common usage, or popular perception. It mostly depends upon the context and purposes of the discussion as to whether the technical distinction is absolutely necessary for clarity or not.[8] For the purposes of this study, *Founders* is used to mean either or both.

So who were these Founders, and what exactly did they found? Each part of the question must be briefly explored. The first part could refer exclusively to the signers of the Declaration of Independence. It could also refer to all patriots who put their lives on the line during the American Revolution. Then, too, the political leaders of the thirteen state governments could be considered Founders. Likewise, certain vocal and patriotic women—Abigail Adams, Martha Washington, Betsy Ross, and Molly Pitcher, for example—and non-citizens such as the Marquis de Lafayette, Baron Von Steuben, Thaddeus Kosciusko, and John Paul Jones—could be considered Founders. The answer could even be simplified to mean *all people* who comprised the first generation of patriots in the United States. The broader the definition, the more difficulties are encountered in discussing this topic, while the more narrow and focused the definition, the more the topic is clarified.

The most common usage of the term refers only to a handful of men who were the main architects of the national government and the ones most responsible for influencing the formation of a uniquely American way of life. These men would undoubtedly be included on anyone's list of Founders, regardless of who else might be included on some lists. They are, in a very loose sort of chronological order: Benjamin Franklin, George Washington, John Adams, Thomas Jefferson, James Madison, and Alexander Hamilton. Their high positions in the United States government in its formative years, their fame both at home and abroad as well as both contemporarily and historically, and their contributions to establishing the nation when lesser men might have caused it to crumble, make them stand out above their contemporaries. Four were presidents, two were vice presidents, two were secretaries of state, one was secretary of the treasury, and one was the most famous and respected representative of America abroad. One was the principal author of the Declaration of Independence, one was the principal author of the Constitution, and one was the most famous and popular author among all American authors in the 1700s. One is called "father of his country," one "father of the Constitution," one "father of the United States Navy," and one "the first American." One was the nation's highest ranking military officer and the symbol of American resistance in the Revolution. One was the principal architect of the national economy. One was among the greatest scientists and inventors of all time. All were Christians of one type or another at one time or another: one was a lifelong Episcopalian, one a lifelong Congregationalist, and four evolved over time into freethinkers, Deists, or Unitarians. Two were thirty-third degree Freemasons. Two were the principal architects of separation of church and state.[9]

Many others will appear on one list or another for some exploit or contribution they made to the survival or establishment of the early United States, but they do not have quite the same stature as the aforementioned. They include, in alphabetical order: Samuel Adams, Ethan Allen, John Dickinson, Elbridge Gerry, John Hancock, Patrick Henry, John Jay, Henry Laurens, Richard Henry Lee, John Marshall, Luther Martin, George Mason, Gouverneur Morris, Robert Morris, Thomas Paine, Edmund Randolph, Benjamin Rush, Roger Sherman, Noah Webster, and James Wilson, just to name a few of the most well known. Among them were signers of the Declaration, the Constitution, their state constitutions, and treaties with foreign governments, as well as vice presidents, secretaries of various cabinet departments, Supreme Court justices, leaders of the Continental Congress, war heroes, and authors of uniquely American works of literature and political science.

For the purposes of this study, *Founders* means mainly (but not exclusively) the six men named previously as the chief architects of the national government and the ones most responsible for influencing the formation of a uniquely American way of life. Of these six, four seem more important: Washington, Jefferson, Madison, and Franklin, for ways that will become apparent in this study. And of these four, two seem most important of all—Jefferson and Madison—because they are the only two men who are completely inseparable from the two most fundamental founding documents of the United States, the Declaration and the Constitution. More like editors than authors of these documents, Jefferson and Madison wrote the words that represented the collective thoughts of all the rest who might be called Founders. It would be nearly impossible to call someone a Founder who opposed the Declaration. It would not be impossible to call someone a Founder who opposed the Constitution of 1787, however, since Anti-Federalists showed their jealousy for the welfare of the United States through their opposition to the proposed new federal system. Patrick Henry and George Mason are perfect examples. No one would question their patriotism or love of their country. Indeed, about the only way for *potential* Founders to be excluded from the list is for them to have abandoned the American cause during or after the Revolution and left the country—Benedict Arnold being the prime example.

Just as there is no consensus about which particular men should be included among the Founders, there is none in answering the question "what exactly did they found?" The obvious answer, "They founded the United States of America," is vague. There are several different possible meanings in that statement. One, they approved the Declaration of Independence, in which they created the entity known as "the United States of America." Two, they approved the Articles of Confederation, which created the initial military alliance and voluntary union of the thirteen states. Three, they approved the Constitution that created the current national system of government. Four, they were original members of the Continental Congress or one of the first administrations of the federal government. And the list could go on.

The work of the Founders in writing the Declaration and the Constitution is more central and important to the establishment and perpetuation of the United States than anything else they did. These two documents are likewise more important than all other founding documents combined. They are in fact more important even than the men who penned them; while their authors live only in our memory, the documents themselves live on as the sustaining lifeblood and the "Holy Writ" of the nation.[10] Considering the importance of the Declaration and the Constitution, an inquiry must be made into their nature, character, and meaning because that is where the illusive original intent that everyone on all sides of the church-state controversy seeks can be found.

The Declaration and Constitution are two very different documents. They had two particular purposes, were written under completely different circumstances, came eleven years apart, and were signed by almost totally separate groups of people. Perhaps the most descriptive definition of the Declaration is to call it the "birth certificate" of the United States of America. Yet for a birth certificate, it is unusual in that it contains almost no information about the baby. Instead, it describes the parents in detail.[11] In this analogy, Great Britain can be thought of as the mother and King George III the father. The actions of the father and mother produced this offspring that is the United States. King George III can be considered an abusive parent. In the "abusive" environment of war, the birth takes place. It is not certain that the baby will survive, but as fate would have it, it does.[12] It experiences its christening or baptism (by fire, so to speak) in the Revolution.

Fast forward in time now eleven years, and the Constitution is written. To continue the analogy of the United States being a child, already christened, the Constitution is to the United States roughly what a traditional confirmation is to a Catholic child. In this analogy, the child is old enough to decide what kind of person he wants to be for the rest of his life, and he takes the necessary steps to make his choice official.[13] The Founders are like the priest(s) who performs the ceremony. The confirmation is put into writing and witnessed/approved by thirteen relatives. It is also disapproved by other relatives (the Anti-Federalists). Thomas Treadwell, at the New York Ratification Convention of 1788, voiced that sentiment, saying, "In this Constitution, sir, we have departed widely from the principles and political faith of '76. . . ."[14] Despite such disapprobation, the Constitution codified what kind of nation the United States would be. While certain specifics in the nation/child's personality and makeup can change over time through amendment/maturation, the basic principles of the nation, like the basic character of a child, are permanently fixed, so long as the child shall live.

What then is the basic character of the United States? What kind of nation were the Founders trying to create? To begin, it seems clear that Jefferson did not believe that he and his colleagues were merely acting in the self-interest of the people of America in creating the United States. He said rather that "we are acting for all mankind."[15] He meant they were founding not only a nation but a *Novus Ordo Seclorum*, or "a new order of the ages," as this motto that appears on the Great Seal of the United States is commonly translated. It might better be translated as "a new order for a new age" or "a new order that begins a new age," but either way, it meant a system of self-rule with no monarchs or tyrants.[16] In this new order, the United States would serve as the example for the rest of the world to follow. This new order would be one that prized individual rights (liberty, democracy, capitalism) and *E Pluribus Unum*, or "from many, one" (religious tolerance and cultural diversity).[17] Each of these prizes should be considered as equals in the minds of the Founders, with religion being no greater but no lesser a consideration than any other.

Concerning religion, "The enlightened founders were eager to produce a universal creed that they could throw like a tent over the diverse church religions," as Martin Marty has put it.[18] That creed would be a principle or set of principles that all religious groups then represented in America could agree on, principles not based on doctrine or dogma, but just on a belief in a monotheistic God who is omnipotent, infinite, perfectly good and wise, who created the universe, and set the cosmos in motion through laws that govern nature. Surely all Americans, they thought, could agree on that creed, regardless of what else they believed. Hence the other motto that appears on the Great Seal, *Annuit Coeptis*, commonly translated to mean "God has favored our beginnings."[19]

It was a worthy goal to aspire to, but one not without its challenges. Many orthodox church leaders saw this creed as an attempt to usurp the traditional conception of the sovereignty of the Christian God and the divinity of Jesus. The Founders were offering a very liberal interpretation of who or what God was, and church leaders were by and large conservative in their disposition. The battle was on. The Founders thus "lived to see the churches regard it [the creed] as just one more tent next to their own, one more competitive sect they must defeat."[20] Church leaders viewed its advocates as the cult of liberty, which worshiped the Goddess of Reason. That brings this inquiry back to the notion that the Founders were the "apostles of liberty," as they have been called.[21] Were they really? If so, this study could be ended here, with the conclusion reached that this land was never meant to be a "Christian nation" but instead a "freedom nation." That conclusion, however, would tell only part of the story. The story is much more complex than that.

From its inception the United States was different from all the nations that existed before it. Its people, when religious at all, were religious by choice, not by force of law. Choice allows movement in and out of churches and religious affiliations as individuals decide. Freedom to come and go as one pleases makes people happy. A happy citizenry makes a strong nation. This system, which benefits the national polity so greatly, has had no negative impact upon religion other than to make it "informal," and it is debatable whether that is a bad or a good thing.[22] On the one hand, it may detract from the solemnity of the worship service, reducing it to the level of any other form of entertainment. Attending church then becomes more like a hobby than a moral duty or an action upon which eternal salvation hinges. On the other hand, it weeds out the less committed and less faithful, leaving a stronger corpus of believers in the churches.

Churches and denominations and religions of all kinds have thrived and prospered under this informal system. It has affected them in one important, unusual way, as well. It has forced religious leaders to work much harder to gather and maintain a following than their counterparts in nations with established religions have ever had to do. The United States government offers them no legal help other than a tax exemption, it even seems antagonistic toward them sometimes, and it grants equal opportunity to their ideological adversaries. Each religion must compete in the free marketplace of ideas with other religions, with atheists and agnostics, and most importantly, with the promoters of carnal pleasure. Ironically, this has actually helped religion in America rather than hurt it. When a religious group survives and grows in America, its leaders can be sure of a devoted corps of followers, whose worship is more intense and personal, and whose loyalty is more tenacious than it would ever be in a nation with coerced religion. What then is the bottom line? In America, God and the devil, Christ and the anti-Christ, share equality under the law. Perhaps better than anything else, that fact exemplifies the great paradox.

Why is it so? Is it supposed to be so? Must it be so? Does the United States suffer from an identity crisis? Can the people not agree on what kind of nation they want, what kind of people they are? Did the Founders of this great country themselves not know what kind of nation they meant to create? Or were they wise beyond all their combined years in deliberately forming a paradoxical nation? Are the people equally wise to support the continuation of the paradox? The answer becomes clear upon considering the words inscribed on the Liberty Bell in the nation's founding city, Philadelphia. It is a Bible verse, Leviticus 25:10, from the King James Version. It says, "Proclaim liberty throughout the land unto all the inhabitants thereof."[23] It needs no explanation, but it begs one anyway. It says in a single sentence what the creed of the United States would forever be. Not *some*, but *all* Americans have liberty, not just those who believe in God or join a church. But it also supports the paradox. It reveals Americans of the 18th-century Enlightenment invoking the Old Testament God of Israel—a God of law and judgment, a God not usually known for his magnanimity toward those who oppose him, a God that many people consider extremely oppressive—as a source of inspiration, toleration, moderation, and liberation.[24]

Once the duality of the United States as a religious-secular nation is acknowledged, there is luminescence by which to view and ponder its national identity, character, and self-image. On the eve of the American Revolution, Edmund Burke, the great Whig orator in Parliament, made the following observation about this strange breed of religious folk that populated the colonies: "The people are protestants and of that kind, which is the most adverse to all implicit submission of mind and opinion. This is a persuasion [of people] not only favorable to liberty but built upon it."[25] In other words, the American people were mainly Protestants—not a particular denomination of them, but a peculiar mutation of them that had no equivalent in the Old World—and this particular species of Protestant loved the freedom to think, believe, and worship as dearly as anyone has ever loved freedom. To say that Christianity and freedom are naturally opposed to one another is thus incorrect. Such may have been the case traditionally in Christian Europe, but it was never the case in America, and some would argue it was not even the case among Christians in Europe prior to the Council of Nicaea in the year 325 (which codified the first rules of orthodoxy in the Roman Catholic Church).

Many of the Founders were not very orthodox in their personal religious beliefs. That fact does not at all mean what some secularists try to make it mean. It does not mean that the Founders were too preoccupied with life on earth, carnal pleasures, and secular concerns to ponder the heavenly and the eternal—far from it. In fact, the opposite is true. Most of them spent so much of their lives contemplating God, the Bible, theology, and the history of Christianity that it became inescapable that they would form their own opinions and conclusions about religion. Their unorthodox religious beliefs factored into the nation's founding, as already mentioned, as just one of several ideals they wanted to inculcate to the United States and its people.[26]

Well knowing the history of Western civilization, the Founders rightly feared the power of churches. They wanted to limit that power in America, but only the churches' power to influence politics. They strongly encouraged, by contrast, the churches' power to shape public morals. Nor did they want to remove its influence altogether and totally from politics; they merely wanted to temper it with Enlightenment-age reason, toleration, egalitarianism, and democracy. The fact that they made a concerted effort to limit the power of the churches implies that the churches had enjoyed a considerable amount of power up to the time of the founding. Indeed, the Puritan-based Congregational churches in New England had exercised power out of all proportion to their membership as a percentage of the population. The Anglican Church had done the same, although to a lesser degree, in the South. Despite their legal establishment and their considerable influence in the colonial, and later the national, polity, they never wielded the power to coerce to the same extent as the Catholic Church had done in Europe or the Anglican Church in England.[27]

## NATIONALISM, THE CIVIC RELIGION, AND PEER PRESSURE

To discover whether the United States was, is, or should be a Christian nation, the word *nation* must be defined. The term has been used as a synonym for *civilization* and *race*, among other terms. It may have more than one meaning, depending upon the context in which it is used. What constitutes a nation lies largely in the eye of the beholder. Some see a nation as merely an enlarged family, clan, or tribe, and certainly the roots of many nations can be traced to that element of kinship. The United States cannot claim such a simple and natural heritage, of course, because its nationality is not based primarily on blood ties among its people. Its complex racial, ethnic, and religious milieu, by default, means its national "identity" must have been artificially contrived.[28] Although it would be tempting to jump to the conclusion that the American "nation" was created by the Declaration and/or the Constitution, that would not be completely accurate because many of its defining characteristics of nationhood were in place before its official birth or christening. Its founding documents are thus more a reflection of its national identity than a creator of it. Yet both certainly codified a part of the nation's identity, making it clearer.

The nation's identity, even if difficult to define, must be recognizable as such upon seeing it. It becomes the thing that, apart from geographic boundaries, distinguishes one nation from all others. It may have evolved over time in the case of older nations (China or India, for example), but it also may have been deliberately "constructed" by its people in the case of younger nations (Germany or the United States, for example).[29] Either way, "Nations, like individuals, more or less consciously continue to present themselves in a certain pattern, a certain formula, which may sit well or ill upon their nature. . . ." This constructed identity may be more for show (such as to attract tourism) than a genuine reflection of the soul of the nation, and "to distinguish between the real and the apparent is . . . no easy matter."[30]

The difficulty in trying to discover the identity of the United States is that it is not nearly as one-dimensional as most nations' identities are. "The notion of national character is one of the vaguest and most mysterious in the history of ideas," and that is true regarding any nation.[31] How much more so the multifaceted United States, which is so large, heterogeneous, and diffuse that it seems to defy a single "national character."[32] Yet there must be something that stands out above all else that identifies one nation from another. To discover what it is requires getting beyond the mere superficial perception, which may or may not be accurate, and into the very soul or essence of a nation, and that takes some serious effort. Famed French writer Ernest Renan once gave a lecture entitled "What Is a Nation?" His basic conclusion: a group of people who share "common memories, sacrifices, glories, afflictions, and regrets" and who recognize a pantheon of heroic "ancestors." English writer John Stuart Mill said much the same thing in different words.[33] Ernest Barker has expanded upon that definition, saying a nation is what results from "a common mental substance resident in the minds of its members—common hopes for the future, and, above all, a common and general will issuing from the common substance of memories, ideas, and hopes."[34]

According to these definitions, the people who compose a nation must have some very basic and fundamental ties holding them together, such as language, religion, culture, and/or traditions. The common ties must have "a certain spread and permanence" as well.[35] Where do such ties come from? Does conscious action produce them, or instinct? Tribal and blood relations can account for only part of the answer because there has been a great amount of interbreeding and cultural exchange among populations over the centuries, especially in the last couple hundred years. And in the case of the United States, blood relations have almost nothing to do with what ties the people together as a nation. Instead, a combination of factors ties Americans together. Examples: a mutual respect between social classes (unlike the intense disdain that rich and poor, cultured and uncouth had for one another in the Old World); a vibrant economy that spans the great geographic distance between states, which keeps them from developing independently of one another in the commercial sense; the development of a public school system with a common set of goals and similar curriculums, which was slow in coming but was always progressing through fits and starts; the evolution of a continental transportation and communication/media network, which always managed to stay within one step of the westward migration of the population; a federal system of government, which made the local politics of any state at least indirectly related to every other; and a unifying religion, initially a liberal form of Calvinistic Protestantism that was accepted as a compromise, if not embraced by all as their ideal.[36]

This last factor, the unifying religion, constitutes what might be called the "national faith," which is the belief in the omnipotent, omniscient, and omnipresent monotheistic God that all Christians, Jews, and Muslims, regardless of the specifics of their doctrinal differences, would recognize as the Creator or Supreme Being.[37] Benjamin Franklin best explained the mono-God national faith when he wrote his own beliefs: "That there is one God father of the Universe. That He [is] infinitely good, powerful and wise. That He is omnipresent. That He ought to be worshipped [sic], by adoration, prayer and thanksgiving both in publick [sic] and private. That He loves such of His creatures as love and do good to others: and will reward them either in this world or hereafter. That men's minds do not die with their bodies, but are made more happy or miserable after this life according to their actions."[38] Franklin, a subtle proselytizer of whatever he believed, whether religious, political, or folk wisdom (as appeared in his *Poor Richard's Almanack*), did not merely state his beliefs for posterity, but surely hoped that by publishing those beliefs he could influence his contemporaries to agree. More than a half-century later, South Carolina Senator John C. Calhoun, one of the most influential second-generation antebellum political leaders, would proclaim in his final public address that "The cords that bind the States together are not only many, but various in character. . . . The strongest of those [are] of a spiritual and ecclesiastical nature. . . ." In other words, Calhoun considered religious ties to be the single most important factor in unifying the many states into a nation.[39]

Whatever causes the ties, they are the offspring, or end result of the forces of "nationalism" in action. Nationalism is difficult to define, but it is a concept that lies beneath the surface of the list of obvious reasons the Founders laid their lives, their families, and their fortunes on the line to create the United States. It is partly a consolidation of distinct territorial regions and their separate governments into one broad political entity that represents all. It is partly a homogenization of various tribal and/or ethnic groups into one large people with a common culture and a unique character. It is more of an ideal than a tangible thing. It is the notion that the state should be organized to reflect the likeness of the people it rules over or represents. It does not value individual rights, nor does it value loyalty to a religion or a royal family. It values the state as the embodiment of thousands or millions of individuals. It seeks its own survival as the ultimate protection of the people it governs. It has been defined as "organized selfishness" on a grand scale, which may use a God or a church to its own ends just as it may use an army or an economic system.[40]

Nationalism has also been defined as "an organic expression of an inward 'spirit'" or "soul" of the people it embodies.[41] According to this definition, a nation exists, like a living body, only as long as a spirit or soul occupies it, gives it breath and consciousness, and animates it for some purpose or purposes. If so, loss of purpose, loss of *raison d'être*, will sound the death knell of a nation. A nation then is dependent upon a purpose for its continued existence. The United States must therefore have a purpose, a reason for being. If true, what is it? What is the soul of America? What is the great animating spirit of this country? Is it to shine the beacon of Christian love and charity to the world? To spread freedom to the world by spreading democracy? To spread prosperity to the world through capitalism? All of the above? Something else?[42]

The answer must begin with the axiom that no one force or factor alone was great enough to give birth to the United States. A combination of forces and factors brought this nation into being and has sustained it to this day. For decades after the country was founded, there was no consensus on the nature of the Union, or on whether the states could or did form a common nation. Problems with continental tariffs conflicting with individual state rights in the 1830s led distinguished American Senators and orators Robert Hayne of South Carolina and Daniel Webster of Massachusetts to debate issues pertaining to the Union, including what created it, what held it together, and what threatened to destroy it. Webster became the champion of American nationalism and/or unionism (at least rhetorically) at a time when serious questions surfaced about the efficacy of continuing the Union. Webster linked nationalism and patriotism in the most effective wedding of the two since George Washington's Farewell Address, explaining the notion of being an "American" rather than a Northerner, Southerner, Bostonian, or Carolinian. Going beyond what Washington had said, Webster formulated a sort of civic religion out of the idea. The unifying faith that Webster brought to life so eloquently was invoked and put into action some thirty years later by Abraham Lincoln in the Civil War.[43] For millions of Union troops and citizens, it became a faith worth dying for. Essentially, embracing this faith required finding more value in preserving an imperfect government and saving a squabbling family of states than in taking the easier course of disunion. The differences that divided the slave South from the free North, and that separated the confederationist Democrats from the federalist Republicans, were real and serious. To choose the unifying faith of the civic religion over local exigencies took equally real and serious courage and fortitude, which Lincoln possessed to a greater degree than anyone since George Washington.[44]

This unifying civic religion that ultimately made American brothers out of Northerners and Southerners, blacks and whites, and Democrats and Republicans, should not be confused with the aforementioned "national faith" in the monotheistic God of virtually all Western civilization. The civic religion is something quite different, although complementary to the national faith. It has also been called the American "civil religion," and it is a force as strong as the belief in the mono-God.[45] It transcends the "intellectual" plane that is the abode of politics and actually rises to the "spiritual" plane where resides belief in God or gods (or other super-ideas).[46]

Although Webster may have been the first to express its existence clearly and openly, the phenomenon of the civic religion has been around since the beginning of the country.[47] It helped create the United States during the dark days of the Revolution, solidly forged the national character in the early

Republic and Jacksonian era, pulled the nation through the fiery trial of the Civil War, and continued to animate the people through America's imperialist phase and two world wars. It led the people and their representatives in government to build shrines and erect monuments to the demigod Founders, such as Washington and Jefferson, as well as their worthy progeny, including Lincoln and Theodore Roosevelt—each of whom fought for the preservation of the Union and rallied the American people to that cause. As Clinton Rossiter has poignantly asked, "Did a new nation ever have heroes quite so satisfying as the Pilgrim Fathers, the men of Jamestown, the Signers, the Framers, Benjamin Franklin, Daniel Boone, and the semi-divine Cincinnatus of the West, George Washington?"[48]

Citizens routinely make pilgrimages to their national sites of civic worship—the Washington Monument, the Jefferson and Lincoln Memorials, Independence Hall, Mount Rushmore, and such.[49] These shrines and the memories of the men they embody and the greatness of America they trumpet "are unchallenged in their broad generality; they are in the possession of virtually all Americans," a far cry from many other products of the national political system that can be "repudiated or accepted as the situation dictates."[50] Examples: political parties (never will the whole country rally around either the Democratic or Republican party); undistinguished presidents (never will there be a national shrine to the greatness of Millard Fillmore or Warren Harding); heroes in unpopular wars (the greatest hero of the Vietnam War *seems* to pale in comparison to the least hero in World War II); and divisive or sectarian religious leaders (never will the whole country embrace a John Hagee or a Jesse Jackson as a spokesman for all Americans).

In the last half-century, the civic religion has faced a host of challenges. The Marxist/Socialist/Communist ideology of the Cold War, the divisive Vietnam War, hundreds of tragic race riots, the sordid Watergate scandal, the counter-culture backlash of the 1960s, and the rise of multiculturalism, moral relativism, and alternative lifestyles, among other things, all contributed to the erosion of the civic religion, causing millions of Americans to lose their "faith" in the nation's purpose.[51] Presently it appears, however, that this falling away was more like a hiccup in the nation's history than a defining moment leading to the destruction of the civic religion. Today, American history textbooks still serve as bibles of the civic religion, preaching the gospel of national greatness.[52] There has been, however, a noticeable change in focus in the civic religion since the 1960s. It now tends to center on one of the founding principles over all the others—that of individual rights. It has come to be synonymous in the popular perception with minority rights, and is often called "civil rights," even though that term is not technically accurate.[53] Rather than the struggles of minorities to gain social acceptance by the majority and equality under the law being portrayed as a weakness of the nation, it is generally portrayed as an example of what is so great about the United States and its Constitution; they are adaptable. The battles for minority rights, which once threatened to gnaw away at the country's foundation like so many hungry termites, now strengthens the same foundation by giving more individuals a stake in the American dream, by giving them a reason to love their country and believe in its civic religion. Thus, the American dream may change over time, and it may be perceived differently by sundry groups of people, and that is a great strength of the United States and a great benefit of the American way.[54]

The indoctrination of the civic religion comes openly, not covertly, through the public schools, and has done so from the nation's inception. As Henry Steele Commager has explained it:

Noah Webster's Spellers, McGuffey's many Readers, Jedediah Morse's Geographies and Peter Parley's Histories—these and scores of books like them conjured up an America past and provided for generations of children, the common denominators, the stories and songs and poems, the memories and symbols. . . . These [and others] were the Founding Fathers of American literary nationalism, and their achievement was scarcely less remarkable than that of the Founding Fathers of political nationalism.[55]

Since then, this indoctrination has rarely been recognized for the propaganda it is. It squelches opposition, and allows only those points of view that toe the ideological line to get a fair hearing. For example, there is scarcely a pro-British or American Tory viewpoint on the War for Independence, a pro-Confederate viewpoint on the Civil War, a pro-Mexican viewpoint on the Mexican War, a pro-Spanish viewpoint on the Spanish-American War, a pro-German or Japanese viewpoint on the world wars, or a pro-Russian viewpoint on the Cold War to be found in the pages of an American history textbook. Why? Because they all opposed the American "nation"—that icon, that god of state, that entity that must be preserved at all costs, or else we get to write no more American history textbooks! Instead, in the name of liberality, comes the glorification of those who did not oppose the United States in the sense that they wanted to destroy it or defeat it, but rather those who petitioned its leaders (sometimes peacefully, sometimes violently) for a share of what it had to offer: women, racial and ethnic minorities, and non-Christians asking for and being given fair treatment and equal opportunity by a male, white, Christian-dominated polity. What is generally called "political correctness" is thus nothing more than the manifestation of the current national zeitgeist, or that which could be called the American way in action—alive, organic, and dynamic.

There are two ironies here. One, the conservatives who oppose political correctness in the name of preserving tradition lead the way in worship of the American civic religion. They and their liberal adversaries actually walk arm-in-arm, in lockstep, in a broad consensus of the ideals that make this nation worth fighting for. They are really only fighting over a few inches of territory near the vital center. Thus, the nation's citizens can disagree over the details of what constitutes the American way, but most still believe in this mysterious thing called "the American way," even if they do not all define it the same. The fraction of the population who do not believe in "the American way" are intellectuals engaged in picking the term apart semantically; the fraction that opposes it, however, are genuine America haters, true radicals and subversives among the citizenry, and they have no welcoming place here. They will generally be silenced, not by law, but by the broad consensus that might best be described as a collective shunning.[56] Two, an even greater irony is that only by preserving United States nationalism can the American people and government fulfill the supposed "national purpose" of spreading the American way or "American dream" to the rest of the globe, thus building the *Novus Ordo Seclorum* of which the Founders wrote and spoke so dreamily.[57] This new order of the ages, which ostensibly is based upon human freedom, can only be achieved by maintaining the ethereal social force of peer pressure on the American people, which is more powerful than any official government thought police or censors could ever be!

This society-shaping peer pressure is nothing new. As early as the 1830s, foreign observers noticed this shunning of unpopular opinions, of points of view out of step with the national zeitgeist, of words and ideas that did not promote the civic religion already alive and well in that day. Alexis de Tocqueville, the famed Frenchman who toured the United States and wrote a much-celebrated account of his experiences and observations here, said, "I know of no country in which there is so little independence of mind and real freedom of discussion as in America."[58] Tocqueville in no way implied that the United States government suppressed freedom of speech or thought—not at all. Instead, he meant that the American way involved majority rule, not just in its democratic political system but, more importantly, in its shaping of public opinion. Those with opinions contrary to the majority are legally allowed to speak up, but rarely will they do so because of the inevitable social castigation that follows. A French contemporary of Tocqueville, Michael Chevalier, agreed, saying that, in the United States, there existed an unwritten but well-understood "public opinion . . . to which all must conform under pain of moral outlawry."[59] The distinction he made was clearly between legal free speech and moral or socially acceptable free speech. The Englishman Lord Bryce concluded the same about freedom of thought in America in the 1880s. He laughed at Americans for thinking they were the freest people on earth. He contended that a British man actually possessed a greater degree of "private" liberty than his American counterpart, meaning a "general liberty of doing and thinking as he pleases."[60] Such statements by disinterested foreign observers, which are clearly incontrovertible, militate against the notion that freedom is America's real religion, as some have claimed.

No doubt there is a "distinction between freedom as a mere political status and freedom as a fundamental human condition."[61] Political freedom can be obtained through legislation or revolution, but freedom of thought cannot. It can still be denied by the majority of one's fellows through a tacit but very real peer pressure. This behavior that causes citizens of a nation to "go with the flow" or "run with the crowd" is neither learned nor conscious. It is instinctive and primal in man. It is a self-defense mechanism. It causes most humans to avoid antisocial behavior and unpopular opinions for their own good. It encourages "civilized" behavior, conformity, and mental homogenization, all of which are conducive to survival of the human species in the natural world. If conflict rather than consensus were the normal human condition, the species would have long ago destroyed itself. Cooperation and compromise are more natural for the vast majority of humans, and the United States exhibits these traits as well as any nation that has ever existed.[62]

"Americanism" consists of "tolerant inclusiveness" but not of the kind that caters to the lowest common denominator of society, not "vulgarity" or "primitive appetites and emotions stirred up from the bottom levels" of man's animal nature.[63] Yet the way the United States achieves the lofty degree of "civilized" behavior it does is very different than how any nation before it achieved conformity. Until the 1800s, conformity was almost universally forced upon the citizens of nations by their government or an established religion. The United States became the first to achieve the same ends without military or police force; it has done it through social peer pressure. American politicians, professors, preachers, pundits, and poets can only make suggestions. That is not to say that public policy has no effect on the way the American people think. It can and does, but again it is indirect, subtle, and unintentional. For example, in giving tax exemptions to churches, the government is sending a message that it values the contributions of religion toward making a healthy nation. Likewise, when it legalizes abortion, facilitates the distribution of birth control devices, and authorizes the teaching of sex education in middle schools, it sends a message that young people are assumed incapable of making wise choices in their sexual behavior without government supervision. So the United States, for good or ill, is and always has been engaged in the "process of belief construction and propagation," just as all other nations have; it has merely done it in a different way.[64]

If it is true that the American people have a certain civic religion and unwritten code of what is and is not acceptable thought and behavior, and it is enforced through peer pressure and only facilitated in a limited way by the government, where did this mindset come from? How did it originate? Who determined what it would be? There is no single source of origin, of course, and no specific event marks its beginning. Clearly it evolved over time but was already fairly well established by the time the United States was founded.[65] Thus, its origins can be found in the colonial era, having been shaped under the Protestant type of Christianity that prevailed at the time.[66] As one scholar put it, "The American mind was shaped in the mold of early modern Protestantism. Religion was the first arena for American intellectual life. . . ."[67] As another put it, Puritanism and democracy were the two essential ingredients in creating the "distinctly American tradition, culture, institutions, and nationality."[68] The Calvinist Puritans' idea of individual responsibility to God also helped create the quasi-democratic form of government that existed under British rule in the colonies. Then this democracy, once born, became like a child who grew up to take care of its mother: "Christianity has formed the basis for American democracy and . . . American democracy in turn has nourished a particularly pure form of Christianity."[69] Hence, Calvinist religious ideas combined with British democratic ideas—particularly (but not exclusively) the Lockean political theories of individual rights—and formed two of the bases for a uniquely American mode of thought that became founding principles of the United States. The cultivation of individuality that results from a Capitalist economic system formed a third base, but discussion of this aspect of the American way is saved for a later chapter.[70]

How much of a role did this unique Protestant mentality play in building the United States? A notable amount, to say the least—enough to prompt objective modern scholars to conclude that American culture was thoroughly imbued with "Christian civilization" and "Christian character," despite its low church membership statistics—also a topic of discussion for a later chapter.[71] As already mentioned, most of the references to God by the Founders were nonsectarian in nature, referring to the mono-God that could be embraced by all types of Protestants, as well as Catholics, Jews, and (theoretically) Muslims—but not all. Sometimes, a clearly Christian message proceeded from the Founders. Consider the following: About 80 percent of all the literature printed in the colonies calling for a revolution in the 1770s was written by Protestant clergymen who largely presented their political views in the form of sermons;[72] In George Washington's first general order to the Continental Army in 1776, he adjured his troops "to live, and act, as becomes a Christian soldier. . . ."[73] And, on the first national day of Thanksgiving called by the Continental Congress in 1777, a proclamation came forth from the United States government (written by Richard Henry Lee of Virginia, Samuel Adams of Massachusetts, and Daniel Roberdeau of Virginia) urging the American people to ask God to forgive their collective sins "through the merits of Jesus Christ" and offering a blessing upon the nation in the name of "the Holy Ghost."[74]

Do such facts prove that the United States was founded as a Christian nation? Not necessarily. They mainly indicate that some Christians played leading roles in causing the Revolution, in waging the War for Independence, and in speaking on behalf of the government and the American people. The fact that they could do these things, however, without causing a backlash or a loud outcry from nonreligious fellow Americans reveals that the peer pressure previously mentioned was already operating with powerful effect at the time of the Founding.

Such statements by Christians on behalf of the rest of the country were not confined to the Revolution years. They also popped up in later generations. Shortly before the War of 1812 began and two years before writing the "Star

Spangled Banner," Francis Scott Key delivered an address to the Washington Society in Alexandria, Virginia, in which he said that a patriotic American should "seek to establish for his country in the eyes of the world, such a character as shall make her not unworthy of the name of a Christian nation. . . ."[75] Shortly after the Civil War, the well-respected, highly popular, and long-lived political periodical *North American Review* wrote that "the American system of government is the political expression of Christian ideas."[76] Do a few isolated quotes like these prove that the United States was established as a Christian nation? Hardly. But they do show the steady continuation of that same outspoken Protestant mentality that had been present in America since its colonial era. Clearly, whether the United States was meant to be a Christian nation or not, from the beginning there were many Americans who *thought* it was. And just as clearly, there was little opposition (although some) from non-Christians to such notions.

What logical conclusion can be reached about all this? Millions of Americans grow up in the "cult of democracy,"[77] worshiping the civic religion, confusing it and intermingling it in their minds with their personal spiritual beliefs, usually of the mono-God, but sometimes a very specific Christian God.[78] While that is not necessarily a bad thing, it could be—if there were a conspiracy of politicians, professors, journalists, and the like to keep the people confused. But no such conspiracy exists (notwithstanding some isolated cases of such from time to time), and if "We, the people" are confused about the facts and are thus creating our own convoluted perception, then "We, the people" must ask ourselves an important question: Which is more important for citizens to have—national pride, love of country, and an emotional attachment/spiritual connection to the nation, or just simply getting the facts right? The one will produce a high-quality citizen body willing to fight and die to preserve the nation; the other will produce an honest citizenry and preserve truth. The former will feed the masses; the latter will satisfy the intellectual elite. One is a national defense mechanism programmed into the collective psyche; the other weakens national defense indirectly by making people question the government, the education system, and the rectitude of fighting to defend a nation entrenched in self-deception about its own character. One seems sure and steady and comforting to most Americans; the other seems to lead to conspiracy theories, chaos, and anarchy. For individual citizens today to feel and think that they are on the same page with their country's Founders, that they are carrying out their will and fulfilling their dream of America's future greatness, that they are their ideological descendants, is a powerful and motivating force for good citizenship. And good citizenship—the kind that accepts its national identity without protest—is an absolute must to perpetuate a nation's existence.

Having now come full circle, this inquiry into the American way ends back where it began: with the national paradox. There is no "one-size-fits-all" definition of the American way, American dream, or American character.[79] There seems to be one for the highly educated and well read and another for the regular folks, but that cannot be changed easily, if at all, and thus must be accepted simply as a fact of life in the United States. All definitions, to be accurate, must include three inches of common ground, which might be called the lowest common denominators: (1) an agreement or concession that the Founders embraced the concept of the mono-God of Western civilization,[80] (2) a recognition of the civic religion as being a vital and integral part of the United States from the beginning, and (3) an acknowledgment that the Founders had a definite purpose in mind for their new country—to make it with a certain character, not so Americans could selfishly possess that character, but so that they could share it with the world, for the betterment of all mankind.

To conclude, "The motivating beliefs of a nation are to be sought in its deeds and illuminated by the words of its leaders, its spokesmen and its key documents. Deeds and words do not always match, but in America they have matched often enough to show a pattern to those who look for one."[81] So while there may be multiple variations of the truth of the American way floating around out there, they all contain the same aforementioned common denominator. All of this common ground will be explored and mapped out in the coming chapters.

## Chapter 2

# The American "Israel"

## Considering the Annuit Coeptis Theory

### A CHOSEN PEOPLE

Fundamentalists tend to have difficulty looking back on their nation's history without seeing everything that happened as events on a pathway to destiny, as if they were meant to happen, supposed to happen, and ordained by God to happen.[1] Countless examples could be supplied, such as the *Mayflower* being blown off its course for Virginia and landing at Plymouth Rock in 1620 where the colony could develop independently of the ne'er-do-wells to the south; the unlikely but timely arrival of English-speaking Indians Samoset and Squanto (also a Christian) to help save the Plymouth settlers; the decision of the British military command in the American Revolution to attack first the New England colonies, which they proved unable to subdue, rather than the Southern colonies, which they could have subdued; and George Washington leading a seemingly charmed life on the battlefield, escaping capture or death against all odds more than once in two different wars. Many similar odds-defying (some would say "miraculous") quirks of fate could be cited that benefited the United States in later wars—the War of 1812, the Civil War, and World War II, particularly. Like Washington, the United States as a whole, despite its many problems over two centuries, has seemed charmed to the religiously minded, almost impervious to defeat in war, and a virtual bastion of security and stability in an otherwise chaotic world.[2]

It has become part of the civic religion not only to assume that the United States is invincible but also to think that all of the Founders were practically incapable of making a mistake in their crucial decisions during the time of nation building. Those who are steeped in the dogma of the civic religion tend to impute to the Founders prescient knowledge, to think of them as so much wiser than the rest of us that they could see the future. As such, the course the Founders charted in creating the United States government must have been, simply *must have been*, straight, true, and correct. And since they knew exactly what they were doing, they "seem to have been aware of their destination and to have been motivated by it." This is a fallacious way of thinking about the past, of course, but millions of Americans succumb to it anyway.[3] Mainly fundamentalists are culpable here, but even some nonfundamentalists are as well. The former tend to explain it in terms of the United States being God's "chosen nation" and themselves being God's "chosen people," or of the American people being "both guardian and beneficiary of a cosmic trust."[4] The latter who believe in "the American way" tend to think of it in terms of "American exceptionalism," of a nation favored by nature, geography, good timing, and other earthly factors, rather than blessed by God.[5] As Joseph Ellis put it, "What in retrospect has the look of a foreordained unfolding of God's will was in reality an improvisational affair in which sheer chance, pure luck—both good and bad . . . determined the outcome."[6] Both points of view are essentially describing the same phenomenon, despite approaching it differently.

Why do so many Americans believe in the idea or "myth," as some scholars prefer to call it, of the chosen nation and/or their country's exceptionalism?[7] Partly because it has been ingrained in Americans to think that way from childhood, through inculcation of the civic religion. For those receiving their early education in private religious schools or Sunday schools, they learn to attribute the establishment and development of this country to God's divine guidance. They find comfort in believing that this nation is special, even chosen of God. It gives meaning and purpose to their lives, or at least a greater sense of it than they would otherwise have, as well as a sense of "mission."[8] Even for secularists, it can be a source of personal pride and self-esteem to identify with such a heroic, mythical past. This "Chosen People conceit," as James Axtell has called it, did not originate after the nation's founding, but in fact can be traced all the way back through American history to Plymouth Rock and even Jamestown.[9]

Consider some examples. John Rolfe, an Anglican Christian who developed tobacco as a cash crop in the first permanent English colony in North America, Jamestown, Virginia, in 1612, believed God had a plan for the English colonizing the New World. The Pilgrims and Puritans who settled Plymouth, Massachusetts Bay, and most of the rest of New England, likewise believed God's hand was in everything they did. Their publications and sermons are full of such references. In 1653, the Puritan Edward Johnson published *Wonderworking Providence of Sion's Savior in New England*, a book whose thesis is clear from the title.[10] Thirty years later, Cotton Mather echoed the belief, and a hundred years later Samuel McClintock repeated it. On through time, many other American writers continued publishing the belief, and not all were sons of the New England Puritans; Anglicans/Episcopalians, Presbyterians, Baptists, Methodists, and others did as well. The Reverend Isaac Keith of South Carolina believed it, as did A. D. Mayo, William Aikman, Joseph Twitchell, George Bancroft, John O'Sullivan, Herman Melville, Albert J. Beveridge, William Stoughton, and the list goes on even to modern times with D. James Kennedy, Jerry Falwell, Tim LaHaye, John Hagee, Pat Robertson, and many others.[11] So much has in fact been written over the centuries about this idea of Americans being God's specially "chosen people," his "new Israel," that today it can be studied as a separate specialty area within American history.[12]

It is clear that contemporary American Christians who hold the belief in the chosen nation do so mainly because it has been passed down from generation to generation, through sermons, Sunday school lessons, and the civic religion. This raises the question, why did the earliest colonial settlers hold the belief? Some scholars find the answer in the combination of William Tyndale's 1530 English translation of the Bible and John Calvin's theology as stated in his book *Institutes of the Christian Religion* in 1536. Both placed an emphasis on the "covenant" that the mono-God made with Moses on behalf of ancient Israel (best described in Deuteronomy chapter 28), and interpreted that the covenant was not merely for ancient Israel but for *any* nation on earth at *any* time in history. Essentially, it called only for a nation to be submissive and obedient to the mono-God in order to receive the divine blessings of world power, wealth, prestige, a healthy and happy citizenry, and the like. This notion that God had offered such a cornucopia of blessings and favors to any nation willing to embrace the covenant became a fundamental tenet of the Puritan doctrine that arrived on American shores in 1630.[13]

It is not difficult to understand the rationale for this belief. Ancient Israel had two unique characteristics that were replicated by the colonists. One, other civilizations prior to the founding of ancient Israel were generally created by people who chose their god or gods. Israel, by contrast, claimed not to have chosen its god but rather to have been chosen *by* its god—and not just any god, but the one Israelites believed was the only god, the true and living mono-God. Two, other civilizations prior to that time were ruled by kings or a king-figure, such as a chieftain, who could make, repeal, and rewrite laws with either semi or total capriciousness. But the god of Israel instructed Moses to set up a government without a king, and to stick firmly to the law he had already handed down. The country would instead be ruled by "judges," who were to interpret the laws already given them by God through Moses (Deuteronomy 1:15-18). The Protestant settlers of New England copied both of those characteristics. They established to various degrees in different colonies semi-democratic, semi-federalist forms of government reminiscent of the judges of ancient Israel. They did not think of themselves as colonizing the New

World out of choice so much as being sent there to do it by God. They, like ancient Israel, were, in their own minds, on a "mission" for God.[14]

The Puritan mission was, at first, only to shine the light of the Gospel to both the Native Americans and to fellow white men. These dedicated folks manifested their sense of mission in every facet of life here, including literature, music, art, education, and technological development. Here, they could start from scratch in the wilderness and build an unadulterated civilization and put their own unique stamp upon it.[15] Over time, the mission expanded, began to merge with the civic religion in the minds of the people, and be embraced by all varieties of Americans, until, by the time of the Founding, it included creating the *Novus Ordo Seclorum*, making it a global rather than merely national mission. The fact that this mission originated during, and as a major part of, the Protestant Reformation of the 1530s, has itself become part of the "chosen people" political theology. "God, according to [Calvinistic] English writers, had delayed the colonization of the New World until after the Protestant Reformation so that America would not fall uncontested into papal darkness."[16] This argument logically concludes with the United States being created as a tool of God for the evangelization of the world. Therefore, no wonder *Annuit Coeptis*.

For the Puritans and Pilgrims, coming to the New World was much the same as the Israelites following Joshua into Canaan in search of a homeland, a place flowing with "milk and honey" (Exodus 3:8). Some of them thus referred to America as "New Canaan," or the "New English Canaan."[17] Others called it a "new Eden."[18] Just as the Israelites had to drive out the Canaanites in order to claim the land, so too did most of these English Christians feel it necessary to drive out or exterminate the Natives of America if they would not convert and assimilate. A shipwrecked crew of Frenchmen who had been captured by a barbarous group of Indians in this region soon to be called New England had supposedly warned their captors that God would take away their land and give it to a more civilized, righteous people, in accordance with Exodus 23:30. As the Natives began succumbing by the thousands to diseases, the survivors among them naturally began to fear the white man's god.[19]

Likewise, "English Separatists, already seeing their lives as part of a divinely inspired morality play, found it easy to infer that God was on their side" in the struggle for mastery over New England, as the Native population was subdued through disease and war.[20] John Mason, a Puritan who gave an account of the 1637 Pequot War in the Connecticut colony, thanked God for his "special Providences" that allowed the English settlers to defeat the Natives, saying, "Thus did the Lord judge among the Heathen, filling the Place with dead Bodies! And here we may see the just Judgment of God. . . . And was not the Finger of God in all this?"[21] John Winthrop, leader of the Massachusetts Bay Colony in the 1630s, naturally assumed that "God hath thereby cleared our title to this place. . . ."[22] With such thoughts came a "feeling of moral superiority" that has characterized American life ever since.

Interestingly, this feeling was not confined merely to the Puritans, Pilgrims, and their progeny but was just as prevalent among the Anglicans who settled America.[23] Indeed, it permeated the thirteen colonies. The only exceptions were the Quaker colony of Pennsylvania and the Baptist colony of Rhode Island, where belief in white superiority to the Natives did not prevail in the early years of settlement.

In 1776, Samuel Sherwood, a Patriot and Congregationalist pastor in Connecticut, wrote a book called *The Church's Flight into the Wilderness*, which postulated that the United States was the child brought forth by the woman named Israel in Revelation chapter 12. The child was to be God's chosen agent for building his true church in the end times. The dragon of Revelation chapter 12 represented Great Britain, which tried to swallow up the child as soon as it was born. God would not allow that to happen, of course, because of a foreordained divine plan. Therefore, the United States must win the *Revolution*; in so doing it would fulfill the *Revelation*. Upon success in the Revolution, the new nation could then proceed to complete its destiny of greatness.[24] Sherwood's compatriot Ezra Stiles agreed, calling the United States God's "American Israel," and boastfully proclaiming that its destiny was to be exalted above all other nations on earth.[25] What such theses fail to account for is that "Only one nation in the history of the world has enjoyed divine favor . . . [ancient] Israel. No nation, including the United States, can be God's 'new Israel'" because the Kingdom of God prophesied in the book of Revelation is international. It is comprised of believers "from every tribe and tongue and people and nation," according to Revelation 5:9.[26] Still, the United States could serve in the capacity of the chosen nation temporarily and, through the *Novus Ordo Seclorum*, help fulfill the ultimate global prophecy of establishing the Kingdom of God on earth.

Most adherents of the "new Israel" thesis, of course, do not mean literally that the United States now holds the exact same status with the mono-God as ancient Israel. But figuratively speaking, the United States, if obedient to the will of the mono-God, is supposedly equally entitled to the promised blessings pronounced over ancient Israel. Regardless, the perception of so many of the political and religious leaders and the public opinion shapers over the centuries that their nation is special has rendered the reality unimportant to the believers of prophecy.[27] Because of this perception, the seeds of the future American world empire—"the righteous empire"—were sown in the minds of colonists, revolutionaries, and Founders of the early republic.[28] Many who guided the destiny of the colonies saw themselves as willing pawns in the great cosmic chess game between God and the forces of evil, in which God *must* prevail and his people *must* become the instruments of the victory. By the time of the Declaration of Independence, Americans "seemingly had grasped that they were something other than [merely] thirteen states, that together they created something greater than themselves, some substitute for the [British] Empire, which they must now needs define."[29]

The Founders themselves propagated the idea of the United States being the mono-God's chosen nation. When the Puritans first arrived, they intended to be the "city set on a hill" of which Jesus spoke in Matthew 5:14. "The eyes of the world were on New England," they believed. One hundred and fifty years later, Thomas Jefferson believed the eyes of the world were still upon the United States. If the Puritans of old were supposed to shine the beacon of Christian righteousness to the world, the Founders of the United States were now supposed to shine the light of religious freedom.[30] Either way, it was up to the Americans, of all the people on earth, to carry the torch. No one else but they could do it. Both Thomas Jefferson and Benjamin Franklin used the religious imagery of Moses taking the children of Israel through forty years of trials on the way to the Promised Land, "led by a cloud by day and a pillar of fire by night," to describe the long, drawn-out, and painful process of nation building in which they were then engaged. Jefferson repeated this analogy in his 1804 presidential inaugural address.[31] At that time, the United States suffered economic hardships caused by piracy committed against American shippers on the high seas. It also felt the side effects of the Napoleonic wars in Europe. Jefferson, a man not known for his orthodoxy, used the religious imagery of which virtually all Americans were familiar to shore up public confidence in the government and his own administration.

George Washington believed in the chosen nation theory, or at least in what might be better described as the "Divine Plan for America" (author's quotes) theory. In his first inaugural address he used the imagery first employed by Adam Smith in his groundbreaking economics book *The Wealth of Nations* (1776), saying an "Invisible Hand" conducted the affairs of all men, and "Every step by which" the American people "have advanced . . . seems to have been distinguished by some token of providential agency." Because of this fact, said Washington, Americans should thank the mono-God with a "return of pious gratitude."[32]

In 1787 and 1788, several political leaders used the public debate over ratification of the Constitution to express their opinions about the nation's chosenness. Benjamin Rush, in the Pennsylvania ratification debate, said of the Constitution that he "as much believed the hand of God was employed in this work, as that God had divided the Red Sea . . . or had fulminated the ten commandments on Mount Sinai!"[33] To which Robert Whitehall replied that he "regretted that so imperfect a work should have been ascribed to God. . . ." Whitehall then offered petitions from some 750 citizens of Cumberland County who opposed ratification unless a Bill of Rights was added that would specifically protect religious freedom.[34] Benjamin Workman of Philadelphia, writing in the local *Independent Gazetteer*, agreed and went a step further. He wrote that God was responsible for the American victory in the Revolution, and God was now on the side of the Anti-Federalists who were fighting for an explicit statement of religious freedom to be added to the Constitution. He warned opponents not to get in

God's way, quoted several scriptures, and employed some very pompous religious imagery to make his point.[35]

But another Pennsylvanian, Benjamin Franklin, offered by far the most powerful argument on the subject. He wrote a letter to the editor of the Philadelphia *Federal Gazette* in which he made an analogy between the thirteen American states and the thirteen tribes of Israel.[36] Just as many among the ancient Israelites rejected the new form of government that Moses brought down from Mount Sinai to them (the Ten Commandments), so said Franklin many in each of the thirteen states now reject this new form of government embodied in the seven articles of the Constitution. He cautioned readers that he did not mean to imply that the Constitution was "divinely inspired," only that "I can hardly conceive a Transaction of such momentous Importance to the Welfare of Millions now existing, and to exist in the Posterity of a great Nation, should be suffered to pass without being in some degree influenc'd, guided, and governed by that omnipotent, omnipresent, and beneficent Ruler, in Whom all inferior Spirits live, move, and have their being."[37] Franklin's words have long rung in the ears of Fundamentalist Christians. This one well-remembered quote is enough to convince them of the correctness of their political theology. To modern secularists, this statement merely shows how un-Christian, at least unorthodox, Franklin and the Founders were. There is no mention of Jesus or any specific Christian doctrine here, just the nature-god of the Deists—a topic covered at length later in this book. For now, suffice it to say that there can be no consensus about the meaning of Franklin's statement.

The United States is, of course, not the only nation in the history of the world to think of itself as special or chosen for some great destiny by some power of the cosmos. Germany, for instance, in the late 1800s and early 1900s, thought of itself the same way and tried to fulfill its supposed destiny by acts of aggression toward other countries. Then it suffered defeat not once but twice in the world wars, and the myth came crumbling down.[38] Not only Germany, but in fact all of the imperialist nations of Europe during the Victorian Age, considered themselves to have, as British statesman Joseph Chamberlain put it, a "national mission," or as French statesman Paul Leroy-Beaulieu proffered, a "great civilizing mission."[39]

Nor does a nation, race, or people even have to be highly civilized and cultivated by modern standards of Western civilization to think of itself as special. As Ephraim Adams has explained, "The sense of destiny is an attribute of all nations and all peoples. If we could . . . grasp the emotions of [primitive] tribes and races . . . we should find that these tribes also felt themselves a people set apart for some high purpose. Possibly even the cannibal, as he sacrifices his victim, satisfies both his physical and his spiritual being," assured of the properness of his actions.[40] No modern, civilized people, of course, can really imagine themselves in the mind of the cannibal, rejoicing over a kill and thanking the gods for the providence of another meal, and feeling that divine favor has smiled on them for one more day. Yet if indeed the individual cannibal did hold that perception, and his community of fellow man-eaters shared it, to them it would be reality. Clearly, the fact that a people consider their nation special and chosen does not make it so. Yet the belief has held on in America longer and more tenaciously than in any other nation. The lack of singularity in the United States' feeling of chosenness does not negate the possibility that *something*, regardless whether of divine or merely earthly origin, is indeed and always has been different about this country than any other, possibly even exceptional. There is no denying the specialness of this young nation.[41] Stripped of all the religious mysticism then, "the true American mission commanded the United States to stand before the world, neither boastfully nor meekly, as a model republic . . . carrying the American message to a doubting world . . . quite simply . . . [by] the force of good example."[42] That is what makes it special. And that is what the *Novus Ordo Seclorum* was all about.

## RELIGIOSITY AND THE NUMBERS GAME

The oddest thing about the belief that the United States is the mono-God's chosen nation is that at the time of the founding only about 17 percent of Americans were church members.[43] Even in the most religious section of the nation, New England, more people were likely to be in the taverns on Saturday night than in church on Sunday morning.[44] In the 1730s, Boston, the hub of Puritannia, was manufacturing, selling, and/or consuming 1.25 million gallons of rum per year.[45] Although the percentage of church membership has gone up steadily ever since—to 37 percent in 1860, 50 percent in 1900, and perhaps as much as 60 percent today—the figure of less than 20 percent in 1776 is stunning to most observers the first time they encounter it.[46] Some scholars think that even the 17 percent, which is a widely accepted estimate, is overly generous. The real figure may be somewhere closer to 15 percent, with the majority of the practicing members being women, not the male pillars of the community of stereotype and legend.[47]

It is impossible to know for certain the exact percentage of Americans who were church members because not until 1850 did the U.S. Census Bureau begin collecting religious affiliation statistics, and even then some scholars have questioned the census records' reliability.[48] Then there is the fact that not all denominations or individual churches kept up-to-date records, and a few kept no written records at all.[49] What can be known for sure is that on the eve of the American Revolution, 3,005 church congregations of all types existed in the United States, serving a population of about 3 million people, for a ratio of approximately one church for every one thousand Americans.[50] Of these three thousand churches, 656 were Congregationalist and 543 were Presbyterian, making them by far the two largest denominations. A scattered assortment of Baptist, Methodist, Anglican, Quaker, and Catholic mainly composed the rest.[51]

On the surface, the numbers do not indicate a highly religious nation or a well-churched population. But then, as Franklin Littell has poignantly noted, "Nothing is more elusive in church history than honest statistics."[52] If one were to look no deeper, one might conclude, as modern secularists typically do, that the early United States was basically a "heathen nation—one of the most needy mission fields in the world."[53] Upon digging deeper, however, it becomes clear that what the numbers do *not* reveal is more important than what they *do* reveal. They do not reveal, for example, *why* the church membership statistics are so paltry. Nor do they indicate anything about the private religious beliefs or practices of the non−church members. They leave many questions unanswered, such as: Could it be that most Americans were actually quite devout, pious, or spiritual in ways that cannot be measured statistically?[54] If so, how can it be known for sure? Since absolute certainty may prove to be an impossibility here, knowing beyond a reasonable doubt ought to be a realistic goal in this study.

To begin, there are facts that mitigate the low percentage of church members being the be-all and end-all in the numbers games. For one, the majority of the books written by Americans during the Colonial Era and Early Republic were authored by Christian ministers and were theological in nature. Of the 496 authors counted in the *American Quarterly Register* in 1833, well over half were Christians writing about religious topics.[55] Certainly, the clergy were generally better educated than the American population at large. As Carl Degler has put it, the Puritans particularly, who counted more than one hundred graduates of Cambridge and Oxford among their number in the first ten years alone of settlement in New England, had produced "a remarkably well-educated ministry." They believed that "learning and scholarship were necessary for a proper understanding of the Word of God." Even during the Great Awakening of the 1730s−1740s, when itinerancy became fashionable, most of the evangelists were literate and educated, and they disapproved of illiterate and "half-learnt" fellow ministers.[56] By the time of the Revolution, there were nine colleges in the United States, eight of which were basically seminaries, and eight of which were located in what came to be called the North.[57] But were New England Christians that far out of proportion to the rest of the American population in the ratio of writers produced, or in literary skills, or even just plain literacy? Or would it be more reasonable to conclude that so many Christian writers must have been representative of the population at large? If only 17 percent of Americans were church members, how could that 17 percent produce 60 percent of all writers in the United States as late as 1833? In earlier years, thanks to Puritan influence, that figure was easily possible. By 1833, however, it seems unbelievable. Since there is no reliable way to quantify literacy rates from that era, one can only speculate that surely there were more Bible readers and believers in the United States than there were church members.

Another mitigating fact is that at the time of the founding all thirteen states had religious requirements for office holding in their constitutions. Variations among the requirements were few and minor, and all fit under the umbrella of the Judeo-Christian philosophy in one way or another. They range from the broadest, that a belief in the mono-God was essential, to narrower—that a belief in Christ was necessary—to even more narrow—that a belief in Protestantism was required—to the narrowest—that a specific church was the only acceptable one. New York became the first to abolish the religious requirement, and Virginia the second in 1786.[58] Such requirements indicate that, to the colonial/Revolutionary political leaders at the state level, the appearance of being religious must have been quite important. They do not prove, however, whether the common people of the states felt the same way.

There are actually several identifiable reasons that church membership probably does not accurately reflect the religiosity of the American people at the time of the founding. For one, the primitive conditions on the ever-moving western frontier, where a sizeable minority of Americans lived and where fewer church buildings stood than the need demanded, made membership and attendance an impossibility for many pioneers. Given the hardships on the frontier, the sparseness of population there, and the lack of communication and transportation networks, it would have been a "major miracle if the majority of colonial Americans had been churchgoers."[59]

For another, some denominations had stringent requirements for membership that included property ownership or some other form of high standing in the community, which effectively disallowed membership of the poor. Essentially, the prerequisites were designed to keep the riff-raff out of the church. The Puritans are the best example of a church group with highly selective criteria for membership. They essentially demanded an outward show of righteousness, which not only included the perfunctory manner of dress, speech, Sunday piousness/Lord's Day observance, and sobriety, but also included thrift, industriousness, and material prosperity. Many Americans who lived among the Puritans did not qualify, mainly for the lack of material prosperity, which according to Calvinist doctrine, was a sign of God's favor, and therefore an identifying characteristic of the Elect. In every other way except church membership these people were Puritans. But they could not be counted as church members. It was a problem since, ostensibly, the idea behind Christianity was to grow the number of people in the Kingdom. How to do that without lowering the standards was a dilemma. In 1662, the Puritans began formulating the solution. They devised the "Half-Way Covenant," which made some people nominal members who otherwise did not qualify, until such time as they could qualify.[60] Even then, they were required to sit in the back of the church and to understand their low station, and then to act accordingly—in humility and deference to the high-standing members.[61] Among the Pilgrims in 17th-century Plymouth, the prerequisites for membership were even more restrictive. The colonists there were divided into four categories—the Freemen, who ran the government; the Inhabitants, who owned property but were not allowed to vote, hold office, or join the church; the Sojourners, who were only welcome in the colony on a probationary basis pending their proving themselves worthy of staying; and indentured servants, who had no rights or privileges of any kind.[62]

This cause of low membership seems the strangest to the modern psyche because today, in most Christian denominations, membership is usually by individual choice. Churches today rarely turn down anyone who wants to join, provided the prospective members are willing to comply with the fundamental tenets of a particular denomination's faith. They are generally open to anyone, regardless of family background, social status, economic class, or similar factors (the notable exception being race in some southern churches, and even that tradition is rapidly dying out). Yet this selectivity and discrimination does not look so strange after all when considering that during the same era qualifications for voting likewise limited the franchise to less than 10 percent of the American population.[63]

A third (and related) reason for the deceptively low membership statistics is that some believers saw hypocrisy in the orthodox church members, which turned them away from organized religion. For example, watching "church officers plucking wealth because of their connections" frustrated the meek and lowly of America.[64] In many cases, however, the nonchurched did not have their own personal feelings toward God or the Gospel destroyed by such hypocrisy, just their desire to associate with the hypocrites. Their collective response to the nationwide Protestant revival of the 1730s and 1740s, called the Great Awakening, is evidence of that. Therein a sizeable contingent of the poor and downtrodden in colonial America thronged to hear the impassioned sermons of George Whitefield and fellow evangelists. So great was the excitement when Whitefield's evangelical show came to town that locals would practically trample one another to get within eyesight and earshot. Nathan Cole of Connecticut submitted in his first-hand account how he was so eager to hear Whitefield that

I with my wife soon mounted the horse and went forward as fast as I thought the horse could bear; and when my horse got much out of breath, I would get down and put my wife on the saddle and bid her ride as fast as she could and not stop or slack for me except I bade her, and so I would run until I was much out of breath and then mount my horse again. . . . every moment to get along as if we were fleeing for our lives, all the while fearing we should be too late to hear the sermon, for we had twelve miles to ride double in little more than an hour. . . .[65]

Whitefield and fellow revivalists did not so much proselytize the already-churched or the wealthy as the unchurched and spiritually disfranchised. The reaction was overwhelming, and it stirred the beginnings of the explosive growth of mainstream Protestantism in the coming decades.[66]

Fourth and fifth, the coercive aspects of church membership in the European countries from whence came these early generations of Americans left many immigrants so glad that they had escaped one church that the thought of joining another had no appeal for them.[67] The Anglican Church in America had the same monopoly in some colonies, technically, as it enjoyed in England and thus the same opportunity to compel membership and participation. But rarely did Anglican leaders do so. They were "lazy church organizers" who, because of their monopoly, saw no benefit in working hard to organize the Americans into a well-oiled church machine. Just knowing they had the power of compulsion seems to have been enough for them. Besides, when they made a concerted effort to compel Americans to do anything, it was to pay taxes to support the Church, not to make them attend services. Undoubtedly, thousands upon thousands of Americans appreciated the Anglican Church's slackness in their missionary and evangelical activities. They did not want to join, and the Church did not make the effort to force them.[68]

Sixth, the skepticism that the Enlightenment bred made many Americans unsure of their beliefs and thus disinclined to attend an orthodox church, although the effect fell far short of turning them completely against religion.[69] While a strong strain of Rationalist thinking was prevalent among the Founders, almost no cases are known of raging animosity toward churches, pastors, or Christianity in the founding generation of Americans—a far milder reaction than what appeared in France to the same stimuli during the French Revolution. Rather, the prevailing state of mind, even in the Puritanical bastion of New England, was one of "marked religious indifference."[70] The same Enlightenment-era writers who influenced France so heavily and violently, most of whom were Deists, agnostics, and skeptics (Voltaire, Rousseau, and Hume, among others), were widely read and discussed in America. Yet their writings did not produce the same type of radicalism or anti-Christian feeling here. Why the difference? Was there something in the American national character that kept the lid locked tightly on that Pandora's box? Or was there something different about the circumstances the French found themselves in?

Actually, both were true. While English political theorists and French *philosophes* were busy formulating the "social contract" theory of government, Americans preferred to focus instead on fulfilling their end of the "covenant" with the mono-God of ancient Israel, as defined in Deuteronomy chapter 28.[71] If the social contract plan would help facilitate the fulfillment of the covenant—and many of the Founders certainly thought it would—then Americans were all for it. The French, by contrast, had no such notion of a covenant with God. They were, if anything, mad at the same God because of the abuses and excesses the Catholic Church in France had indulged in over the centuries.[72]

After considering all these mitigating factors, the great American paradox once again surfaces, demanding consideration. The nation was not Christian through and through at the time of the founding. It had a strong element of Christianity in it, but that religion's orthodox churches had nothing like an absolute grip upon all the people. While it is true, for example, that General George Washington ordered compulsory church attendance for the Continental

Army, it is equally true that not all soldiers appreciated it. Joseph Plumb Martin, a private under Washington's command, recalled with disdain the Thanksgiving church service he was forced to attend. The meal consisted of a bowl of rice and a spoonful of vinegar. The sermon consisted of admonitions for the soldiers to be honest and to commit no unprovoked acts of violence against anyone. Martin resented the mandatory meeting, the modest message, and the meager meal.[73]

Likewise, while it is true that there was only one church for about every 1,000 Americans at the time of the founding, it is equally true that the American people had a propensity for throwing together a new church edifice every chance they got, just as they still do. As the French visitor to the United States Hector St. John de Crèvecoeur wrote in his *Letters from an American Farmer* in 1782, "When any considerable number of a particular sect happen to dwell contiguous to each other, they immediately erect a temple, and there worship the Divinity agreeably to their own particular ideas. Nobody disturbs them." He was struck, moreover, with the American Christians' "zeal" for going about this religious business, which certainly was not the case in France.[74]

Just how religious, nonreligious, or sacrilegious, then, was the average American at the time of the founding? Did such a creature as an "average American" even exist? Does one even exist today? Clearly there are diversities among the American people, and always have been, that are as starkly contrasting as night and day—it is the great American paradox. Yet, as already shown, there have likewise always been ties that hold the American people together. These ties do not make them think as one on every single point of politics or religion, but they provide a basic set of principles that are shared widely enough to constitute a common American frame of mind. The basic principle concerning church membership and attendance was, as it still is, that both are good and fine, and they are always good and fine for the other person, but not necessarily for "me." In other words, almost all Americans of the founding generation would have agreed that churches served a high and worthy purpose in this nation, but not all would have agreed that becoming a member was in their personal best interest at the moment. The bottom line? "There is ample evidence that most Americans are and long have been religious in the rather undoctrinaire way that . . . [is] beneficial for democracy."[75] It is an idea that Clinton Rossiter has called quite accurately "Christian rationalism."[76]

"Christian rationalism" indeed seems a fitting description of the predominant American frame of mind at the time of the founding. It does not, however, continue to describe the American mind-set far beyond that inaugural generation of the United States. By the mid-1800s, a different mentality had emerged. Church membership had more than doubled, and it had happened among a generation not born in European nations with compulsory church attendance. It had happened among a generation born and raised in the United

States under the First Amendment's separation doctrine—a topic covered in depth later in this study. By mid-century, the United States boasted a population of 23 million people and 14.2 million seats in its churches. That was roughly a 65 percent accommodation capacity, larger even than England's impressive 57 percent at that same time.[77] The churches had gone from "virtual extinction" at the time of the Revolution (and largely because of the Revolution) to the bulwark of a thriving religious enterprise, perfectly in keeping with the capitalist economic system and democratic political system of the United States—chosen people or not, new Israel or not.[78]

## Chapter 3

# The American "Pie"

## *Considering the History of* E Pluribus Unum

### INGREDIENTS

The United States has been called the "great American melting pot." For decades that description went unchallenged. It seemed to make sense. It sounded appropriate. It became part of the civic religion to think of the country that way. Eventually, however, it became just a cliché, and people began to question whether the metaphor of a melting pot was accurate. A melting pot, after all, would homogenize various ingredients into a uniform new substance. Perhaps the United States did not really do that, at least not since the civil rights movement and the advent of multiculturalism from the 1960s on. Perhaps a more reasonable description of the United States would be "a boiling cauldron of conflict."[1] Or, perhaps the United States was actually more like a stew kettle. Throw in an assortment of disparate ingredients and come out with a new dish, but one in which each ingredient is still identifiable and has a flavor of its own.

The popular song of the early 1970s called "American Pie" by Don McLean has provided yet another descriptor of the United States. Technically meaningless in that song, the term *American pie* nevertheless can be used as a literary device for the purpose of this discussion.[2] Perhaps the United States is the great American *pie* rather than the great American *melting pot*. Although dissection of clichés such as the "melting pot" and "American pie," and of metaphors that compare nations to food dishes, may seem so trite as to border on absurd, such language surgery can actually be quite instructive, and should therefore be indulged in briefly. Whatever terminology one chooses, there can be no doubt that the United States is composed of many various ingredients. Discussion of these ingredients and how they came together over more than 150 years of Colonial American history is central to answering the question, "was the United States meant to be a Christian nation?"

If the United States were a real food dish—be it a pie, a stew, or whatnot— the nation's government and constitutional structure would be the container holding all the ingredients together. The national character and purpose would be the sauce, the civic religion and the orthodox religions would be the spices, and the people and ethnic groups would be the meat, potatoes, and assorted vegetables. The United States is thus dependent upon its diversity for its existence, but it is equally dependent upon the compatibility of its individual parts. In a food dish, cooks would not likely put a cup of salt in a chocolate cake, or a scoop of ice cream on a pot roast; those ingredients are not compatible. The various ethnic and religious groups of the United States have often seemed just as incompatible over the centuries. Yet, unlike the food metaphor, the ingredients have developed a tolerance for one another over time, if not a compatibility. Is it because the ingredients have changed? Or is it because the taste of the cooks has changed? Maybe the taste of the American cooks (the Founders) was always different from that of most other cooks (the government builders in the Old World). Or maybe this metaphor is being employed altogether incorrectly. Perhaps the Founders decided the ingredients do not necessarily have to mix; they can be taken one at the time like a seven-course meal, and yet still be part of the same meal.

Any metaphor or analogy if dissected this way will eventually break down. Besides, getting caught up in the semantics and technicalities of the melting pot or American pie terms is not helpful in this discussion. When focusing on the actual issue of American religious, cultural, ethnic, and intellectual diversity, it seems clear that the United States is a nation built upon the principle of *E Pluribus Unum*, which was part of the Founders' grand design to help fulfill the *Novus Ordo Seclorum*. The Founders, however, were essentially cooking without a recipe. They had no pattern to go by and no guarantee that the final product would actually be found desirable to the palate—the intellectual and spiritual taste of the consumers. They were in fact experimenting. Practically the whole history of the world before them pointed to the impossibility of the success of their experiment. Yet, that same history compelled them to try it. If it worked, it really would usher in the *Novus Ordo Seclorum*. If it did not, would the American people really be any worse off for the effort?

The problems with developing compatibility or even tolerance among the smorgasbord of Americans was painfully evident from the beginning. First, not every Founder even agreed on how to define the problem, much less on its solution. Conventional wisdom said that the majority, whether Christian, agnostic, atheist, or otherwise, must tolerate the minority. Thomas Paine, the great American patriot famous for writing "Common Sense" (the pamphlet most responsible for persuading the Founders to declare independence from Britain in 1776), disagreed. He once said "tolerance" is not the polar opposite of "intolerance," as it would initially seem. Tolerance of someone or something is only slightly different and barely better than intolerance because, while they produce dissimilar fruit, both stem from the same root. Intolerance obviously results from people believing they have a right to withhold freedom of choice from others, while tolerance is the result of people claiming to have the power to allow others freedom of choice. Paine, a true Enlightenment-age secular Rationalist who believed firmly in Lockean "natural rights," thought no man could control another's conscience, and therefore, no man should try to control another's words or actions. If nature gave freedom of choice, only nature could take it away.[3]

A second problem was that "toleration is at least a cousin of indifference" in the minds of many devout Christians.[4] How could true believers make such a concession without compromising their own beliefs? How could they tolerate unbelievers, or believers of strange doctrines, and stay true to their own understanding of their responsibility to God? Essentially this was a problem of insecurity in the spirit and immaturity in the mind of the believers. They lacked the spiritual maturity, the inner mental fortitude, so to speak, to cope with those beliefs or lack of beliefs that challenged their own.[5] The notion that they must tolerate those unlike themselves rather than change them or at least try to proselytize them seemed anti-Christian, and specifically anti-"city set on a hill" and anti-"light of the world" in their immature thinking. Yet the Founders intended to force them by law to accept having their light snuffed out and their city razed from the hillside. They would now get what they had been giving. Not surprisingly, they did not think this was a positive development.

Although most Americans today take it for granted that a diversity of religions is a good thing for society, colonial- and Revolutionary-era Americans, by and large, did not agree. As early as 1704 the South Carolina Assembly stated that "It hath been found by experience that the admitting of persons of different religious persuasions hath often caused great contentions and animosities in this Province and hath very much obstructed the public business."[6] To the Anglican establishment of South Carolina, non-Anglicans were like a cup of salt in the cake. Nor were the Carolinians or the Anglicans exceptional in that regard. The Puritans of the various New England states were of like mind. Each church group, especially the larger ones like Anglicans and Puritans, believed in only "a single correct moral code," and to compromise on it was to frustrate the will of God.[7] "Whatever men believed" in the Colonial era, "they believed with greater devotion than is common today," or so it seems.[8] This straightjacket of right and wrong made religious fanatics of otherwise sane men and turned them automatically into theocrats. As the Puritan pastor of Ipswich, Massachusetts, Nathaniel Ward put it, "If the devil might have his free option, I believe he would ask nothing else but liberty to enfranchise all false religions and to embondage the truth."[9]

It has been said that a fanatic is "a man who does all God would do if God had all the facts."[10] Fanaticism is both the breeder of theocracies and the offspring of them. The remedy for fanaticism is, of course, to take away the power of the fanatic and subject him to persecution, for only then will he plead for tolerance, and then only for his own sake. Once toleration takes hold in a land, the people themselves will not easily relinquish it. To do otherwise would be to cast away the power to keep the peace and to breed a whole new generation of fanatics. Getting the concept of nationwide toleration to take hold in the new United States was the challenge for the Founders. Even getting it to take hold at the state level proved difficult, although that is ultimately what made it possible at the national level. The change was a slow process, and one not complete even at the end of the 18th century and beginning of the nineteenth.

It would be a stretch to say that "most" Americans were guilty of the spiritual immaturity of fanaticism at the time of the founding, but certainly not everyone had the progressive mindedness of Nathaniel Ames on the issue of toleration. Writing in his *Almanack of 1767*, Ames wryly remarked that "To defend the Christian religion is one thing, and to knock a man on the head for being of a different religion is another."[11] Indeed. But as common sense as that statement sounds to modern ears, it was practically a radical statement to the established church crowd of that era. Basically, the American people divided over toleration and where to draw the line on it, although a precise breakdown of the people in these opposing camps by percentages is impossible to ascertain.

## RECIPE

Continuing the metaphor of making an American pie, toleration is analogous to the cooking time. After all the ingredients have been mixed, the food dish must be cooked—slowly over a low flame for many hours. Likewise, the United States did not simply spring to life in 1776 with toleration already a *fait accompli*. It had to be developed over a matter of a century and a half, and patience was the key to getting it right. There was little in the history of Christendom from which colonial Americans could draw inspiration in developing toleration. What colonial Americans had instead—particularly the Puritans— was a set of directions for establishing a theocracy. The term *theocracy* originated with the Jewish scholar Josephus in the first century of the Christian era. He used it to describe the blending of government and monotheism that ancient Israel implemented under the Mosaic law. It called for draconian punishments for both sins against God and crimes against one's fellow man. It served as an example for virtually all Christianity-based nations for roughly the next 1,750 years. Intolerance was thus deeply rooted in the hearts and minds of most colonial Americans.[12]

The great irony and tragedy of intolerance among Christians over the millennia is that the interrogation of Jesus on the day of his crucifixion became the "prototype for all heresy trials" in Western civilization thereafter.[13] Most

of the original Apostles were murdered for being Christians, as were multi-
tudes in the first few generations. Notable martyrs include Polycarp, murdered
by Jews and Romans in concert in Smyrna in the year 156, and Justin Martyr,
killed in Rome by the Roman prefect in the year 165.[14] Although a few coura-
geous souls arose to advocate tolerance in the early years of the church, such
as Tertullian, Lactantius, and Ambrose of Milan, they always constituted a
decided minority.[15] Toleration of Christianity came slowly and in small incre-
ments. In the year 261, Gallienus issued the first Edict of Toleration in the
Roman Empire, Galerius reiterated it in 311, and Constantine legalized Christianity in the Edict of Milan in 313.[16] Once the Roman Catholic Church
became entrenched as the arbiter of power in Europe, the way of the heretic
grew even harder. Male heretics were commonly disemboweled and quartered,
while females were burned . . . since, after all, burning was a more merciful
death![17] The crusades of the 1100s and 1200s showed the determination of
the popes, bishops, and their subordinates to root out opposition, as did the Inquisition, which lasted from the early 1200s to the late 1700s (and was still
burning heretics at the stake to the very end), and the Counter-Reformation
headed up by the Jesuits in the 1500s. Although an occasional heretic, such as
Marsilius of Padua, author of *Defensor Pacis*, pleaded for toleration during
those centuries, it mattered not to the Church.[18]

The Protestant Reformation did almost nothing to reform intolerance. It was
designed initially (if it can be said to have had a design) to reform the corrupt
aspects of Catholicism, not to break with the Roman Church completely. At
least that was true in the case of Martin Luther in Germany. The Reformation
of course had several different components. There were actually four distinct
dissenting movements going on simultaneously in the early-to-mid-1500s:
Lutheranism, Calvinism, Anglicanism, and Anabaptism. The first three can be
lumped together and called the "conservative" wing of the Reformation, while
the Anabaptists comprised the "radical" wing. What this means in essence is
that the first three basically accepted one another's legitimacy (with notable
exceptions) at the same time that each was seeking its own legitimacy via recognition from the Roman Catholic Church. The Anabaptists were never
accepted, however, by either the three conservative Protestant groups or the
Catholics. This mutual disrespect of Anabaptists by Catholics and other Protestants gave everyone a common enemy, so to speak—a common focus for
continued intolerance.[19] It should be pointed out that "The term 'Anabaptist'
was applied to a wide range of small, fluid, quite diverse groups, some with a
strong biblical orientation, others mystically inclined."[20]

Some early Protestant theologians, including Martin Luther, Menno Simons,
and Erasmus of Rotterdam (who was not a "Protestant" per se but a Catholic
"protester" of the corruption in the Church), believed that to force Catholicism on
people by way of law was to follow the spirit of Anti-Christ.[21] Referring to the
popes of the high Middle Ages up to his own time who used their spiritual authority for temporal power, Luther said, "the very Anti-Christ sits in the temple of

God and the Roman Curia is the synagogue of Satan. . . . What is Anti-Christ if such . . . is not?"[22] That does not mean Luther tolerated other dissenters, however. He certainly did not. Once he succeeded in gaining a wide acceptance of his own brand of Christianity, he sought to help the Catholic Church wipe out other Protestants in Germany.[23] Meanwhile, Simons asked, "Where did the Holy Scriptures teach that in Christ's kingdom the Church, conscience, and faith, should be ruled by the sword of the magistrate?"[24] Whether he too would have turned intolerant over time cannot be known for sure. He never received the same level of acceptance for his faith as Luther and thus never got the opportunity.

Other early Protestant theologians, including John Calvin, were intolerant of other dissenters from the beginning. Concerning those "subversives" who "stir up disorder," Calvin urged the English Duke of Somerset to coerce them to comply with the Calvinist tenets of the faith "by the avenging sword which the Lord has committed to you" because "God Himself . . . set the king upon his throne and installed you as Protector. . . ."[25] Calvin wrote these words in 1548. One can only wonder how he would have felt when the temporal powers of England used the "avenging sword" to try to root out his followers in the 1593 "Act Against Puritans," which authorized imprisonment for Puritans "until they shall conform and yield themselves."[26] Meanwhile, Calvinists in Geneva used the "avenging sword" to burn the Anabaptist and anti-Trinitarian Michael Servetus at the stake. The "Sentence Pronounced on Michael Servetus," October 27, 1553, affords a glimpse into the thinking of the Calvinists, which undoubtedly carried over into the brand of Calvinism that flourished in the American colonies a century later:

You have [with] malicious and perverse obstinancy sown and divulged . . . opinions . . . by which many souls have been ruined and lost, a thing horrible, shocking, scandalous, and infectious. . . . and so you have obstinately tried to infect the world with your stinking heretical poison. . . . we now in writing give final sentence and condemn you, Michael Servetus, to be bound and . . . attached to a stake and burned with your book to ashes.

The stated purpose of this harsh punishment was to make him "an example to others who would commit the like."[27] Thus Calvinists showed themselves to be censors of speech and press, as well as judges, juries, and executioners of the violators from the beginning.

At the same time that Calvinists were burning Servetus, Calvinism was being grafted into the Anglican Church by young King Edward I, son of Henry VIII, the church's founder. Intolerance was nothing new for Henry VIII or the Anglicans even before Calvinism arrived on the scene. Henry VIII put some twenty-three people to death for various types of heresy just to get his denomination started and stabilized. He undoubtedly would not have tolerated the Calvinism of his own son, Edward, had he been alive to deal with it. Edward's reign did not last long; he died at age fifteen. The crown then passed to his Catholic half-sister, Mary, whose reign was equally short, and especially noted for its intolerance of all types of Protestantism. In 1558, her Anglican half-sister Elizabeth took the throne and tried to purge both Catholicism and "hot" Protestantism (Calvinism and Anabaptism) from the Church of England. She considered the Anglicanism of her father Henry VIII to be a middle-of-the-road religious option that both Catholics and Calvinists could accept—at least reluctantly, if not enthusiastically. It kept relative peace for many years. It allowed the Puritan faith to grow, so long as the Puritans did not cross the line and challenge the orthodoxy of the Church, which did happen occasionally.[28]

Around the same time as the Anglican Elizabethan government passed the 1593 "Act Against Puritans" (which mainly just compelled church attendance and conformity),[29] England began its quest to colonize North America. The timing was perfect. Shortly after English colonization proved a successful enterprise in Virginia under the Anglican King James I, who wanted to "harry" the Puritans "out of the land," religious dissenters began looking at the New World as a potential home.[30] The government of "High" (Catholicized) Anglican King Charles I, who came to the throne in 1625, was glad to rid Albion of the unwanted minority by supporting their colonial dream. In 1630, seventeen English ships brought over about two thousand Puritans to settle the Massachusetts Bay Colony. Over the next eleven years, some 21,000 Puritans would come over in what came to be known as the "Great Migration."[31]

Then the English Civil War broke out in 1641, and the migration stopped abruptly. Charles I caused the war, which was mainly political in nature, but it pitted Catholics and High Anglicans against Protestants of all other types. There were Presbyterians—Calvinists who merely wanted to restore the power of Parliament after Charles I had destroyed it and to purge the Anglican Church of Catholic rituals; Independents—Calvinists who likewise wanted to restore the power of Parliament and purify the Church but also wanted to execute Charles I for crimes against his country (neither favored toleration of other religious groups); and Levellers—who were the most liberal, and who wanted both political and religious changes, including complete toleration for all the various Christian sects in England. In 1648, as the Civil War came to an end, and as the various groups sought to find their place in the coming new sociopolitical order, the leader of the Levellers, John Lilburne, wrote *The Foundation of Freedom, or an Agreement of the People*. It was too far ahead of its time in espousing the democratic "social contract" idea soon to be made famous by later Rationalists in the Age of Reason.[32] The social contract, and thus codified religious tolerance, would have to wait another forty years, until passage of the English Bill of Rights.

The leader of the Protestant parliamentary majority (and especially of the Independents) was Oliver Cromwell, who was tolerant enough of all types of Christianity that critics accused him of being an Anabaptist. He was not really an Anabaptist, but he and the Independents, who were the prototypes for later American Congregationalists, did share certain commonalities with Anabaptism, favoring the localization of power in church affairs and lacking a broad institutional structure or hierarchy.[33] Victorious in the Civil War, Cromwell enjoyed a short tenure as leader of England, serving not as a king but as "lord protector" (a king substitute), during which time he made Puritanism legal and fashionable. After his death, the crown passed to a legitimate or traditional ruler, Charles II, in what was known as the Restoration. He once again tried to purge both the Anglican Church and Parliament of Puritans. He passed the Test and Corporation Acts of 1673 for that purpose, but his efforts failed as he conflicted with the Latitudinarians of the Church, who favored widening the tolerance of Puritans ever so slightly. Control of the government then passed to the Protestants William and Mary in the Glorious Revolution of 1688, and within two years the English Bill of Rights and the Toleration Act were passed. England's long, bloody, and ugly struggle over religious freedom was finally just about over . . . although the Test and Corporation Acts stayed on the books until 1829, unenforced and unenforceable, yet present, and a source of irritation for English people seeking true separation of church and state.[34]

## MOVE TO AMERICA, SHAKE WELL

Meanwhile, the Puritan experiment at creating a city set on a hill continued. Puritans, to state the obvious, never wanted an American pie. Nor did they envision a seven-course meal. They wanted bread and water for themselves and for everyone else too. For about one hundred years, they "banned, whipped, harangued, and hanged" dissenters in a futile "effort to preserve and protect" their peculiar way of life in New England.[35] The irony, of course, is that the Puritans were themselves dissenters.[36] They were even called the "Dissenters" and the "Nonconformists" back in old England.[37] They were "protestants" among Protestants. It was, in fact, their unwillingness to accept the carnality and materialism of the Orthodox Anglican Church in England that made them a distinct sect.[38] They did not even approve of the Anglican practice of observing Christmas because they saw it as just one more excuse for half-hearted professing Christians to get drunk and rowdy.[39]

The Puritans could dish it out, so to speak, but they could not take it. They suppressed dissent at every turn throughout the 1600s. Roger Williams is the most famous dissenter among them who suffered the consequences of his beliefs. He is a study in contradictions. Although a Puritan in name and a resident of the Massachusetts Bay Colony initially, he was closer to the Separatists of Plymouth Rock in doctrine, in the sense that he did not want to purify the Church of England, which he labeled a type of Anti-Christ.[40] While generally considered the founder of the Baptist Church in America, he was only temporarily a Baptist himself. He spent the last years of his life as a "Seeker."[41] Williams is often thought of today, like so many other Protestants over the centuries, as a hypocrite because he called for freedom of religion for himself and his band of believers while denying it to others. Yet, he actually set an example of the most primitive form of toleration by demonstrating civility toward his opponents. His goal was to achieve mutual respect between antagonists. He did not base his opposition to the Quakers, for instance, on what they believed or said or how they worshiped, but rather on their attitude (as he perceived it) toward other Christians. He considered them condescending and sarcastic in tone when arguing the Bible. When he tried to debate them in a civil way, they got emotional and began shouting him down and throwing out *ad hominem* attacks.[42]

In 1636, Williams left Massachusetts Bay to form his own colony, Rhode Island, along with a like-minded fellow named John Clarke, who was just as influential in formulating the idea of separation of church and state as his more famous associate Williams.[43] There Williams wrote his famous 1644 treatise *The Bloudy* [sic] *Tenet of Persecution*, which outlined his views on separation of church and state. He made a subtle distinction between the first four commandments of the Decalogue, which deal with man's responsibility toward God, and have no place being mixed with governance, and the last six, which deal with man's responsibility toward man, and which form a basis for civil law.[44] As he saw it, people could disagree over how to interpret or apply the first four commandments, because they were a matter of conscience, as long as they did not violate one of the other six commandments in doing so. Violation of one of the last six commandments meant automatically that someone had been hurt, defrauded, or victimized, and government had a responsibility to prevent victimization or make recompense for it. Needless to say, the Puritan theocrats of Massachusetts Bay could not appreciate Williams's argument. John Cotton, the preeminent religious figure of the colony in the 1630s and 1640s, countered Williams in his *The Bloudy Tenet Washed and Made White in the Blood of the Lamb*, saying that the first four commandments should indeed be enforced by the government. Williams responded to Cotton with *The Bloudy Tenet Yet More Bloudy*, and the feud over separation of church and state was on.[45] (Here we are now, nearly four centuries later, and it obviously still rages as strong as ever.)

After Williams came Anne Hutchinson, whom John Winthrop described as an "American Jezebel," after her 1637 heresy trial. This 45-year-old wife, mother of fourteen, and devout Christian did not champion separation of church and state but rather became the most famous victim of the lack of it in colonial America. Believing that God had spoken to her personally—in spirit only, not in an audible voice—she shared her own unorthodox version of the Gospel with those who would listen. She was charged, tried twice, found guilty, excommunicated, and banished from Massachusetts. Moving to Rhode Island while pregnant, she gave birth to a stillborn baby. Cotton, Winthrop, and their sycophants used the stillbirth as evidence of God's punishment of this woman for her pride and rebelliousness, thus justifying their own theocracy. Nor was Hutchinson's time on earth thereafter any better. Her husband died, and then she and five of her children were murdered by Indians on Long

Island in what was then part of New Amsterdam, to which the Puritan theo-crats gave a loud see-we-told-you-so.[46] Meanwhile, Hutchinson's brother-in-law John Wheelwright, who also believed and preached that God spoke directly to him, was likewise tried, convicted, excommunicated, and expelled from Massachusetts.[47]

Hutchinson and Williams were the first and therefore most famous dissent-ers among the Puritans, but by no means the last. In 1648 in Connecticut, a second generation colonial New Englander named John Rogers was born. He was destined to inherit the mantle as the next great dissenter in Puritannia and the next great protagonist for separation of church and state. Giving rise to a cadre of followers known as the Rogerenes, he suffered imprisonment for his outspoken views.[48] But by this time, the late 1600s, disenchantment had arisen toward the theocracies of both of the major Protestant groups in America, the Puritans and the Anglicans. This led to the rapid increase of Antinomian sects (those who believed God spoke directly to them as opposed to merely speak-ing through the Bible), such as Quakers and Rogerenes. Antinomianism grew slowly, and it never quite caught up with the orthodox Calvinists (who took the view that God speaks only through the scriptures) during the colonial era. Yet it grew fast enough and in large enough numbers in the early 1700s to begin to soften up the rigidity of the mainline churches. Indirectly, it helped pave the way for the emergence of all kinds of new heretical doctrines, sects, and practices, such as intellectually based Unitarianism and Deism, the emo-tionally based Methodists and evangelical revivalists of all stripes, and the Great Awakening of the 1730s–1740s. Likewise, it helped lay the foundation for the American dissent that caused the break with England in 1776.[49]

The growth of Antinomianism alone probably would not have caused such radical changes in such a short period of time. The Puritans contributed to their own demise and to the abolition of theocracy in America by their attempt to purge dissent in the form of witchcraft in the infamous Salem witch trials of 1692. The Puritans did not invent the witch hunt, of course. Witch hunts can be traced in history as far back as the Roman Empire in the year 373. About fifty years after that, Rome began the practice of burning witches. In the Middle Ages, the Spanish Inquisition hunted witches along with other dissenters. In England, King Henry VIII, founder of the Anglican Church, made witchcraft an official and separate form of heresy in 1541. King James I published a book about witchcraft called *Demonology* in 1603, but it never rose in celebrity quite the same as the *Malleus Maleficarum*, first published in Germany in 1486. Even so, in July 1645 alone in England, more than thirty people were executed for alleged witchcraft.[50] Puritan Massachusetts thus drew from a long history of intolerance toward witchcraft in the Salem episode of 1692.

These trials, where the accused were guilty unless they could prove them-selves innocent, seemed to confirm Roger Williams's notion of the church-state union making both the church and the state "more bloudy." They became the most notorious of the fifty separate heresy trial episodes in American history.[51] It is interesting and ironic that the Salem witch trials occurred in America amid the backdrop of an unprecedented time of enlightened religious thinking abroad in England, as the English Bill of Rights and the Toleration Act had just been created. Thus, as the old country sailed forward, the new country moved backward. A few Puritans in good standing with both the church and the colonial government of Massachusetts, such as Thomas Brattle, a wealthy Harvard administrator, shook their heads in dismay at the "Salem superstition," and adjured that "it is not fit to be named in a land of such light as New England."[52] Brattle and fellow critics of the trials were right, of course, and after nineteen innocent people had already been executed, the truth came out. Apologies were issued to the victims' families, but it was far too little and much too late. Thereafter, Puritanism fell into disrepute and suffered a rapid erosion of power in the New England political arena. By 1720, a separation of spiritual and temporal powers was well under way. In that year, Daniel Neal published *The Present State of New England*, which proclaimed of the "New-English Man": "Happy People! as long as Religion and the State continue on a separate Basis; the Magistrate not meddling in matters of Religion any further than is necessary for the Preservation of the public Peace; nor the Churches calling for the Sword of the Magistrate to back their Ecclesiastical Censures with corporal Severities."[53]

Much more common than persecuting alleged witches in the colonies was the persecution of Quakers, Catholics, and Jews. Nor were the Puritans the only practitioners of it. The Society of Friends (Quakers) had been in existence only since 1646, but within twelve years the Separatists of the Plymouth Colony had passed a law banning Quakers from living there.[54] New Amsterdam, the Dutch colony that became English New York in 1664, likewise banned Quakers, calling them in Dutch Reformed Church terminology the "instruments" of Satan and attaching stiff fines even to giving temporary shelter to the Antinomian sect.[55]

While the Quakers represented an unwelcome minority in most of the colonies, a great majority of Americans considered Catholics the greatest threat to the colonial experiment. The Puritans blamed Catholic missionaries for stirring up the Indians of New England in 1675–1676 in what came to be known as King Philip's War. Indeed, French Canadian Catholics did have a good bit of interaction with the New England natives, but blaming them for the rebellion is an exaggeration of their impact upon the tribes and an oversimplification of the problem. Whatever caused it, the war resulted in fifty-two Puritan villages being attacked, twelve razed, and hundreds of Puritans killed. It bred animosity in the Puritans toward Catholics similar to what had existed in England for a hundred years, but since there were virtually no Catholics in New England, there was no meaningful way to vent the hard feelings, and eventually they dissipated. But anti-Catholicism did not disappear from the colonies altogether. It soon appeared in Maryland, and more than a half-century later it cropped up again, this time in South Carolina in 1739 and New York in 1741. In both cases Spanish Catholics conspired with African-Anglo slaves—unsuccessfully—against the English colonies, although political rather than religious reasons mainly motivated them.[56] In early 18th-century Virginia, one of the most vile epithets one could hurl at a foe was "Jesuit," which some Virginians lumped together with "Dog, Rogue, Rascal," and "Villin" [sic].[57]

That is not to say no one ever attempted to reconcile Catholicism with the English Protestant colonial experiment. The northern frontier of Puritan Massachusetts, which is today Maine, issued a "Declaration of Religious Toleration" in 1649 allowing Catholics to settle there.[58] With Maine located so close to French Canada, this declaration seems as much a self-defense mechanism as a genuine olive branch of religious peace. In the same year, the formerly all-Catholic colony of Maryland (the only Catholic colony among the English colonies), extended settlement rights to Protestants in its famous Act of Religious Toleration, which was in reality only partly tolerant. It began with a detailed explanation of what sacrilegious speech and behavior would *not* be tolerated. "Blasphemy," a crime that was largely in the eye of the beholder, was to be "punished with death."[59] Also a defense mechanism, this act shielded the Catholic proprietors of Maryland from a potential hostile takeover by the new Cromwell government. It turned out just as damaging for Catholics in the long run, however, as Protestants and noncommitted semi-Protestants poured into Maryland over the next three decades. By 1675, non-Catholics accounted for eleven of every twelve inhabitants of Maryland. With this overwhelming majority and with Protestants firmly in control of England, in 1692 Maryland established the Anglican Church, and within another dozen years it had outlawed holding mass and infant baptism, and within another decade it had disfranchised Catholic voters. That did not make Maryland particularly strange, however. New York expelled all Catholic clerics in 1700, and in most other colonies they had never been welcome in the first place.[60]

The trend in the Protestant English colonies in the 1700s certainly was not toward more toleration of Catholics. If anything, it was toward more intolerance. The outbreak of the French and Indian War in the 1750s only increased the anti-Romish feelings. But the onset of the American Revolution forced the English Protestants to make an abrupt about-face in their attitude toward Catholics. Desperately needing the help of France, desiring the aid of Spain, and hoping for an alliance with Canada, the patriots suddenly welcomed Catholics with open arms. Upon France's alliance with the nascent United States in the midst of the Revolution, American political and military leaders began to show utmost respect and reverence for institutionalized Catholicism in Europe—the same kind they would have spit upon just a few years earlier. George Washington routinely addressed King Louis XVI as "His Most Christian Majesty," a label that stuck and became semi-fashionable in the 1780s, until the French Revolution ended the happy alliance with the United States and ultimately the king's life.[61] Catholic Americans felt caught between the two opposing sides in the American Revolution and had to choose which was the lesser evil. Most ultimately became patriots.[62]

As for persecution of Jews, so few practicing Jews lived in most of the colonies that it was virtually a nonissue. There were laws excluding Jews, or excluding the practice of Judaism, and laws barring them from holding public office. There were also isolated cases of persecution committed by individuals and mobs, but anti-Semitism in the traditional European sense of staging "pogroms" (government-sponsored murders of Jews) never reared its head in America. The few Jews in America at the time of the Revolution had been as quiet and unassuming as to be almost completely ignored by the Founders. Rarely before the debate over the Constitution in 1787–1788 did the question of the Jews' place in the national polity even arise.[63] Famously, the Philadelphia Jew Jonas Phillips entreated his friend George Washington to ensure the right of his people to live in the new nation without fear of persecution. He even pronounced a blessing upon the Framers at the Constitutional convention, saying, "May God extend peace to them and their seed after them as long as the sun and moon endureth. And may the Almighty God of our father Abraham, Isaac, and Jacob endue this noble Assembly with wisdom, judgment and unanimity in their councils. . . ."[64] Washington not only assured Phillips and the Philadelphia Jews of their safety, but also Jews in New York, Charleston, Richmond, and Newport (Rhode Island) on other occasions.[65]

The Constitution in its original form did not offer any specific protections to Jews or any other religious minority, but with the addition of the First Amendment, Phillips and other Jews saw their wish granted. They may well have supported the Constitution without the Bill of Rights, however. According to James Madison, the Quakers of Philadelphia did.[66] Jews tended to see the Jeffersonian Republican party, rather than the Federalist party, as their great protector because of its more enthusiastic embrace of the *E Pluribus Unum* concept. As Benjamin Nones of Pennsylvania expressed it in 1800, "I am a Jew, and if for no other reason, for that reason am I a republican."[67]

## SERVE HOT

In the years leading up to the American Revolution, toleration of minority religious groups showed no sign of increasing. If anything, American society as a whole had grown more intolerant. The Baptists, for instance, had become the most persecuted sect in America in the 1760s and early 1770s. In fact, the years from 1768 to 1774 were known as the time of the "Great Persecution" in Virginia, when the Anglican establishment arrested, beat, fined, imprisoned, and virtually tried to exterminate the Baptists. As late as the eve of the American Revolution, the Anglicans still considered themselves the "only true church."[68] The effect this persecution had on Baptists was extremely positive for the development of separation of church and state in the coming decades. Baptists became some of the main proponents of tolerance and separationism in the Early Republic.[69]

When the American Revolution broke out, "The battling churches ceased fire against each other just long enough to unite against England. . . ."[70] Even though nothing in their collective history indicated that they would be able to maintain solidarity even to the end of the war much less permanently, they shocked everyone, including themselves, by doing so. The Presbyterian Church led the way in developing and formalizing a policy of toleration of rival denominations. Others soon followed. Nowhere was the mutual toleration more evident than in the old Puritan stronghold of Boston. By 1785, the Boston area had multiple Congregational churches, three Episcopal, two Baptist, one Presbyterian, and one Quaker church. They all lived in relative peace side by side, despite the continuation of the legal establishment of the Congregational faith—a major advance for a region that less than a century earlier had burned alleged witches.[71]

By the mid-1700s, the Puritans had already morphed into other sects—mainly Congregationalists—and thus ceased to exist as a separate, identifiable group. By the 1770s, essentially only three basic types of Protestants could be found in America. Anglicans (soon called Episcopalians), Presbyterians (nearly pure Calvinists), and Dissenters (Congregationalists, Baptists, Quakers, and numerous smaller sects).[72] The first group fell into disarray because of the American Revolution. It proved difficult to divorce the American Episcopalians from the Anglican Church. The Presbyterian denomination, although smaller in number, exercised a notable amount of influence in the formation of the United States government. The Dissenters, however, composed the largest group and became the one most influential in shaping the American view of separationism in that first generation.[73] But the splintering of this third group into more various sects continued unabated during and after the Revolution. Some of the offshoots were fairly large and influential, such as the Unitarians, who descended mainly from the Congregationalists. They will be discussed in a later chapter. Others, such as the Shakers, were small and considered more like cults (to describe them in modern parlance) than orthodox denominations.[74]

The Shakers began in England as a spin-off of the Society of Friends, where they were called, amusingly but not surprisingly, the "Shaking Quakers." Ann Lee, one of the group's founders, came to America in 1774, just in time for the Revolution. She had a peculiar twist on the idea that America was God's new Israel. She believed that God certainly had a chosen people in America, but not all Americans were chosen. Basically, her group, the Shakers, an exclusive and communal little sect, were the chosen ones. They built twelve separate communes from New York to Kentucky from 1787 to 1792. The interesting thing about this building campaign is that it occurred just as the United States went through its Constitutional changeover. While the rest of the nation at the time, like historians ever since, were all enthralled with the ratification struggle and the beginning of the Washington administration, this little body of believers went about what they perceived as the Lord's work, almost totally oblivious to political issues. As time went on, that changed. By 1808, they had come to consider the United States a special place of refuge for God's people, despite the fact that they were occasionally persecuted here. They sang as they worked, and one of their songs was an ode to the American civic religion that began: "Here we see what God has done, by his servant Washington." Their doctrines centered on hard work, being set apart from the carnal world (including from marriage and sex), and focusing on the coming millennial Kingdom of God.[75]

It was virtually a foregone conclusion that, as a celibate group, the Shakers could not last more than a couple of generations. But of course in the early 1800s, a plethora of new religious groups came along to replace them, including similar communal sects like the Oneidaists, and other groups that drew their doctrines from sources other than or in addition to the Bible, such as the Millerites (or Adventists), the Mormons, and the Transcendentalists.[76] In every case, these groups arose after the creation of the United States, after the addition of the First Amendment, and therefore under the auspices of separation of church and state. That fact is the first piece of evidence supporting the assertion that separation of church and state did not damage American religion but rather helped it thrive and multiply. More evidence is supplied in the coming chapters.

As already mentioned, the Baptists, who had previously been the most persecuted group in America, became the most vocal proponents of separationism in the formative years of the United States. John Leland, a Baptist pastor, who developed a friendship with Thomas Jefferson, became the poster child for separationism. He came up with eleven reasons why state-controlled religion was evil, the most important one being that it actually drove people away from religion rather than drew them toward it. Interestingly, he made a study of French history from 1751 to the outbreak of the French Revolution in 1789 and discovered that 39 Princes, 148 Counts, 234 Barons, 147,518 other Nobles, and 760,000 Commoners had been put to death in France just for being in opposition to the unified church-state consortium.[77] Although these numbers sound incredible, they could have easily been matched in the early United States, had it not been for the aggressive and progressive leadership from some of the key Founders.

Lest it seem as though the United States stood head and shoulders above all other nations in the development of religious tolerance in the late 1700s, it should be pointed out that a movement to reform the French system had been gradually fomenting thanks to Enlightenment *philosophes* for decades. Voltaire, among other *philosophes*, pleaded for religious toleration in France akin to what England already enjoyed at that time. The Bourbon monarchs, however, steeped in the Divine Right of Kings doctrine, could not see the wisdom of separation of church and state. Yet, King Louis XVI finally did see the light in 1787, issuing a too-little-too-late Edict of Toleration. He was partly responding to the mounting forces of revolution but also partly to the zeitgeist of religious tolerance that had already overtaken England, the United States, and even Austria under Emperor Joseph II. A year later, the zeitgeist would arrive in Prussia, as Frederick II issued a toleration decree. It gave legal standing to three denominations—Catholic, Lutheran, and Reformed, but granted the right of existence to smaller sects.[78]

In conclusion, the United States certainly stood in the vanguard of separationism but by no means initiated the movement for it. England, for all its faults, more than any other nation, did that. The United States merely did it better, eventually, than any other nation. The American idea of *E Pluribus Unum* actually enhanced its chances of success. The proof is, so to speak, in the pudding. Circumstances, chance, fate, and/or excellent political and religious leadership determined that this particular nation would become the main one to combat the establishment of religion, as is discussed in the next chapter.

## Chapter 4

# The American "Magna Carta"

## *Congress Shall Make No Law . . . So Neither Should the Supreme Court*

### DIVISION OF LABOR

One aspect of the American way that "has often been rated as our most distinctive contribution to modern statecraft" is separation of church and state. "The churches have thrived on it, and the government has flourished under it. Freedom of thought *and* freedom of faith have progressed under it."[1] Many observers believe that, of all the good examples that the United States has set for the rest of the world to follow, its separation of church and state is the greatest.[2] The jury of public opinion in Western civilization deliberated upon that issue for many years, however, before accepting separationism. As late as the 1830s, some foreign visitors to the United States, such as English writer Frances Trollope, were still convinced that lack of an established church created "unseemly vagaries" in the American conception of morality. Churches of various denominations and strange doctrines sprang up on "individual whim" and carried off thousands of Americans into the gray area of moral uncertainty. Trollope believed an established church could act "as a sort of headquarters for quiet unpresuming Christians, who are contented to serve faithfully, without insisting upon having each a little separate banner, embroidered with a device of their own imagining."[3] Likewise, the Catholic Church still stood adamantly opposed to separationism even in the 1860s, as Pope Pius IX published his "Syllabus of Errors," in which he called separation of church and state one of the most egregious "errors" in modern history.[4] Yet such opposition did nothing to restrict the growth of separationist sentiment in most of the Western world.

The phrase "separation of church and state" has been employed so frequently in the last century in America that it has become entrenched not only in the collective national lexicon but also in the subconscious thought processes of English speakers everywhere. The result is that those five words have become fairly well fused together in people's minds, such that the unique meaning and importance of the two nouns therein seem to be lost. A brief dissection of the phrase is thus in order. If the "church" and the "state" are considered according to the actual function of each entity rather than according to the traditional philosophical debate surrounding their relationship, then it becomes clear that each has a specialized job in American society. There is, in essence, a division of labor between the two in the United States, in which the state deals with public issues through the political process and the church (or more precisely "churches") deals with them through the social process. This division has never been codified in these terms but is nonetheless real and understood by both. It was much more noticeable in the pre-20th-century era of American history, before the federal government got into the business of providing and supervising social services, such as public education and retirement benefits. But the division is nevertheless still evident today, if not as sharply defined as before, as the government now plays the role that the churches once played exclusively.[5] Whether this has been a wise change is a large topic that lies beyond the scope of this study and thus must be debated elsewhere. In this division of labor arrangement, the state holds the upper hand and the churches the lower. In other words, the state is in the supervisory position and the churches in the subordinate. Yet the churches have the ability to coerce the state into doing their bidding in many cases through subtle (and sometimes not-so-subtle) influences they infuse into the political culture, and occasionally through direct electoral action. Ultimately then, even though the state holds sovereignty in its relationship with the church, it has little meaningful control over the churches and is in fact beholden to their members just as it is to all voting blocs in varying degrees.

The relationship is partially analogous to that of the national government and the various state governments. The former holds sovereignty but must be cautious in how it deals with the individual states lest it incur the wrath of the voters living there and thus destroy its current management team in the next federal election. It is even more analogous to an old-fashioned Christian marriage. The husband (government) was/is the head of the household, and the final authority to make decisions affecting the home and family rests with him, but the wife (religion) had/has more direct influence over the structure of the home and family than the man. In this arrangement, the husband or government rarely goes against the wishes of the wife or church because he understands all too well that doing so causes unwanted friction in the home or nation. Rather, the husband or government is very aware and sensitive to the mentality and emotions of the wife or church, and consequently makes decisions based on her wishes, whether expressed or implied.[6]

To get a mental handle on the phenomenon of American separation of church and state, we must begin with some definitions. The terminology in the "church" and "state" debate is somewhat confusing in the previous analogy in that the national government *is* the "state," while the state governments are in the same subordinate but potentially powerful position as the "church." We must also keep in mind that, in the United States, there is no "church" in the same sense that there has traditionally been in Europe for most of the Christian era. What the term *church* designates in the United States is the collection of the various religious groups that, other than sharing the same position within the American sociopolitical system, have little in common.[7] Using the European terminology to describe an American phenomenon is thus imprecise at best and deceptive at worst.[8] Yet we all use it for three reasons: (1) because others before us did; (2) everyone knows instinctively what is meant by it; and (3) it has become entrenched in our lexicon. Consequently, we will undoubtedly continue using it regardless of its semantic difficulties, although this study uses *churches* when that term is necessary or more accurate.

Not until 1674 was the phrase "church and state" actually coined, and it happened in England, not America. In 1694, it made its first appearance here, in the Maryland colony, where it was used not to describe a separation of the two but their union. The phrase is always used in current discussions of the First Amendment despite the fact that it is not used in the amendment itself or in any other part of the Constitution. The phrase "establishment of religion" is, however, used in the First Amendment. It is likewise of fairly modern origin. Not until 1660 in England was the term *established* church used, and not until 1731 was the proper noun *Establishment* of religion used, while the term *disestablishment* did not appear until 1800.[9] The terminology as we know it today is thus hardly older than the nation itself.[10] Contemporary Americans by and large do not clearly understand what "an establishment of religion" is or what the phrase means exactly in the Constitution. This lack of understanding would be a problem no matter what, but once the courts get their hands on the First Amendment and start interpreting it and expanding its original meaning, the difficulty increases considerably.[11]

To understand how the relationship between church and state came to be what it is, its development must be traced throughout history. To begin, it is ironic that the roots of separation of church and state can actually be found in the Old Testament nation of Israel, which was a theocracy. Even though it was a theocracy, it had a separation of powers initially between the civil and ecclesiastical leaders. Moses and Aaron jointly led the nation during the forty years of wandering in the wilderness after the exodus from Egypt. Moses, the main political authority, held the dominant position over his brother Aaron, the main religious authority, but each had a job equal in importance within the theocracy.[12] Moreover, inasmuch as Moses derived his authority from God and could hardly make any decisions for himself but rather merely passed along what God told him, it is fair to say that the "church," figuratively speaking, ruled the "state" in ancient Israel.[13]

The ancient Israeli model was, for all intents and purposes, never used again in any other nation, although Jesus indirectly reaffirmed the idea of separationism even within the Roman Empire with his famous utterance, "Render to Caesar the things that are Caesar's, and to God the things that are God's" (Mark 12:17). The Apostle Paul echoed that sentiment in his letter to the Roman Church, when he wrote, in essence, that Christians should not disobey the political authorities in the name of religious dissent (Romans 13:1-7).[14] With the coming of the Roman Catholic and Byzantine Church/Empires, separationism was abandoned. Christians in those early centuries quite naturally assumed that union of church and state was God's vehicle for bringing about the prophesied millennial kingdom on earth. Besides, they had the scriptural admonition to pray that God would provide wise leaders—and if they prayed for that, they must have believed they would get what they asked for (Matthew 7:7–11).[15] Thus, "sacralization" (the unification of religion with politics) occurred. For about a thousand years thereafter, the idea of separation of church and state basically gathered dust, although the idea of a separation of powers or division of labor between church and state was broached by, among others, anti-Trinitarian dissidents in Italy called the Socinians in the 1500s, and by Baptists such as Leonard Busher in England in the early 1600s. This concept of dividing the two powers according to spheres of responsibility was called "jurisdictionalism," and it served as a stepping stone on the path to modern separation of church and state.[16]

Modern separationism actually began with the American colonists in New England. The Puritans did not come here with the intention of initiating desacralization (separating religion from politics) but rather to establish a new relationship between the two.[17] Only through time and experience did that begin to change. In 1661, a Puritan pastor named James Noyes published *Moses and Aaron, Or the Rights of Church and State*, which, along with what Roger Williams and others were already practicing and teaching, served as the basis of the idea of separationism in America.[18] For the next century thereafter, not much changed in terms of the liberalization of church-state relations. Rhode Island and Pennsylvania continued with separationism, while the other eleven colonies retained/created unionism. Most had to pass through the stage of unionism modified by increased toleration of dissenting groups. Maryland actually regressed to unionism and religious intolerance.

By the eve of the American Revolution, every colony except Rhode Island and Pennsylvania still had a union of church and state. What had changed, however, was the number of dissenters in the colonies—enough to pose a serious challenge to the established churches. In Virginia, for instance, in 1763, the Anglican Reverend James Maury complained that the colonial judges held a "striking . . . loyalty, impartiality and attachment . . . to the Church of England in particular, and to religion at large," which could plainly be seen in their rulings and pronouncements.

Yet, he noted, the people of Virginia themselves, from whom juries were selected, held the established church in contempt. Lawyers, such as the young Patrick Henry, made their names and reputations by pandering to the juries and the people and thumbing their noses at the judges. In one particular case, Henry allegedly lambasted the Anglican clergy, saying, "the community have [sic] no further need of their ministry, and may justly strip them of their appointments." Henry then privately apologized to Maury for his caustic remarks, which supporters of the church called "treasonous." Maury later claimed that Henry's "sole view in engaging the cause, and in saying what he had, was to render himself popular." To Maury, the way to political advancement in Virginia in 1763 lay in trampling "under foot the interests of religion, [and] the rights of the church."[19]

Despite Maury's story, the Anglican/Episcopal Church generally dished out the harassment in the southern states rather than received it. By contrast, it routinely stood in the receiving line in New England. In the 1760s, as the tension leading to the American Revolution mounted, the Anglican minority in New England begged and pleaded with the British government to step in and force the establishment of their denomination there. If the government had responded to this supplication, it would have put a stop to the harassment on paper only, because physical enforcement measures to stop it in actuality would have proven difficult, if not impossible, to carry out. During those tenuous times, the British government, which suffered from religious dissent itself, certainly could not justify such a strong action even if it could have mustered the ability to do so. However, had it done so in the 1760s, the question arises as to whether there would have ever been a Revolutionary War in the 1770s. If there had been, it certainly would have taken on a different form and character. The southern colonies, overwhelmingly Anglican, likely would not have joined with the Congregationalists of New England against the mother country.[20]

Even before the tumult of the 1760s, the idea of establishing the Anglican Church in every colony seemed appealing to Church of England leaders in the mother country. In 1758, Thomas Secker, the Archbishop of Canterbury, wrote to Dr. Samuel Johnson, the Rector of King's College (now Columbia University) in New York City, with a plan to establish bishoprics in America. He opined that "the establishment of Bishops of our Church in America" was "what we must ever pray and labour for, till we obtain it. . . ." He noted the "vehement" opposition to the idea from a majority of Americans, which was the only thing, as he saw it, that constrained the Crown and Church from going ahead immediately with the plan. "Therefore," said Secker, "the principal point is to convince them, that whatever the Bishops were, from whom their ancestors fled into the New World, those of the present age are, and have always been, most sincere patrons of extensive toleration."[21] The fact that church leaders and government officials in England had such a plan before King George III ascended to the throne and started the taxation and concomitant policies leading to the Revolution indicates that under different circumstances the Anglican Church may well have been established in all the colonies eventually, regardless of opposition to the idea. In that sense, the coming of the Revolution may have been the best thing that ever happened for proponents of separation of church and state.

As late as 1767, Secker's plan still sat on the table as a serious possibility. The Reverend Charles Chauncy, pastor of the First [Congregationalist] Church in Boston, as would be expected, opposed the plan. He did not for a minute believe that the Anglicans had reformed themselves since earlier generations of colonists had fled from them. Not only did he not trust the Anglicans, but more importantly he feared that having an established Church of England in the colonies would lead to rapid and rampant conversions for the wrong reason, for political expediency rather than sincerity. He wrote, "if Bishops should be sent to the Colonies, the people . . . would generally turn Churchmen. . . . Episcopalians would quickly exceed the other denominations of Christians, as much as [we] now exceed them. This, without all doubt, is the grand point aimed at. . . . if these Bishops should make use of their SUPERIORITY, as they most probably would, sooner or later," they would take "measures to force the growth of the church."[22]

## DEVELOPMENTS IN THE REVOLUTION AND EARLY REPUBLIC

How did the Founders view separation of church and state? Were they monolithic in their opinion? Or did they disagree over it just as the American people still do more than two centuries later? To answer such questions requires delving into that most murky of all historical inquiries—original intent. Even knowing the Founders' original intent is not a panacea for clearing up all controversial political questions, mainly because various Founders said and wrote contradictory statements on the subject over the course of their lives and because they did not always practice what they preached anyway.[23] In other words, each Founder did not even agree with himself all the time, much less with his fellows. Still, knowing what they wrote, said, and did is helpful, and besides, "there are far worse intellectual exercises" that a student of history could be engaged in.[24] One must enter into such an exercise, however, with the axiom that the Founders were not divine or infallible, and therefore their work on the subject must not be considered "canonical" (meaning unalterable over time because it was perfect to start with). Indeed, their work has been interpreted by the courts organically (meaning changeable over time because it was never meant to be set in stone).[25] So while the temptation is certainly ever present to call the Founders demigods and elevate them to superhuman status, it would be better to admit that they were just mortals who realized from all they had witnessed, experienced, and read about in history that separationism was the only prudent option in creating their new nation. The fact that their work has been vindicated so convincingly by history does not mean they had prescient knowledge. What is today experiential was to them merely experimental.[26] As Jack Rakove has put it, "Nothing would have struck the Framers as more unrealistic than the notion that their original intentions must be the sole guide by which the meaning of the Constitution would ever after be determined. They did not bar future generations from trying to improve upon their work, or from using the lessons of experience. . . ."[27]

Getting back to the questions at hand then, it seems accurate to answer that both are partly correct and incorrect. The Founders did not automatically or instinctively agree that separating the mechanism of government from the mechanism of religion was a good idea, much less the brilliant idea that it is generally thought to be today, but they arrived at the conclusion that it was a necessity (some would have said a necessary evil) in order to keep the peace and give the country a better chance to survive.

The way the various states dealt with this issue in their constitutions helps illuminate the Founders' original intent. Of the thirteen states at the time of the founding, twelve had constitutions that either required, or at least encouraged, Christianity in one form or another. Only Rhode Island did not. No other religion besides Christianity is mentioned specifically in any of those original state constitutions.[28] It is evident, however, that a particular religion/philosophy—Deism—although not named in any of the constitutions, was targeted as the common enemy of all the orthodox churches—churches that supplied most of the state representatives who wrote those constitutions. Most of the state constitution makers, regardless of which church they attended, did not feel threatened so much by other Christians of different denominations as by Deists, who were often portrayed as just dressed-up atheists. To Episcopalians in Virginia or Congregationalists in Massachusetts, Quakers, for example, were misguided but sincere in their faith, but Deists were sinister, maybe even diabolical, in their subversiveness. The orthodox churches certainly felt uncomfortable with the growth of dissenting religious groups in their midst, but felt no immediate, imminent danger from them, whereas they saw Deists as potentially dangerous in the 1700s, not only to their own vicinity but to all Western civilization—to roughly the same degree as Americans of the 20th century saw Soviet Communism. The state constitutions, by promoting Christianity, thus reacted to and defended their respective polities against this perceived threat.[29]

That is not to say that minority denominations in any particular state were not also targeted for exclusion; they certainly were. Examples include Baptists in Virginia and Quakers in Massachusetts. But such dissenting sects could not be painted with a broad brush throughout all the states the way Deists could. Nonetheless, Deists and minority denomination church members found themselves in a similar situation in the founding generation. Both were loathed by the large, powerful, orthodox churches. This put them in an alliance with one another by necessity on the issue of separating the jurisdictions of church and state in America. Pietists—members of several different minority denominations who were some of the most devout, spiritual people in the United States—and Deists started from practically opposite ends of the religious spectrum and arrived at the same middle ground, agreeing that only by segregating church and state into separate spiritual and temporal spheres would either be protected from the other.[30] Such unholy alliances were not unheard of, of course, for as early as the 1740s during the Great Awakening the revivalists and the Rationalists had already discovered that they had a mutual interest in opposing the established Anglican and Congregational churches.[31] More will be discussed about Deism and similar free-thinking philosophies in a later chapter.

State constitutions and local political/religious issues stand as one major pillar in understanding the Founders' original intent, but the other pillar, which gets far more coverage in history books and contemporary debates, is what the Founders said and did at the national level. Beginning with the First Continental Congress in 1774, its Declarations and Resolves mentioned only one thing about religion; it expressed opposition to the English government's Quebec Act, one of the Coercive or "Intolerable" Acts passed in 1774 to punish Boston rebels for their revolutionary activities that had culminated in the famous Tea Party of December 1773.[32] The act recognized Catholicism as the established/preferred religion of Canada, a region in close geographical proximity to the Congregationalist New England colonies, and which the people of the lower thirteen colonies considered to be their fellow "American" colony at the time. New Englanders in particular, but all of the lower colonies to some degree, considered this nod to the Catholic Church to be dastardly, dangerous, and representative of everything wrong with the government of King George III.[33] Not to single out the Catholic Church for discrimination, New Englanders would have undoubtedly felt the same disdain had there been a Virginia Act or some such thing propping up the establishment of the Anglican Church in the South.

A year later, the second Continental Congress seemed to be more religiously minded than the first. This Congress opened daily with prayer; invoked the name of the mono-God in at least twenty different ways (seven using the word *God*, four using *Providence*, two using *Creator*, two using *the Supreme*, and one each using *Lord*, *Christ*, *Divine*, and *Jesus*); passed fasting proclamations for July 20, 1775, and May 17, 1776; passed laws against Continental soldiers swearing, cursing, or blaspheming; and ordered the publication of 30,000 Christian Bibles in the United States or the importation of 20,000 from other countries in 1777. By 1780, this Congress had passed a resolution requesting that the states help pay for the printing and distribution of Bibles to alleviate the shortage of them, proclaimed a day of Thanksgiving, and offered a prayer that the United States might "cause the knowledge of Christianity to spread all over the earth."[34]

Even after the Revolution had ended, this Congress did not cease with its heavenly mindedness. In the Northwest Ordinance of 1787, it said "Religion, morality, and knowledge being necessary to good government and the happiness of mankind, schools and the means of learning shall forever be encouraged."[35] In summation, the position of the Continental Congress "may be described as one of sympathy with religion in general and the Christian religion in particular," but "there was a similar disposition to encourage religion without special reference to any particular religion."[36]

The overt religiosity of the Continental Congress seems odd considering the secularism of the document that created the government structure under which it labored through the Revolution. This document, the Articles of Confederation, drawn up in 1777, "just tactfully ignored," said historian Thomas Hall, the whole issue of church and state. The delegates to the convention who wrote the document did, however, open the convention of 1777 with prayer, over the objections of John Jay, who would go on to become the first Chief Justice of the U.S. Supreme Court. The Articles, Hall continued, were "as completely secular as the by-laws of an insurance company."[37] The Articles also served the nation adequately in terms of religion, and the new Constitution of 1787 did little to improve upon them (except for the new document's Article VI) until the Bill of Rights was added. Indeed, the subject of religion seems conspicuously absent from discussion at the Constitutional Convention of 1787. The one time it came up, when Benjamin Franklin moved to begin business each day with prayer, was summarily dismissed with no serious consideration.[38]

Ironically, once the new federal government began operating in 1789, both the Congress and the president did so with, again, overt religiosity. On April 30, 1789, in his first inaugural address, George Washington invoked the name of "that Almighty Being, who rules over the universe, who presides in the councils of nations," who was "the Author of every public and private good."[39] Six days later, the House of Representatives welcomed Washington to his new elective position as president with the statement, "We feel with you the strongest obligation to adore the Invisible Hand which has led the American people through so many difficulties" and made "fervent supplications for the blessings of Heaven on our country. . . ." Washington responded in kind, asking for the continuation of "the blessings of Heaven on our beloved country." Two days after that, the Senate welcomed Washington to the presidency in a similar formal address, saying, "We commend you, sir, to the protection of the Almighty God, earnestly beseeching Him" for good health and a prosperous administration. Washington replied that he felt himself "inexpressably [sic] happy in a belief that Heaven, which has done so much for our infant nation, will not withdraw its providential influence" from the United States.[40]

Again it appears that the Founders wrote one thing into their legal documents and practiced quite another thing in their actual day-to-day activities. This seemingly contradictory (some would argue hypocritical) behavior is undoubtedly the source of most of the confusion over the church and state debate today. But it is what it is, and historians can only deal with it as best they can—rationalizing the irrational.[41]

## THE PHILOSOPHY OF SEPARATIONISM

"The United States furnishes the first example in history of a government deliberately depriving itself of all legislative control over religion. . . . But it was an act of wisdom and justice rather than self-denial."[42] It was equally an act of virtual desperation rather than of brilliant forethought. The liberalization of religion in America came in stages over a couple hundred years. Before separationism could be achieved, simple toleration had to become widely accepted, as it did in the thirteen original states, despite the establishment of churches in some of them.[43] In other words, the philosophy that ultimately resulted in separationism had to emerge through an evolution of thought. It would be wrong to attribute this evolution of thought to the genius of the Founders. They were merely born into a particular stage of the evolutionary process and proceeded accordingly in their thinking on the church-state issue. They were the beneficiaries of good timing and used it to become some of the world's most notable ideological benefactors. Those nations that followed the American evolutionary example exhibited wisdom, those that resisted suffered from a lack of it, and those that sought to skip a step or two in the evolutionary process displayed utter foolishness.[44]

The significance of separationism resulting from *evolution* rather than *revolution* cannot be overstated. In nations where such religious changes have occurred by revolution, skipping the intervening steps, the changes have never worked well, if at all. France after 1789 is the prime example. That traditionally Catholic nation went straight from unionism to a new artificial god worship—from government imposition of a certain type of traditional religion on the French people to government imposition of Robespierrean religion, which amounted to worship of the state. The same could be said of the Soviet Union in the 20th century. It went from established orthodoxy to militant atheism in a single giant leap, and the shock to the people proved too great.

For the United States, the problem with this evolutionary thesis is that separationism itself may not be the final stage of development. Indeed, it is one step beyond toleration and two steps beyond unionism, but it may be one step short of the ultimate destination—complete secularism. The adoption of the First Amendment in 1791 did not mark the end or culmination of the evolutionary process, just the codification of one step within it. It did not, therefore, even check the speed of the evolutionary process, much less stop it. Indeed, it seems to have accelerated the process. Within a century, a majority of the American people had gone from asking for simple toleration of dissenting religions to claiming freedom of religion as an "inalienable right."[45] Within another hundred years, they had gone from espousing freedom *of* religion to emphasizing their right to enjoy freedom *from* religion. If each marks a step in the continuing evolutionary process, what should the final stage be if not complete secularism?

This is a doomsday scenario for the religious right in America today, and it is why many forward-thinking Christians work relentlessly to keep separationism intact. This seems ironic because, before and during the founding, the orthodox Christians (religious conservatives and church-state unionists) tried to arrest the evolutionary process, while the liberal, nonfundamentalist, dissenting Christians of the same era embraced the evolution of thought, as did atheists and Deists, and as their ideological progeny have ever since. The third group, the counter-conservative fundamentalists and Antinomian dissenters, meanwhile embraced it out of necessity at the time but have since then slowly inched backward away from it. Hence, a tug-of-war has existed throughout American history between the various types of Christians over whether to accept or reject the evolution. It should be noted that the truest kind of fundamentalists shun political affairs with the notion that God's kingdom is not of this world, while other so-called fundamentalists find justification in the Old Testament or some New Testament scriptures taken out of context for trying to control the government. Liberal Christians, by contrast, think it far better for their own moderate, educated, humanitarian breed to run the government, or at least to have a voice in it, than to leave it to either the atheists or radical fundamentalists. It is important to understand that most of the Founders fall into this category of liberal (enlightened/rational) Christians rather than fundamentalists or atheists or otherwise. More will be discussed about this topic in a later chapter.

Assuming in advance, for the sake of argument, that this thesis is correct, the Founders must not have intended separationism to be the total divorce of politics and religion, but rather, in a manner of speaking, a cautious wedding of the two. It would be like the marriage or partnership described earlier in this chapter in which each would have an equally important role to play, each would respect the other's function, neither would try to usurp authority over the other, and a healthy balance could be achieved and maintained. "All reasonable men recognize that, somewhere between . . . the complete union of church and state and their complete divorcement, Americans must find a middle ground of adjustment and understanding that will preserve a free church in a free society and simultaneously protect the liberties of the nonreligious."[46] The Founders were indisputably "reasonable men." So have their ideological progeny been, although there seem to have been more of them in the 19th and early 20th centuries than in the post–World War II years. These "reasonable men" (and women) over the past two hundred years, far from leading the drive for a secular America, have led some of the most important religious movements in American history (chiefly Abolition, Prohibition, and Civil Rights). These movements have come to fruition and achieved their ends neither through dictatorial and theocratic power nor merely social peer pressure, but mainly through the democratic legislative process.[47] Such politically charged religious movements (or should we say religiously charged political movements?) bear witness to the statement that "Our heritage is in the main vitally Christian although the nation is not committed to any one faith. Church and State are legally separated but the state is friendly to religion and cooperates ungrudgingly with churches and other religious bodies."[48]

Herein lies the great beauty of the First Amendment: while the pendulum of public opinion may swing back and forth from national espousal of religion to a national thrust toward secularism over a matter of centuries, the minority is protected from the majority either way (although disputes between the two are sometimes not resolved without resorting to litigation, and then it may take years to see the results). When outwardly religious zealots, such as Abolitionists or Prohibitionists, hold sway over the majority and are thus able to affect national legislation, at least secularists can retreat to their freedom "from" religion philosophy, knowing that even if the zealots manage to force some aspect of their religion upon the nation, they cannot force the religion itself upon those who do not want it. Likewise, if the secularists become the majority and are thus able to affect national law, the godly can hide under the protection of the freedom "of" religion philosophy, realizing that even if the ungodly or nongodly force some aspect of secular humanism upon the nation, they cannot close down the churches, burn the Bibles, or outlaw private prayer. To illuminate the brilliance of the First Amendment further, it must be pointed out that while no church or religious group can rule the American government, churches are composed of individuals who can. It is thus fair and pertinent for voters to ask candidates in federal elections to proclaim their religious affiliation or lack thereof openly. Not to inquire into candidates' beliefs and worship practices or lack thereof is arguably an abdication of the responsibility of citizenship.[49]

Often a candidate's personal religious beliefs become common knowledge before he/she runs for high office, especially at the national level. Voters can be tempted to prejudge the candidate based upon such information rather than give him/her a fair hearing. Such was the case with Thomas Jefferson, whose unorthodox religious ideas were well known before he ever ran for president in 1796 or 1800. The orthodox church crowd at the time belonged overwhelmingly to the Federalist Party, and they made much political hay out of Jefferson's Deism/Unitarianism. A related point that must be made here concerns the great amount of debate over the past two hundred years about Jefferson's important, but generally misunderstood, "wall of separation" between church and state.[50] Hardly can one discuss or read about the history of church-state relations in America without bringing up or confronting that phrase. It is, like the phrase *separation of church and state*, not mentioned in the First Amendment or anywhere else in the Constitution. President Jefferson merely mentioned it in a letter he wrote to a Baptist preacher and his congregation in Danbury, Connecticut, in 1801, and by using it tried to craft a metaphor that would capture the spirit of the First Amendment. He did this to set the preacher and his congregation's minds at ease. They expected nothing from the government but to be left alone by it.[51] They feared that the new, alleged maverick, philosopher-president Jefferson would somehow use his position at the head of the federal government to outlaw or make more difficult their style of worship. Jefferson assured them that their fear had no basis in fact, for even if he wanted to, he could not touch their church because the First Amendment put a wall of separation between the government and the church. This much-celebrated "wall of separation" was thus designed to keep the "government out of the church—not church or church people out of the government!"[52] The irony of the "wall of separation" metaphor is that the religious crowd for whom Jefferson intended it rarely invokes it, but the secularists routinely employ it, and employ it improperly, to say that the church people must stay out of politics.[53]

Objective scholars remind us that the Jeffersonian metaphor is just an expression, that it has no actual legal authority, or at least it should not, and therefore that the wall technically does not exist.[54] As Sidney Hook put it, "There has never been a wall of separation between church and state in America, although it is true that efforts to build such a wall have been made and have been crowned with a modest success."[55] Sydney Mead, meanwhile, laments the fact that this Jeffersonian expression got stuck in the collective memory of the nation, when a much more accurate term, James Madison's "line" of separation between church and state, has been all but forgotten.[56] Madison coined this term in a letter to Episcopalian preacher Jasper Adams of Charleston, referring to the thing that separates religion from the civil authority as a movable, imaginary line. Madison admitted that it seemed impossible to draw the line once and for all in a place where everyone could agree it should be. Just as in his own day there were "collisions & doubts" as to where to draw it, said Madison, so would it ever be.[57]

The difference between the "wall" and the "line," although merely a semantic distinction, is full of symbolic importance. Picture a physical brick wall: it is unmovable, unmistakable, and permanent. Now picture a line drawn on a piece of paper: it may be faint or bold, it may be erasable or not, and it may be straight or curved. This is a far more accurate description of the fluid and flexible First Amendment than the Jeffersonian wall. Americans would thus do well to stop talking about separation of church and state in terms of a wall and start talking about it in terms of a line. If, however, people must continue using the wall terminology out of habit, then they should at least start thinking of the wall not as straight but as crooked. In fact, one can visualize it as looking like the famous "serpentine" wall on the campus of the University of Virginia, which Jefferson designed. This actual, physical brick wall follows a wavy path, goes nowhere in particular, and serves no specific function other than an aesthetic one. It bears a striking resemblance to Jefferson's imaginary church-state wall.

When religion scholar James H. Hutson looked at what Jefferson actually said in his famous letter to the Danbury, Connecticut, Baptist Church, he concluded that the president never intended to divorce the church from the state completely or to set the state over the church as a watchdog of their behavior, but merely to distinguish between "active" and "passive" relations between the two. Active government involvement in religion is impermissible under the First Amendment. Examples of "active" government include: promoting a particular religion or denomination over the others; establishing a church by law; allowing one church to be supported with tax dollars while the rest are not; requiring or coercing the people to attend a certain church; forbidding people to attend a certain church; punishing people with fines or imprisonment or otherwise for their religious beliefs; confiscating Bibles, hymnals, and religious literature; and collecting a tax from those who attend church while not taxing those who do not attend. Allowing all religious groups, however, to enjoy an equal tax-exempt status is not active but passive. Allowing all religious groups equal access to use of government buildings and property is also passive.[58] Many Americans believe that allowing nondenominational prayers on public property is likewise passive and therefore acceptable, although such a belief takes for granted that all people pray to the mono-God of Western civilization—a belief that has been successfully challenged in federal court in recent years. So far, therefore, the United States has arrived at the point in its national evolution where a collective moment of silence is the only solution that is largely acceptable to all sides—the church crowd, the secularists, and the courts—although it may not remain unchallenged much longer.

Where then should this serpentine wall be built or this imaginary line of separation be drawn? Historians, theologians, politicians, lawyers, and judges get to hash out the answer for each succeeding generation. The Founders were well aware that it would be a moving target, and they must have intended it to be so.[59] Were they worried about in which direction the target would move—toward more government control of religion or toward more religious control of government? They apparently thought that there would be enough give-and-take that the two would balance each other out. In his old age, Madison, in a letter to Edward Everett in 1823, addressed the issue of government ruining religion by controlling it. He wrote, "There are causes in the human breast which ensure the perpetuity of religion without the aid of law."[60] In other words, regardless of what the United States government ever did for or against religion, the American state would never extinguish the light of religion from this nation.

Concerning a religious group taking over the government, there seems not to have been much concern over that possibly happening in the founding generation. Indeed, when the topic came up at all, which was rare, the fear expressed was just as much toward some type of secularist anti-religion being forced on the nation. Thomas Treadwell, in a speech at the New York Ratification Convention, explained that he feared equally a "religious establishment . . . tyrannizing over our consciences" and "profane scoffers . . . who will tell us that religion is in vain," à la the French Revolutionaries of his day. He wanted the middle road in which each man could determine his own beliefs without government aid or interference. "Our Bibles," he said, which have been "handed down to us by our forefathers" would prove quite sufficient to guide the American people in terms of religion.[61] Essentially, Treadwell was arguing for the privatization of religion, still a novel concept in the 1780s–1790s.

Privatization was the wave of the future, however, and the Constitution's almost complete silence on the subject shows that the Founders ultimately arrived at it as the middle road approach, as a way to keep either extreme—forced religion or forced secularism—from holding the American people hostage. History has vindicated this approach. Indeed, history shows that if there is a creator-God, this deity does not automatically side with nations that profess allegiance to "God" or use "the name of the Lord" to justify their existence or cause. Take for instance the constitution of the Confederate States of America, written in Montgomery, Alabama, in 1861. The framers of that government, which is renowned as the great defender of slavery, inserted a reference to "Almighty God" in their preamble, "but that constitution died with the Confederacy in 1865," said Philip Schaff. "The name of God did not make it more pious or justifiable."[62] Likewise, the example of the atheist Soviet state of the 20th century stands as a reminder of how removal of the church did not lead to positive results for Russia or Russians.

## EXPLORING THE FIRST AMENDMENT

The United States Constitution should be understood today as a product of its times. The Founders did not contrive it in a vacuum. The Constitution not only reflected the ideology of the age of rationalism, as has been well documented, but also showed a reaction to the late war and the fear of falling back under British rule. Just because the new nation had been independent technically for four years did not mean Americans need not fear losing that independence by some future mishap. Indeed, freedom from Britain could potentially open the United States to attack from other countries. Or a weakened and divided American nation could be gobbled back up by Britain one bite or state at a time. The British, after all, never evacuated the forts they held in the western Indian territory, despite the terms of the Treaty of Paris of 1783. The United States was still in the process of negotiating that issue's resolution in Jay's Treaty twelve years later, and British occupation (or more precisely, the threat it posed and fear it induced) served as one of the underlying motivations to write a new national constitution in 1787. The issue lingered unresolved until 1796, and thereafter continued British trespassing on American territory contributed, at least indirectly, to the outbreak of the War of 1812. The Founders thus had good reason to fear falling back under British or other foreign control in the pivotal 1780s. The best way to avoid that fate lay in fashioning a constitution that not only all the states could endorse but that all the various religious groups in America would also approve. Neutrality on religion was about the only conceivable way to make that happen. No church group could feel threatened, and especially not singled out for threatening, by the Constitution of 1787. So neutral was this document, in fact, that its deafening silence on religious issues caused paranoia among many Christian Anti-Federalists. Their perception of what the Constitution implied through omission far outweighed any factual exegesis that James Madison or any other Federalist could offer as to what they actually intended, as Madison himself admitted.[63] As the Baptist preacher John Leland expressed it, the Constitution may not have openly threatened his church, but neither did it protect it: "If oppression dose [*sic*] not ensue," he opined, "it will be owing to the Mildness" of those men running the government, "not to any constitutional defense" that he could see.[64]

With the addition of the First Amendment, which has been poignantly called the "Magna Carta" of American religious freedom,[65] the paranoia subsided, and a relative feeling of security replaced it. In that security rested the best hope for lasting unity among the thirteen states and survival of some denominations that might otherwise have become extinct. Anti-Federalists at the Virginia ratification convention took the lead in getting such an amendment added to the Constitution, with George Mason being the catalyst for it.[66] The wording of the resolution ratifying the Constitution is interesting. It said nothing about protecting the right of freedom *from* religion, only the freedom to fulfill "the duty which we owe to our Creator" and freedom to choose "the manner of discharging it." North Carolina's resolution said verbatim the same thing.[67] While this is merely a technicality, it is an important one because such technicalities often provide the basis for the arguments of radicals on each side of the Christian nation debate. Being careful to steer clear of appearing to take sides in this study, points of fact must be acknowledged when they are obvious, and this is certainly one of them. Representatives of these two states at their ratifying conventions took great care to express clearly what they intended *for* the Constitution to say when they approved it—that there was/is a "Creator" (the mono-God), and men are *not* free to disbelieve in this Deity, but only free to make a personal decision about how to worship or serve this God. This was, in other words, freedom *of* religion, not freedom *from* it that they were endorsing. They definitely presupposed the Constitution would not fundamentally alter the axiomatic notion that theirs was a religion-based society, even if they did not have or want a religion-based government. Superficially, this technicality seems to contradict the aforementioned constitutional protection of people to enjoy freedom *from* religion. Therein, however, lies the brilliance of crafting a flexible Constitution. Although the Anti-Federalists' original intent was limited to freedom *of* religion, time and common usage have broadened the meaning, which would have undoubtedly pleased James Madison and the Federalists, who comprised the majority at the time of the ratification.

In the summer of 1789, the first United States Congress debated how to word the First Amendment. Some delegates, such as Roger Sherman of Connecticut, thought it redundant and superfluous to have a free religion clause in the Bill of Rights, because, quite obviously, nothing in the Constitution gave the new federal government the right or power to create an established church in the first place. Several congressmen submitted proposals for such a clause anyway. Madison, understanding perhaps better than any other member of Congress the paranoia of those Anti-Federalists who were jealous to guard their own respective religious faiths, submitted a proposal that ironically contained the word *national*, the implications of which he must not have considered very carefully in advance. Elbridge Gerry of Massachusetts strongly objected to Madison's choice of words for its implication that the Constitution had created a "national" rather than a "federal" form of government. Better to have no religious clause at all in the First Amendment than to saddle it with the word *national*, which would undoubtedly provoke a violent reaction from untold numbers of Americans.[68]

Needless to say, just as the Founders haggled over how to word the amendment to say precisely what they meant—nothing more, nothing less—lawyers, judges, politicians, pundits, and the general public have argued over precisely what they meant ever since. And although the amendment is sovereign law, it was/is not worded to make adjudication of its principles easy. It was thought necessary and included in the Constitution to quell a fear, not to incite a legal revolution, to answer the questions of religiously minded Anti-Federalists at the time based on their knowledge of religious bigotry in the past, not to lay a foundation for some abstract new theory of church and state. And yet, that is precisely what happened.[69] The Founders, as smart and careful as they were, could hardly have avoided creating this situation. Had they spent years rather than mere days refining their syntax and diction in the First Amendment, it probably would not have prevented people from arguing over what they meant still today.[70] Such cynicism is inevitable. Does it not quickly become dreary to debate the meaning of one clause in one sentence in one legal document? With that said, in a study of this kind, a brief dissection of the First Amendment is perfunctory at this point.

The clause, as the Founders finally agreed to word it, reads: *Congress shall make no law respecting an establishment of religion, or prohibiting the free exercise thereof.* It limits Congress's involvement in religion, not the president's or the judiciary's. It is written in active voice, and is the only one of the first ten amendments to be so worded. Why? Did Madison and company intend, by omission, to say that the executive and judicial branches could, should, or must have power over religion? All evidence points to the contrary. Was it then merely a mistake, a poor choice of words? That seems more likely, but it still leaves much to be desired as an explanation considering that Madison put so much thought into the wording. The truth is, no one knows why this Amendment is worded in active voice, with Congress specifically made the subject of the sentence. It seems odd because the main fear of the Anti-Federalists was not the power of Congress but of the president, whose job title and description appeared similar to a king, and whose office did not exist under the Articles of Confederation. It can only be assumed that the rationale behind the wording was that only Congress could make a law, and only by a law could a religion be established. The president, barring a misuse of military power that would essentially make him a dictator, could not establish a religion and compel the people to accept it, whereas a simple majority in Congress could theoretically do it with the stroke of a pen—and might, at certain times in the nation's history, have been so inclined if the president happened to be in agreement with it (lest a presidential veto should kill the bill). Thus the First Amendment specifically targets Congress, limiting its ability to tamper with religion, either by promoting it or harming it.

The First Amendment as it pertains to religion looks to modern observers, just as Roger Sherman said at the time, like overkill. With the large variety of denominations already in America in the 1780s, it seems unlikely that any one group would have been able to take total control of the machinery of the new federal government. However, as United States Supreme Court Justice and Harvard Law School founder Joseph Story later explained, adding the Amendment was still a brilliant idea because, suppose one denomination somehow grew in such number, wealth, and political influence that certain ambitious citizens thought it necessary to convert to that faith in order to move up through the ranks in government? With enough insincere, sacralized converts, such a church group could easily, in time, attain a *de facto* control over the machinery of the federal government, which they could, in turn, use to change the law to allow for *de jure* control. That possibility, as strange and "un-American" as it sounds today, was not at all inconceivable in the 1780s.[71]

Now assume that the Founders' intentions in framing the First Amendment the way they did were what has just been presented herein: (1) to prevent Congress from establishing one religion in discrimination of all others, and (2) to prevent any single religious group or consortium of believers from gaining control of the federal government. And why is it so important to keep any particular group or alliance from gaining control? Because it would lead back to the possibility of establishing one religion in discrimination of all others—circular logic. The question then arises whether that is all the Founders meant. Or should Americans, as so many secularist lawyers, judges, pundits, and professors have done over the last fifty years, read between the lines and expand the meaning to include a proscription against the president, the judiciary, or the state and local governments interlocking religion and politics? Surely, as has already been noted, the Founders intended the Constitution as a whole to be flexible and organic in order to meet the changing needs of successive generations.[72] But what about this particular clause? Would they have approved of the modern expansion of its meaning?

There is, of course, no way to know the answer to such questions for certain, but one way to get an important insight on the topic is to look at not only what the Founders wrote but also at their actions—that is, to look at how the Founders applied the religion clause of the First Amendment to real life in the 1790s and early 1800s. To do this and then to juxtapose it to contemporary secularist propaganda and most late-20th-century court rulings (which often go hand in hand) causes a clearly black-and-white issue to emerge out of what would otherwise be one with many shades of gray. So, what did the Founders actually do and not do? For one thing, they did *not* apply the modern expanded definition of the religious clause in their own day. Presidents were free to proclaim national days of thanksgiving or fasts, to offer prayers, to swear their oaths upon the Bible, and such—and most did. Likewise, state governments were free to continue holding to their traditional religious establishments and only to part with them when the locals deemed the time appropriate, not when Congress used federal compulsion. Moreover, local governments then, unlike in some highly publicized instances today, had no fear whatsoever that a local religious custom—such as praying a sectarian Christian prayer to open a town meeting—would be condemned as unconstitutional by a federal court. Most important of all, however, is the fact that even Congress, which is supposedly the only piece of the federal government puzzle that is denied the right to wed politics and religion, opened (and still opens) each day with a prayer![73]

Now take this line of thought a step farther down the road to its logical conclusion. For the sake of argument, it can be conceded hypothetically that Congress is proscribed from weaving religion into the fabric of our political institutions in any way, shape, or form. If the modern expanded interpretation of the religious clause that secularists use to try to deny a president or state/local government the right to weave politics and religion together (the same as is herein conceded it does to Congress) were applied with no double standard, then it *must* deny the same right to the judiciary. This means first that it must disallow all references to religion in the courts, including opening prayers, swearing in judges and witnesses on Bibles, or having the Ten Commandments and such stripped from all court buildings—and not just the federal buildings, but every one down to the smallest local court. Second, and most important, it must abolish the practice of federal judges "legislating from the bench," as modern parlance calls it, which is in effect what is happening when a court expands the meaning of the religious clause beyond how the Founders themselves applied it! And therein lies the rub. The courts, once in the business of expanding the meaning to suit the contemporary cultural disposition, arguably forfeit the ability to be impartial. By default they become radical, liberal, and uncontrollable. In other words, they *must* use a double standard to justify their power and their actions. They must tell all other parts of the federal government in effect, "You have no say-so in how the First Amendment is interpreted; we alone do. We choose to interpret it broadly to deny your power to interpret it at all, and we cite the Founders' words to prove we are correct."[74]

Legal scholar Mark DeWolfe Howe once complained that the Supreme Court has power both to "interpret history" and "to make it," and chides the Court for too often making it poorly by misinterpreting it. In failing to understand the theological dimensions of the wall of separation metaphor, and trying to make it merely a political cliché, "the court has dishonored the arts of the historian and degraded the talents of the lawyer." And yet, the power the Court wields leads inevitably to the conclusion that whatever it says *is* the truth about history *becomes* the truth in the minds of the American people at large. Indeed, since "the justices have the power to bind us by their law they are also empowered to bind us by their history." Thus has been the effect of the federal courts, particularly the Supreme Court, from the mid-20th century onward. They have "codified" a mere "figure of speech" using their own misinterpretation of history for the purpose of legislating from the bench the gradual secularization of America.[75]

Yes, for guidance in interpreting the First Amendment everyone (including federal judges) should look at what the Founders wrote, but everyone should also look at the Founders' actions—how they actually applied it. When this is done, it becomes obvious that the Founders did not always do as they said to do. People today could dismiss them as hypocrites, or apologize for them as being merely flawed mortals like themselves. Or, they could recognize that these "reasonable men" gave modern man an *ideal* to aspire to and a *real* to live by. A strong argument can be made that contemporary judges would do well to consider the *real* before prescribing the *ideal* in church-state cases.

The inevitable result of dissecting the First Amendment and playing legal word games with it is to end up in a quagmire. It is much the same as the mathematical formulas used to contrive "string theory" in physics. Although the formulas start off making sense, if followed to their logical conclusions, they break down.[76] And what then? Where do physicists go then? Back to the drawing board, which is where this study must go now to give a clearer understanding of church-state relations in America and to answer the question of whether the United States was, is, or is supposed to be a Christian nation.

## Chapter 5

# The American "Orthodoxy"

## Nonconformity among the Founders

### FREETHINKERS AND FREETHINKING

Historically, the orthodoxy of any of the Christian nations of Europe was generally specific and well defined. There was little gray area, and anyone posing an unorthodox idea knew they were doing so, knew what the consequences would likely be, and rarely turned out to be wrong. The opposite holds true for American history. With the exception already noted of attempts by Puritans and Anglicans to establish an orthodox mentality in America during the Colonial era, virtually all the rest of the United States' history has been characterized by "freethinking" of one type or another.[1] Deism, Masonry, Unitarianism, Transcendentalism, and a host of smaller sects and movements spring to mind as examples. Likewise, "freethinkers" of several varieties are among the most famous of American leaders. Indeed, "Almost all great Americans have been called infidels," including Washington, Jefferson, and Lincoln.[2] While it is true that certain freethinkers during the founding generation, such as Elihu Palmer, author of *In Defense of the Age of Reason*, might well be considered "infidels" because they had an anti-Christian agenda to promote, others such as Abner Kneeland, author of the *Bible of Reason*, should not be called infidels merely because they possessed unorthodox religious opinions.[3]

The fact that freethinking permeates American history presents the illusion— which many modern secularists are either deceived by or see through, yet readily exploit to their own advantage—that the United States government was founded in deliberate opposition to traditional orthodox Christianity. The sources, however, do not bear out that belief. The erroneous assumption that leads to this inaccurate conclusion is that freethinking automatically and invariably results in a rejection of Christianity. The truth, however, is that a freethinker is not necessarily an atheist or even an agnostic. A freethinker, it has been said, is one who refuses to set limits in his thoughts; to him or her nothing is taboo, nothing is beyond the realm of imagination.[4] This includes the possibility of a God, and the equal possibility of no God—and if a God, then possibly the mono-God of Western civilization.

Prescribing clear definitions to not only *freethinking* but also *Deism* is necessary herein, because both terms have been used incorrectly by well-meaning people historically and contemporarily. Both terms are often used synonymously, or practically so, with *atheism*, which is nebulous at best and totally incorrect at worst. While freethinking may or may not result in atheism, Deism is, as the name implies, the belief in a deity, and therefore cannot accurately be substituted for *atheism*.[5] If modern students of history find these words used synonymously in old historical sources, it is only because the authors of those sources were equally confused about their meaning. People of the founding generation often referred to Deists *and* atheists as two separate groups, but also lumped them together with several other groups as "persons of bad principles."[6] To them, knowing the subtle distinctions among these various unorthodox groups was unimportant.

Undoubtedly, the most celebrated freethinker of the founding generation was Thomas Paine. He is also, unfortunately, the most misunderstood, although his friend Thomas Jefferson comes in a close second. Paine, the renowned American Revolution patriot and author of *Common Sense* and *The American Crisis*, was no atheist. Despite his oft-repeated statement that his "mind" was his "church"—which has served as a freethinker's motto for generations—he was in fact just as opposed to atheism as he was to orthodox Christianity. Born into a Quaker family in England, he grew up in a minority Christian sect of the Antinomian variety, which means he imbued the freethinking mentality early in life. Abandoning both Christianity and his English homeland, he moved to America just in time to become the loudest voice of the Revolution. The first person on record to use the phrase "The United States" as a description of the thirteen English colonies, Paine fell into disrepute in the new country he had helped to name by showing increasing radicalness in his writings thereafter. His *Rights of Man*, published in England in 1791, a defense of the American Revolution, was censored in Britain and snubbed in the United States by none other than George Washington himself (for political, not religious, reasons).[7]

The reception of Paine's book as a criminal treatise in England caused the controversial author to flee to France at the very height of its revolution, which had begun in 1789. There, in 1794, against the advice of his friend Benjamin Franklin, he published his masterpiece of Enlightenment thought, *The Age of Reason*, which garnered the opprobrious sobriquet "the atheist's bible" from the

Federalist press in America. Again Paine proved to have an uncanny knack for rubbing influential people the wrong way with his writing. Just as Washington, of all people, should have been appreciative of *The Rights of Man*, the French leader during this time, Maximilian Robespierre, should have been, but was not, appreciative of *The Age of Reason*. Robespierre had Paine jailed. President Washington in the United States, fully committed to neutrality in regard to the sparring factions in France, refused to call for Paine's release, considering him something other than an American citizen. The American ambassador to France, James Monroe, bailed him out, however, and Paine then denounced Washington in the strongest terms, as he did many of the highest-ranking Federalists in the United States, including John Adams and John Jay. Thomas Jefferson and fellow Republicans meanwhile embraced the caustic Paine.[8]

With the publication of *The Age of Reason* in 1794, Paine became the poster child for Deism in both Europe and America. He rejected all parts of the Christian religion that were based upon divine revelation. He mocked with equal fervor those who preached it and those who merely believed it. He claimed that most of the atrocities committed by one group of people against another throughout history had been caused by someone claiming God had spoken to them. He believed in God, to be sure, and the mono-God of Western civilization, but this God to him had simply started a plan of creation and time in motion and then left it to run without interference. While this message was anathema to the orthodox Christians of the United States, the publication of *The Age of Reason* became a sort of blessing in disguise for the critics of Deism. Before the book appeared, the orthodox in the United States could cite only Voltaire, a few other Europeans, and some lesser-known Americans as evidence of the dangers of Deism.[9]

Thereafter, Paine, a man every American knew well, and his book, could be pointed to as the epitome of that supposedly diabolical religion/anti-religion. The timing could not have been more perfect for them either. By 1795, the French Revolution had mostly run its course, but it had also already turned upside down the thousand-year tradition of Catholicism in France, and American Christians could declaim that this is what happens to nations that abandon orthodoxy. Such declamations could hardly stand up to historical scrutiny, of course, because the whole Protestant Reformation, which had produced most of the forms of Christianity present in America at the time, was a grand test of unorthodox theology and anti-orthodoxy with respect to Catholicism. Rarely are theologians bothered by such arguments, however, and that was certainly the case with American church leaders in this circumstance. They had their minds made up that Paine and Deism were sinister, and nothing could change that. By the time Paine returned to the United States (as Jefferson's guest in 1802), he was a pariah on the order of Benedict Arnold. Whatever good he did for the country in days gone by had been erased by his more recent radicalism. Indeed, if Arnold was a traitor to his country, Paine was equally a traitor to the Christian religion, at least to his orthodox critics.[10]

The problem with the popular perception of Paine as anti-Christian is that it is simply not accurate. If judged against the backdrop of modern right-wing American Christianity on the one hand and left-wing atheism on the other, Paine falls somewhere in the middle, and both sides can equally claim him as their own. Consider some of the statements of this man whom Alexander Hamilton once called an "enemy of Jesus Christ"[11] from *Common Sense*, such as "we [Americans] claim brotherhood with every European Christian." He called his Deistic God "the Almighty," and proclaimed in the best Puritan and modern fundamentalist fashion that this God had a "design" for the United States. Moreover, he believed the Reformation had been orchestrated by this God deliberately around the same time as North America's colonization in order "to open a sanctuary to the persecuted in future years. . . ." He likewise referred to "the Devil" as the force or personage that caused wickedness in the world. He quoted Old Testament scriptures copiously, specifically those regarding the nation of Israel being an example for the United States to follow. He clearly saw the United States as a "chosen nation," if chosen for the purpose of spreading democratic and egalitarian ideas rather than religious ones.[12] Consider also what Paine wrote in *The Age of Reason*: "I believe in one God, and no more; and I hope for happiness beyond this life."[13] Contrary to Hamilton's opinion, Paine clearly had respect for Jesus, just not for most of Jesus' modern professing followers.

Another notable freethinker among the famed patriots of the Revolution was Ethan Allen. The leader of the Vermont militia, the Green Mountain Boys, in the early years of the Revolution, Allen was self-educated, inasmuch as he had any education at all. During the Revolution, he became such a Francophile as to be labeled thoroughly "Frenchified" by some of his contemporaries. He claimed never to have read the writings of fellow Deists and Rationalists, but arrived at the same conclusions independently. He rejected orthodox Christianity and specifically abhorred Calvinism because of the straightjacket it placed on freedom of thought.[14] He may have had personal animus towards the Calvinists who surrounded him in New England as well. On at least one occasion he had a run-in with them in a court of law for, among other reasons, making a vow on the name of "Jesus Christ."

To say that because Allen was a Deist he was really just an atheist by another name does not ring true. It is in fact patently false. Consider that after his famous capture of Fort Ticonderoga at the beginning of the Revolution, Allen demanded the British surrender (according to legend) in the name of "the Great Jehovah," one of the monikers for the mono-God that every Christian and Jew at that time would have recognized as a synonym for their own God. Whether he actually said that or not, his writings leave no doubt as to what he believed. In his one treatise on Deism, *Reason: The Only Oracle of Man*, he denied that he was a "Christian," questioned the accuracy of the Bible as a historical document, ridiculed miracles, prayer, and the trinity, and criticized "Armenian" theology. Yet he consistently stated his belief in a

"God," which he defined as "something superior to ourselves in wisdom, power, and goodness. . . ." It is clear that his frame of reference in arguing his case for Deism came from belief in the mono-God. Consider this passage: "The Christian believes the gospel to be true and of divine authority; so that the Christian and the Deist are both of them believers . . . and a Deist may well retort upon a Christian and call him an infidel, because he differs in faith from him, as a Christian may upon the Deist . . . both are believers. . . . Why then may there not in both denominations be honest men, who are seeking after the truth, and who may have an equal right to expect the salvation and favor of God."[15]

Allen herein made a couple of points that should raise the eyebrows of those who would lump him in with atheists. He claimed to believe in the same God as the Christians but disagreed with their approach to worshiping that God. He considered Deism a "denomination," like, for example, Baptists, Methodists, or Presbyterians. One may rightly conclude, therefore, that when Allen denied that he was a "Christian," he referred specifically to the orthodox version of Protestantism practiced widely in America—and particularly New England Calvinism—in his day. He most likely also meant that he rejected the divinity of the historical Jesus, certainly not that he disbelieved in the existence of the "man" named Jesus.[16]

The United States was nurtured as a nation in its infancy by several freethinkers like Allen and Paine, but of various degrees and stripes. Yet their freethinking had limits, and it still trapped them within the confines of the intellectual parameters of belief in the mono-God. None thought in terms of Eastern mysticism, religions, or philosophy. Allen, for instance, named Islam as the most starkly contrasting religion to Christianity, which shows his lack of a genuine worldview. His view passed through the occidental lens of Judeo-Christian monotheism. The same was true for Paine. If such was the case, did Deism in general merely represent another manifestation of that same Western religious tradition? The answer is yes. Deism can rightly be considered the 18th-century intellectual's version of Western monotheism. The God of the Deists had created all things seen and unseen, including possibly other worlds with intelligent life. This God was a "he," and a being that required worship from his creation. He would judge men in an afterlife and reward them or damn them according to their earthly mortal deeds. He was a God who could, but rarely would, intervene in human affairs, but when he did it was to guide the affairs of nations, not to answer the prayers of individuals for personal or selfish reasons.[17]

## DEISM

Defining Deism accurately is central to this study. Without a definition that both the secularists and fundamentalist Christians can agree on, trying to answer the question of whether the United States was, is, or should be a

Christian nation becomes a futile endeavor. For help with this definition, the Founder who is generally considered the greatest authority on the subject of Deism, Thomas Jefferson, should be consulted. If one gives any credence to the words of Jefferson on the subject—and surely everyone does—18th-century Deism was nothing more than a synonym for *monotheism*. In a letter to Benjamin Rush in 1803, Jefferson called "Deism . . . the belief in one only God." He added that Jesus "corrected the Deism of the Jews, confirming them in their belief of only one God, and giving them juster notions of his attributes. . . ."[18] Two important implications emerge from this statement: (1) Jefferson believed the historical Jesus was a Deist, and (2) Jefferson merely tried to imitate Jesus in being a Deist (monotheist) himself.

It should be noted that Deists were never an organized body in the sense that they established an institution such as a church, with a hierarchy, head-quarters, or branches, although a few tried. While the earliest strains of a De-istic form of thought appeared in America with Cotton Mather's *Reasonable Religion* in 1713 and *The Christian Philosopher* in 1721, Deism did not really begin to take root in American culture until the critical decade of the 1760s, when revolutionary political fervor first erupted. As a sort of sidebar or con-comitant to the political upheaval, Deistic thought seemed to be the religious/philosophical/intellectual complement to the thuggery of groups like the Sons of Liberty. Deism came into vogue (meaning a sizeable number of American leaders embraced it) only in the post-Revolution years.[19]

It is true, just as modern secularists would have it, that the United States Con-stitution of 1787 was written, debated, and ratified in the very midst of the big-gest outpouring of freethinking ideology in American history. Needless to say, some Deistic and other freethinking ideas thus went into that document. Ortho-dox Christian leaders of the time naturally saw the new Constitution as a Deistic conspiracy to de-Christianize the new nation. One professing Deist defended the new Constitution, proclaiming triumphantly that it represented the culmination of years of efforts to free "uninformed minds" from "incredible tales" in the Bible and religious "darkness" and "fable" in general.[20]

Ratification did nothing to end the debate. Rather it intensified in the 1790s with the eruption of the French Revolution, the Citizen Genet episode, and the development of the two-party system in the United States, in which one party represented orthodoxy (Federalist) and the other free thought (Republican).[21] These first two American political parties "advanced distinct visions of American nationality. . . ."[22] Whereas the Federalists opposed the French Revo-lution and saw their own role as keeping the young United States unadulterated by its freethinking radicalness, the Republicans supported it and hoped it would spark revolutions throughout the world to overthrow monarchy, religious tyr-anny, and all else that kept people from liberty of mind and body. The Federal-ists were in power throughout the time of the French Revolution, and preached against it to the American people, who they wrongly saw as just "one big con-gregation that would, they hoped, sit contentedly in the pews."[23]

The Republicans, meanwhile, though out of power at the national level, gained increasing power at the state and local levels by organizing clubs known alternately as "Democratic," "Republican," or "Patriotic" societies, from Maine to Georgia. By 1800, forty-six societies had been organized in all, with memberships ranging from twenty to four hundred each. These societies routinely drank toasts to the French Revolution (and thus against monarchy and tyranny in general), expressed a globalist vision for peace to "The Great Family of Mankind," spoke of the mono-God (by various names), alluded to Bible passages, met at Lutheran or Presbyterian churches, and even listened to "patriotic" sermons delivered by ministers ordained by those denominations.[24] Yet, despite all this, they were anti-orthodox, anti-Federalist, and overwhelmingly secular in most of their writings and speeches.

Because of the French Revolution, and the quick rise of the Democratic-Republican societies, the 1790s became the pivotal decade for American Deism. In the 1790s, the Tammany Society of New York began as a Deist organization before evolving into a nonreligious (but not an antireligious) political body. A "Druid Society" also formed in New York but did not last long. The Deistical Society of the State of New York, founded by the blind former preacher Elihu Palmer, stood in the vanguard of the movement, which proved, like so many other religious movements in American history, quite ephemeral. Palmer, who began his career as a Presbyterian, but then became a Baptist, then a Unitarian, and finally a Deist, first appeared as a public figure by contributing "Thoughts on the Christian Religion" to the book *Defense of the Age of Reason* in 1794. In 1800, he started a weekly newspaper called "The Temple of Reason." He also sought to build a Temple of Instruction and Temple of Nature for his followers, but such grandiose plans came to naught amid the changing religious climate of the early 19th century, falling victim mainly to the Second Great Awakening.[25]

Deists never codified their beliefs into a single document that could serve as a manifesto for all future adherents (such as, for instance, John Calvin's *Institutes of the Christian Religion* did for most Protestants), although any of several Deist books could vie for that honor. Deism was more like a convenient label for a hard-to-categorize ideology than a structured belief system.[26] Contrary to popular misconception, Deists did not uphold nature as the deity. The fact that all the deity's creation acted according to the laws of nature gives the impression that nature itself was the sovereign power in the universe. In reality, nature was/is merely the instrument through which the Deist's God manifested his sovereignty. Benjamin Rush, the Philadelphia physician of the founding generation, who has been called a Deist by some observers and a Christian by others, pronounced that "In religion and morals as well as in medicine, nature leads to error and destruction. When we worship the sun, a cat, a crocodile, or the devil, we follow nature. When we lie, steal, commit murder or adultery, we follow nature."[27] Rush certainly did not speak for all Deists in stating his views on nature, but, again, there is no single and official statement of the Deist philosophy, so Rush's thoughts may be considered as valid as anyone else's.[28]

Moreover, consider the words of New Yorker John Jay, one of the authors of the *Federalist Papers*, the first Chief Justice of the Supreme Court, a key member of George Washington's administration, an Episcopalian who founded the American Bible Society, and a Deist of the same type as Rush. He tried to explain the Deist philosophy succinctly when he said of the United States winning the American Revolution against incalculable odds, "They who ascribe all this to the guidance and protection of Providence do well; but let them recollect, that Providence seldom interposes in human affairs, but through the agency of human means."[29] This quote sums up what might best be described as the "mild" Deist philosophy in a nutshell: not that the laws of nature as set forth by God are so rigid and unalterable that God could never intervene in human affairs through miraculous means, but that God directs the affairs of nations and hence the whole human race through chosen vessels that perform his supernatural will in natural ways. When seen in this light, the mild Deist philosophy looks quite similar to Calvinist predestination.[30]

In its glory days of the 1790s, Deism and other forms of freethinking, mainly Unitarianism and Freemasonry, made such inroads into the previously all-Christian colleges of New England that, by the end of the decade, there numbered no more than one, two, or three professing Christians in the graduating classes of Dartmouth, Princeton, and Bowdoin. This sudden flourishing of freethinking among America's intellectual elite convinced many observers and participants in the Founding generation that Christianity would soon go the way of the dinosaurs.[31] Jefferson's oft-quoted statement that he trusted no young Christian in America in his day would die as anything other than a Unitarian sums up that notion nicely. A generation later, the tide had turned away from Unitarianism, but one of Jefferson's ideological progeny, John C. Calhoun of South Carolina, repeated the prediction anyway.[32] It might be concluded that Calhoun was just a Southerner who blindly followed his ideological father Jefferson in religion the same as he did in politics (specifically in the state rights doctrine of nullification).[33]

The intellectual elites turned out to be partly correct—their prediction held true by and large for members of their own social class. William Ellery Channing of Harvard, for instance, managed to guide his institution of higher learning about as far away from its repressive Puritan roots as could be thought possible. His Unitarianism gave rise to the Transcendental movement of the early 1800s, which in turn gave the world some of the classics in the corpus of American literature. Timothy Dwight of Yale stood practically alone among the old bastions of Christian education in opposing the new-fangled intellectualism. He considered Unitarianism to be a "half-way house" between righteousness and infidelity, and he had more of the common people on his side than did Channing or other Unitarian leaders.[34]

The ideological battle between Channing and Dwight shows that the great debate in the Founding generation was not between religion and atheism or orthodox Christianity or Deism, but between two different strains of Christianity. The two strains were not Catholicism and Protestantism, as had traditionally been the case in Europe, but rather Trinitarianism and Unitarianism. If so, the question of whether the United States was originally a Christian nation seems to take on a new meaning. Moreover, the question that should be asked is whether the United States was ever a "Trinitarian" nation. Put in modern terms, the question equates roughly to whether it was a "fundamentalist" nation. Put in a more accurate historical terminology, it equates to whether it was ever an "orthodox" nation. The answer to the question, no matter how it is phrased, is "no," although it can be argued that the answer is "partly." This would be true in the sense that a much larger portion of the American people considered themselves Trinitarians than Unitarians in the Founding generation.

The intellectual elite of the late 1700s and early 1800s—who held sway over colleges, the media, and government, and who led the Deist and Unitarian movements—garnered attention for themselves out of all proportion to their numbers within the general population. They thus failed to consider several points that, with the benefit of hindsight, look obvious to modern observers. One, the democratization of America was rapidly occurring and would put down deep roots within one generation, ironically resulting from the egalitarian policies and principles of the main group promoting freethinking—the Jeffersonian Republicans. Two, the transforming power of the religious revival during the Second Great Awakening was about to steer the majority of common Americans in an anti-intellectual direction. Third, the frontier would soon become the main outlet for these commoners, with their anti-intellectual religion and their demand for equality under the law *vis-à-vis* the coastal elites who ran the state and national governments at the time.[35]

As the Deism fad evaporated in the early 19th century, most erstwhile Deists settled into the "half-way house" Unitarian churches rather than make a complete break with religion and become atheists. Although this made them "Christians" of a sort, this they could handle because it required neither that they sacrifice their faith in the mono-God nor offend too terribly the senses of their fellow Christians, the Trinitarians. The Trinitarians, although certainly not enamored of the Unitarians, at least did not feel threatened by them to quite the same extent as they did the Deists, and not nearly to the same extent as atheists. The Unitarians simply did not have the numbers to cause alarm. Some Deists, such as John Randolph, later in life found their way back to the Trinitarian orthodoxy of their youth, and others, such as Edmund Randolph, converted to Trinitarianism for the first time only after disestablishment made joining an orthodox church a voluntary affair.[36]

## FREEMASONRY

Meanwhile, the one freethinking institution that managed to survive and thrive while the others either languished or became mere country clubs for wealthy and educated elites was Freemasonry. In Richard Brookhiser's words, the Founders' "Freemasonry is a difficult subject, not because everyone cares about it, but because hardly anyone does. The only people interested in Free-masonry are Masons and Anti-Masons; almost everything written about it is either self-infatuated or loony. . . ."[37] Like Unitarianism it was ecumenical in scope and outlook, but unlike Unitarianism it was never considered a "reli-gion" according to the common usage of the term. It was rather a fraternal order that served to bridge the gap between intellectual philosophy and emo-tional religion, between natural science and metaphysical mysticism. Stripped of all its trappings, such as secrecy, esoteric rituals, and thirty-three different degrees (levels) of membership—all of which tend to cloud what it was really about—this fraternal order emerges as a fairly important organization in American history. In it from the beginning were the elements of *E Pluribus Unum*, *Annuit Coeptis*, and the *Novus Ordo Seclorum*. In scope and outlook it was international, not national, and in America it was continental, not regional or local. In religion it was Unitarian, not Trinitarian or sectarian. Thus, it defi-nitely helped shape the type of nation the United States became.

Having started before the Revolution in Scotland (at least in its modern form), it quickly spread to the United States. Sources differ as to the actual or-igin of this brotherhood, but at least one form of it can be traced back to a medieval craft guild of actual stone cutters and builders. From this seemingly humble beginning, it evolved into a professional union of men who would today be called architects and engineers rather than mere masons. By the time of the Revolution, Freemasonry had spread throughout the thirteen colonies, from Boston to Savannah. In some cases, Americans living in such disparate parts of the country as Massachusetts and Georgia felt more of a kinship through their Freemason membership than they did through their political opinions, national defense exigencies, or church affiliations. In short, Freema-sonry served as a unifying force in American life at a time when unification was sorely needed.[38]

Why did Freemasonry prosper when so many other freethinking institutions did not? Perhaps because it was totally acceptable for a man to be a Freema-son and an orthodox church member simultaneously, at least from the Freema-sons' point of view. Various church groups took different stances on their members belonging to the Freemasons, as they still do. But mainly, the two were not seen as mutually exclusive or incompatible. A man could view his church affiliation as his religion while thinking of Freemasonry as his philosophy—one as his spiritual guide and the other as his intellectual guide. No other major freethinking institution could make that fine distinction. One could not, for instance, call oneself a Christian in the Trinitarian sense and a Deist at the same time.

In conclusion, freethinking came in several varieties, from the hardcore Deism of Elihu Palmer and Ethan Allen to the mild Deism of Benjamin Rush and John Jay, from the Unitarianism of Thomas Jefferson and William Ellery

Channing to the Freemasonry of George Washington and Benjamin Franklin. It came among famous people such as Cadwallader Colden, one of the true Renaissance men of the American colonial period, who took his freethinking to the extreme of embracing hedonism, and Jonathan Mayhew, the first great Unitarian minister in New England. It likewise came among those who ranged from the less well known, such as Freemason William Bentley and Unitarian John Murray of Massachusetts, to totally obscure common citizens, such as Joseph Barrell, who wrote letters trying to convert his brother Nathaniel to Deism.[39] This lineup shows quite an array of free thought for a nation that was, in the words of Jefferson's friend John Trumbull, "a country professing Christianity."[40]

Finally, a smattering of various underground societies existed in the United States that have not been mentioned, such as the Bavarian Illuminati, which seemed practically Satanic by comparison to their milder counterparts.[41] The numbers and influence of such groups made them a negligible factor in early American history, although those who are so inclined today can find all kinds of conspiracy theories behind their existence (just as orthodox Christian Federalists did at the time). The recent Hollywood movie starring Nicolas Cage, *National Treasure*, springs immediately to mind as an example. Conspiracy theories make interesting reading and entertaining movies but rarely make accurate history. Although professional historians are trained to know better than to speculate upon the plausibility of conspiracy theories, it seems reasonable to say that most claims of diabolical intentions among Founders with connections to sinister organizations are highly exaggerated at best and utterly baseless at worst. The facts, however, that several of the Founders were Freemasons, that Masonic symbols can be seen on some of the nation's currency, that Freemason Pierre L'Enfant's city plan for Washington, D.C., seems to have been imbedded with Masonic symbols, and that some of the most influential American political leaders since the Founding generation have been Freemasons, will keep the conspiracy theorists actively pursuing their craft in perpetuity.[42]

## Chapter 6

# The American "Irrationalism"

## The Founders and the Reasonableness of Religion

### THE DECLARATION OF IRRATIONALISM

Having established a basis for understanding freethinking among the Founders, an inquiry into how they put their free thought to use in creating the United States government is now in order. If freethinking did not lead to atheism in most cases but rather to differing views of who or what the mono-God was, the Founders, it can be concluded with certainty, did not leave this God of theirs out of the nation's governmental charters. Although modern secularists contend that the Founders were motivated merely by a secular philosophy of natural law and natural rights, the fact is that most of the Founders did not believe this system of nature operated without the guidance of a deity.[1] "It was . . . the Founding Fathers' faith in the reality of the higher law that enabled them to speak so confidently of the self-evident truths which they accepted as axioms. . . . What God had given God could take away, but divine gifts were not to be taken away by one's fellow men. . . ."[2]

Two examples of men in the Founding generation who held this view are Thomas Jefferson and Samuel Langdon. In the Declaration of Independence, Jefferson called the deity "Nature's God," and then used the synonyms *Creator*, *Judge*, and *Providence*. This deity was not nature itself but the one who ruled over nature, as evidenced by the wording he used: "Nature *and* Nature's God." This deity could be prayed to and an answer could be expected, as long as the things prayed for were not self-serving. Asking for a blessing, for instance, upon the new United States, a nation founded with the intention of having a positive impact upon all mankind, would be considered an acceptable prayer.[3] An American Loyalist named Samuel Langdon said during the Revolution, "Thanks be to God that he has given us, as men, natural rights independent [of] all human laws whatever. . . . By the law of nature any body of people may form themselves into a civil society. . . ."[4] This statement indicates that Langdon believed in God and nature as two separate entities, with the former controlling the latter.

The confusion over the question of whether the Founders viewed God and nature as one and the same comes most directly from the words of John Locke, who wrote such things as the Creator made man to be a social creature, and thus it is ingrained in man "to enter into society by a certain propensity of nature."[5] In this phraseology, God designed man to obey nature, thus making man subservient to both nature and God. If subservient to both, does that not make nature a type of "lord" over man as well? So it would seem. Today it is understood that genetic coding is what gives man most of his natural propensities. When people say colloquially nowadays that it is in someone's "nature" to be a certain way, they mean it is in his or her genetic composition. Locke certainly meant the same thing but lacked the scientific knowledge of genetics to explain it in anything other than the most primitive, rudimentary terms.

Moreover, to be perfectly clear and precise about this issue, Locke's words must be used in a political rather than metaphysical or abstract, philosophical context. By doing so, it can reasonably be concluded that Locke intended (just as Jefferson and most of the Founders interpreted it), that a hierarchy existed in the universe that flowed from top down in this order: God, nature, mankind, government—with each the creator of, and thus the one in control of, the one directly beneath it. This idea had enormous consequences for the Founders who realized, as Locke had a century earlier, that mankind and government had gotten backwards in relation to one another in other nations through monarchies and other despotic political systems. The job of the United States, therefore, was to correct this imbalance and put man back in charge of government, in other words, or to put government to work for the good of man, rather than government lording over man. This idea seemed, to the Founders, "self-evident." When Jefferson and other Founders applied this rationale to the new American man-and-government relationship, they did so with the understanding that unless they declared clearly and forcefully that man's rights are "unalienable" because they come from nature rather than government, someone someday would surely get the hierarchy out of order again and use government to try to take away man's "natural rights."[6]

According to this interpretation, the wording of the Declaration of Independence begins to take on a new meaning and make better sense. When Jefferson wrote that "governments are instituted among men" to "secure these rights," he meant that governments are instituted *by* men to ensure that the laws of nature are followed, which are in turn subject to the will of the unseeable, unknowable creator. The creator, who is otherwise hidden from man, is revealed in the creation—nature—and in order to make certain that all mankind gets the opportunity to appreciate the creator through the creation, governments must keep the peace between individuals and nations but otherwise not interfere with the hierarchy. Without government, every man would be a law unto himself. Hence, the hierarchy in reverse works like this: government protects man's right to observe nature and thereby observe the creator through that creator's handiwork called nature. Thus the formation of the United States of America was for the purpose of protecting and enforcing the will of an unseeable, unknowable entity. If this interpretation is correct, it must be concluded that the Declaration, which is generally seen as an almost exclusively Rationalist document, contains a strong strain of the religious, the mystical, and/or the metaphysical.[7]

Although this interpretation of the Declaration makes it appear quite irrational, and at first glance that would seem strange, it actually should not be thought unusual. When scrutinizing carefully the ideology that is called Rationalism during this Age of Enlightenment, we find that there is a great deal about it that does not seem at all rational. Consider the French Revolution, undoubtedly the zenith of Rationalism so-called. It was based upon a deliberate intellectual rejection of the orthodox religion of France (Catholicism), any unorthodox religious ideologies (as defined by French tradition and/or law) such as Protestantism and Judaism, and the monarchy that claimed to rule by "divine right." Yet it resulted not from a thoughtful, plodding, intellectual appeal to the masses, but from an emotional, knee-jerk reaction to the excesses and corruption of the monarchy and clergy. When the mob stormed the Bastille, that was not a "rational" action. Likewise, when Robespierre instigated the reign of terror and instituted the new, artificial civic religion through dictatorial power, those were not "rational" actions. Revolutions, whether French or American or otherwise, while possibly being conceived intellectually, are invariably carried out irrationally. Thus, it should not be surprising that the Declaration, which was conceived by rational thought, relies upon irrational, primitive ideas, such as beginning with an acknowledgment of a creator-God and ending with an appeal for that deity's "Protection" and "Providence."

The Founders' interpretation of natural law, natural rights, self-evident truths, and unalienable rights came mainly from John Locke's philosophical musings, of course, but it came more precisely from a combination (primarily) of Locke and his many disciples, Isaac Newton's scientific formulations, William Blackstone's political commentaries, and Scottish Enlightenment religious skepticism.[8] The first three sources mentioned here were distinctly Christian in orientation. Hamilton Long has proffered that everywhere one reads the phrase "unalienable rights" in writings or speeches of the Founders it should be interpreted "'God-given' rights, because the only basis for considering them to be unalienable is the fundamental and uniquely American

concept of their origin—that man possesses them solely by reason of endow-
ment by his creator."[9] Lockean philosophy may have been the bedrock under-
neath the thinking of the Founders,[10] but Newtonian science was almost as
important for them, if not as often noticed by observers today. Bernard Cohen
has concluded that "Lest any reader think it far-fetched to suppose that Newton's 'axioms, or laws of motion' should be cited in a political context, let it
be noted that a few years after the Declaration, John Adams would be citing
Newton's third law of motion in the course of a political debate with
Benjamin Franklin over the optimal form of the legislature." He also noted
that "James Wilson introduced one of the definitions relating to Newton's first
law in the context of a lecture on the principles of government."[11]

Concerning Blackstone, the great English Whig, whose *Commentaries on the
Laws of England* was perhaps the most widely read and discussed political book
in late-18th-century America, the Founders considered his views on natural law
and rights to be practically indisputable.[12] Blackstone said the "law of nature"
was "dictated by God himself," and therefore was "binding over all the
globe, in all countries, at all times: no human laws are of any validity, if contrary to this; and such of them as are valid derive all their force and all their
authority . . . from this original."[13] Two points are notable here. One is that
Blackstone considered God to be above nature, not synonymous with nature,
and the other is that he considered natural law within the global, rather than
merely national, context. It seems obvious that Jefferson's terminology in the
Declaration utilized this whole-of-humanity view when he said that "all men
are created equal," not "all Americans are created equal."[14] If so, the Declaration, which has been called the "charter of the American Dream," is actually
the charter for the dream of all humanity, regardless of nationality.[15] It is consequently a romantic (idealistic) rather than rationalist (realistic) document,
smacking of utopianism, which makes it irrational in some ways, just as it is
rational in others.[16]

## THE IRRATIONAL CONSTITUTION

If the Declaration of Independence contains irrational ideas and words, might
the Constitution as well? This question demands investigation. Modern secularists contend that "the principal architects of our national government" were so
thoroughly rational in their thinking that they "envisioned a godless Constitution
and a godless politics."[17] This statement, however, does not hold up to scrutiny.
It does not even come close. It is in fact utterly false and misleading. The main
pieces of evidence this "godless" group of scholars point to for proof come
mostly from James Madison's notes on the convention and on the Constitution
itself—(1) that the delegates at the Constitutional convention in 1787 did not
make religion a topic of discussion, (2) they did not pray over their deliberations
(and ignored the idea to do so when broached by Benjamin Franklin), and
(3) they made almost no mention of anything of a spiritual nature in their final

document. Alexander Hamilton, who was not only present but took a leading role in the discussions that produced the Constitution, explained that this omission of religion was not by design but by accident.[18]

Some respected historians, such as Catherine Drinker Bowen, have accepted that explanation, adding such apologies as "there sat no delegate whose ideas of government or political philosophy were not profoundly influenced by his religious beliefs and training."[19] Hamilton's explanation, however, sounds weak and doubtful at best and ridiculous at worst. How could the Founders have overlooked such an important topic by accident, especially considering that Madison himself later stated his own personal belief that "a finger of that Almighty hand" helped guide him and his fellows in crafting the Constitution?[20] If it is true that the delegates did not discuss religion and made no overt gestures favoring Christianity either in the convention or in the Constitution, regardless of whether intentionally or unintentionally, there is no doubt that religion became a topic in the ratification debates in the various states, in the national press, and among the citizenry in general. Likewise, it became the main point of argument leading to the creation of the Bill of Rights.[21] New England Congregationalists in particular lamented the "sinful omission" of any acknowledgment of God in the Constitution and made sure the states heard about it in the ratification process.[22]

The various ratification debates reveal much more about the thinking of both the Founders and the American citizenry on the topic of religion than does the Constitution itself. To the delegates at the Virginia convention Richard Henry Lee wrote, "I pray Sir that God may bless the Convention with wisdom, maturity of Counsel, and constant care of the public liberty; and that he may have you in his holy keeping."[23] At the Virginia convention itself, governor Edmund Randolph, soon to be appointed George Washington's first attorney general, called religion "the dearest of all interests," and believed that supporting the Constitution was showing obedience to God.[24] James Iredell of North Carolina supported the Constitution, using much biblical imagery, speaking of the "Supreme Being," and calling on God to give wisdom to the various ratification conventions.[25] At the South Carolina convention, David Ramsay proclaimed that "Heaven smiled on their deliberations [in Philadelphia], and inspired their councils," and he gave "Thanks to Heaven" accordingly.[26] Benjamin Rush at the Pennsylvania convention used biblical imagery to make his point that God was the real framer of the United States government.[27] Someone from Rhode Island using the pseudonym "Phocion" called on "gracious Heaven" to grant the American people the wisdom to ratify the Constitution.[28] Someone at the New York convention using the pseudonym "Brutus IV" likewise employed a great deal of religious imagery, quoting the Apostle Paul, and taking for granted that the Bible provided the common ground for both Federalists and Anti-Federalists to stand upon to make their cases for or against the Constitution.[29] An anonymous New Yorker commented that the new Constitution was a "blessing of Heaven," and called on God to "avert" the efforts of the Anti-Federalists, urging his fellows to "pray" that God stop the intentions and designs of such evil men.[30] John Stevens, writing as "Americanus VII," compared the Anti-Federalist idea of calling a new convention to repair the defects in the Constitution to the biblical story of the gathering of people that created the tower of Babel.[31]

Anti-Federalists, who were "spokesmen for an important alternative constitutional heritage," believed equally that God was on their side, or they on God's.[32] James Winthrop of Massachusetts, writing as "Agrippa XII," called on "Heaven" to direct his state's delegates to reject the Constitution.[33] Charles Jarvis echoed those sentiments, saying that "Heaven" or "Providence" would bless the United States if it accepted the Constitution, but would bless it even more if it rejected the document.[34] John Hancock agreed that, pending amendments, the Constitution should be defeated, but called on the "Supreme Ruler of the Universe" to "continue to bless and save our country" regardless of the outcome.[35] Luther Martin of Maryland recalled how the several states had invoked the "Supreme Being" to be a "witness" and "avenger" if they should break the union made in the Articles of Confederation.[36] Martin also wanted a religious test for holding public office put into whatever government charter should be used, calling the United States a "Christian country."[37]

Many others likewise hedged their bets, choosing not to try to speak for God in stating opinions on the Constitution. They focused their attention instead on creating a righteous people in the United States, regardless of what form of government the ratification process produced. A Rhode Islander calling himself "Plough Jogger" referred to God as the "great Governor of the Universe" and the civil authorities of the United States as "God's ministers" no matter how they voted on ratification.[38] Governor Samuel Huntington of Connecticut believed that whether the Constitution was ratified or not, the fate of his country rested with the "great body" of the people being "acquainted with the duties which they owe to their God," among other things.[39] John Dickinson of Pennsylvania, writing as "Fabius," said, "Our most gracious Creator . . . *demands*— that we should seek for [good government] in *his* way, and not in *our own*." The way to which Dickinson referred lay in creating a government that would function according to the Golden Rule. Man is never happier, said Dickinson, than when he strove to "correspond with the Divine designs, by communicating happiness, as much as we can, to our fellow creatures." He called God "our Maker" and observed that the "*perfect liberty*" for which the Constitution's Framers were striving was nowhere "better described" than in the "Holy Scriptures," particularly in the work of the "inspired Apostle Saint Paul."[40]

The previously cited evidence, and many similar examples that could be cited, suggests that the Founders were just as adept at quoting scripture and calling upon God to guide their nation as they were at citing Locke, Blackstone, or anyone else.[41] It shows the Founders and their colleagues as not merely semireligious men but extremely religious men, at least in the sense that their worldview lay almost completely within the parameters of Western

Judeo-Christian thought. So despite their obvious omission of any overtly Christian statements or terminology in the Constitution, they were not atheists, and they were not bereft of all concern about religious matters. Besides, in Article I, Section 7, they did set aside Sunday as a nonwork day for the president. In so doing, they gave tacit approval to the observation of Sunday as the traditional day of rest and/or worship for the United States. This initial action would later be supplemented by legislation that apparently reiterated the Founders' intent. For example, the president is never inaugurated on Sunday, Congress does not meet on Sundays (except in emergencies), federal courts do not open on Sunday, national holidays are not observed on Sunday, and voting never occurs on Sunday.[42] Granted, this has as much to do with the fact that every nation and people needs *some* regular day of rest, regardless of whether it is used for worship, as it does with practicing Christianity. If, however, that is all there was to it, why did the writers of the Constitution not choose Tuesday? Thursday? Saturday? Clearly, out of deference to the nation's Christian heritage they chose Sunday. Likewise, they chose to end the Constitution with the words "in the year of our Lord," another Christian tradition that they could have easily chosen to abolish but did not.[43]

Even without such indirect nods to Christian heritage and tradition, the Constitution can be construed to imply Christian principles such as the Golden Rule and "love thy neighbor as thyself." It is all about having respect for authority, respect for the law, respect for one's fellow man, and all such ubiquitous humanitarian principles. It allows for no individual's pride to be rewarded, or any individual's political office to grow too powerful. It is, some observers have said, the perfect example of "doing" the word of God rather than preaching it. It makes no outright proclamations of righteousness, but it silently exudes righteous ideas and pure motives. As such, the Constitution could be said to be "Christian in substance, though not in form. It is pervaded by the spirit of justice and humanity, which are Christian."[44] Foreign commentator James Bryce of England agreed in the 1890s, saying the Constitution is pervaded by a Puritan sense of right and wrong. Those who would claim otherwise, he said, are not measuring it by the correct yardstick. If measured by the French Constitution, which is not only secular but absolutely antireligious, then the American Constitution suddenly looks quite religious, if not specifically Christian.[45] But if it is indeed so different from other national government charters that are openly antireligious, and yet it does not profess Christianity, what religion then does it exude? Although the religion does not have a name, it could be said to be some type of humanitarianism. This should by no means be confused with "humanism" or "secular humanism," which implies atheism or agnosticism to many adherents. No, the Founders were deeply religious, believing firmly in the mono-God; that much is sure. If their belief in the deity is coupled with their humanitarianism, they could rightly be said to have adhered to "Monotheistic Humanitarianism," if it must be given a name.

## A UTILITARIAN FAITH?

Some important questions that inevitably arise in discussions about the Founders' religion or lack thereof are: (1) Did they *really* believe in God, or did they merely mimic the sociopolitical orthodoxy of the day (being politically correct, in other words), for the sake of winning elections and appealing to their constituents in the biblical language they could understand? (2) Moreover, did they *really* apply biblical or otherwise ascetic principles in their own private lives, or did they merely act religious in public for the sake of appearances? (3) Did they *really* believe the religious faith they professed, or did they merely want to set an example for the citizenry, with the notion that fostering the fear of God among the people would keep law and order and produce a stable society?

If the answer to the first part of any of these three questions is "no," then it can be concluded that the Founders were all hypocrites and some of the most gifted con-artists of all time, and that they entered into a secret conspiracy with one another to fool the masses. It frankly stretches the limits of the imagination to think this could be true. As Clinton Rossiter has expressed it, the Founders all in all seem "to have been entirely sincere. I have never found . . . any evidence to suggest that these men and those who echoed them throughout the land did not mean exactly what they said."[46] Besides, the inadvisability of using conspiracy theories as bases upon which to write history has already been noted. Keeping in mind that it is impossible to prove conspiracy theories false, it is not fruitful to engage in defenses against them. Rather, they should be dismissed as anti-history, because they rely not on written documentation but on speculation. That said, it is impossible to know for sure what was in the Founders' hearts, whether their faith was genuine, or whether some of their religious words and deeds were for show. Most likely, their seeming hypocrisy and ideological contradictions stem from vacillation between faith and doubt rather than from deliberate deceitfulness. Each modern observer can judge only by the Founders' writings and what contemporaries wrote about them. When doing this, it can easily be deduced that the two parts to each of the three previous questions are not mutually exclusive, meaning even if one answers "yes" to the first part, that does not preclude the second part from being answered in the affirmative as well.[47]

Jefferson serves as the prime example of a Founder who wanted it, and had it, both ways. Although modern secularists routinely laud him as the president who took religion out of the public square after Washington and Adams had put it in, his actions as war-time governor of Virginia show quite the opposite. He called for days of fasting, prayer, and thanksgiving, and seems to have done it to shore up the morale of his constituents rather than because he personally thought it necessary or proper.[48] He thus believed in the mono-God, but thought it a waste of time to pray, yet called for prayer for the benefit of the people. Therefore, he was both a *believer in* and a *user of* religion. He agreed with the basic Enlightenment philosophy of Locke and others that the government's role was to do the greatest good to the largest number of people. This philosophy was later codified by Jeremy Bentham in England under the moniker "Utilitarianism." Certainly Jefferson and the rest of the Founders shared a belief in the utilitarian principle, and inasmuch as religion could be used to promote the greater good, they all used it.[49] Madison, for example, wanted to find or fabricate a "common core of useful religious truth" for that purpose.[50]

The possibility must now be explored that the Founders indeed wanted to "use" the belief in God to help instill morality and stability in American society. The use of religion for such social and political purposes is often called "Functionalism." Whether the religion being used is real or artificial is beside the point to a Functionalist; any belief system can serve the function of helping to create a well-ordered society as long as the people buy into it.[51] As one American theologian put it, "Our national life would be a shambles if there were no . . . consensus on matters of justice and public morality. . . . The decisions of the state depend upon [a] broad moral consensus."[52] In a Functionalist system, theoretically, anyone or anything can substitute for God. It may be nature, reason, a nation, a race, an ethnic group, a king, or an ideal. If the Founders were Functionalists, they could have chosen any of these substitutes. Yet they chose the mono-God. Why? Did they know then what people surely know now: the problem with these substitutes is that none are infallible, incorruptible, or undefeatable, and that once corrupted or defeated, these substitutes lose their power to hold the allegiance of the masses. This seems unlikely for three reasons. First, nothing in their writings yields any evidence that they probed for a substitute or discussed one among themselves; instead, they seem to have accepted axiomatically what the Reverend Caldwell stated at the North Carolina ratification convention: "even those who do not regard religion acknowledge that the Christian religion is best calculated of all religions to make good members of society, on account of its morality."[53] Second, since the dawn of the Christian era and the end of the Roman Empire, no Western nation had tried such a substitution before the birth of the United States, so the Founders had no pattern to follow or examples from which to learn. Third, it smacks again of the conspiratorial.

Immediately after the Founders made their American Constitutional experiment, France staged its own, in which the Robespierre regime substituted devotion to reason and allegiance to the state for the traditional worship of God and adherence to the Catholic Church. Needless to say, French "reason" quickly became extremely unreasonable to those many thousands murdered in its name, and the French state immediately proved incapable of maintaining the order, stability, and control (or "liberty, equality, and fraternity," as the revolutionaries put it) that was the object of the revolution. It failed, according to Wilson McWilliams, because the "creed of liberty, equality, and fraternity is intelligible only in relation to the idea of a Creator, a Divine 'father' who established fraternity among men."[54] Later, worship of the state and/or its leader(s) was tried again and again in various formerly Christian nations, such as Germany, Russia, and Italy. Each time, the effort failed miserably.[55] Modern observers can look back confidently and say that none of these substitutes for God can quite fill the deity's shoes. To think the Founders had the prescience or forethought to know that in 1787 seems a little much.

It has already been shown in this study that the Founders did not intend to create a secular state. Clearly, creating a nation *without* a God or *with* some kind of God substitute never entered their minds, at least not for serious consideration. The question arises, however, whether secularism itself could have been a substitute for God in their plan. That is, was their desire to keep an established church from forming in the United States so strong that they would be willing to discard worship of the mono-God and replace it with worship (veneration) of freedom of choice? If so, secularism itself could be considered the religion of the nation.[56] This is an intriguing idea that harkens back to this study's earlier discussion of the civic religion. Some observers have concluded it impossible that secularism and/or freedom of choice could be considered a religion.[57] Yet, belief in nothing is still belief. Atheism is a creed. Secularism is a philosophy of life. Institutionalized antireligion makes antireligion the new religion. Nazism, Fascism, and Communism, for example, elicited in their followers "a depth of conviction and a fervor of devotion usually found only among persons inspired by a transcendent faith."[58] Moreover, "Like a religion . . . it [such examples] creates true believers, who feel that they are participating in a great cause—a heroic fight against evil—that gives meaning to their lives."[59] Winston Churchill recognized the religious fervor that Nazism raised in the German people, for example, arguing that it pitted the religion of "barbarous paganism" against "Christian ethics" and "Christian civilization."[60]

Such ideas about the need for mankind to have some kind of religion and some kind of God, whether real or artificial, have long been known. Consider the words of French psychologist Gustave Le Bon in his 1895 tome *The Crowd*: "A person is not religious solely when he worships a divinity, but when he puts all the resources of his mind, the complete submission of his will, and the whole-souled ardour of fanaticism at the service of a cause or an individual who becomes the goal and guide of his thoughts and actions."[61] Consider also the thoughts of Lev Kopelev, a Ukrainian Jew living under the Stalin regime in the 1930s–1940s:

We were raised as the fanatical [believers] of a new creed, the only true *religion* of scientific socialism. The party became our church militant, bequeathing to all mankind eternal salvation, eternal peace and the bliss of an earthly paradise. It victoriously surmounted all other churches, schisms and heresies. The works of Marx, Engels and Lenin were accepted as holy writ, and Stalin was the infallible high priest.[62]

In seeking a replacement for God, nations tried not merely such ideologies that made war in the early 20th century, but war itself as a substitute. As

French writer Georges Sorel noted in 1908, "In default of paradise, there is [military] glory, which is itself a kind of immortality."[63]

After two world wars and a cold war against atheistic communism, American psychiatrist Scott Peck determined that "humanity might be better off without a belief in God. . . . God is not only pie in the sky by and by, but a poisoned pie at that. It would seem reasonable to conclude that God is an illusion in the minds of humans—a destructive illusion—and that belief in God is a common form of human psychopathology that should be healed. So we have a question: Is belief in God a sickness?" Peck concluded that the generalized answer is "no," because *something* serving as God exists within every person. However, some people's versions of "God" are healthy and some are not, so belief in God may lead to mental illness in some humans.[64]

Some theologians and philosophers have questioned whether it is possible to have "morality" in a completely atheistic state. Laws against murder, theft, rape, and such exist in atheistic states just as they do in traditionally religious nations, which seems to answer the morality question in the affirmative, if the fact be discounted that the impetus for enforcing such laws may be lost in cases where the atheist sees no benefit for himself or herself in the action. Fear of government officials who hold higher positions of authority provides the impetus in many cases, of course. The question then should be rephrased to ask whether it is possible to have morality in the individual conscience without fear of someone (man, government, or God) in a higher level of authority. To many religious observers, the answer would seem to be "no," but there is no way to prove it. To many atheists and agnostics, the answer would be "look at me. I have morality without fear of God, and I would live right and do righteously of my own accord, even if there were no laws against harming my fellow man." Therefore, one can only speculate about this question, and no consensus seems possible.[65]

The Founders did think about such questions, although they did not have the luxury of time to ponder them in depth and let insights seep into their minds slowly. They had to make choices relatively quickly during and after the American Revolution, so dynamic was the pace of change during those years. By the time they entered the Constitutional Convention of 1787, their views had to have been already fairly well forged and set. Even if they had enjoyed the luxury of time, there is a high probability they would have opted to take an old European concept called "Erastianism" and put an American twist on it anyway, rather than attempting to concoct an elaborate new civic religion of their own. Erastianism is the practice of a government utilizing and manipulating the church for the benefit of the state. The American twist would have been that the United States government would use not "the church" per se but the "church*es*." The Founders could have looked to the example of several European nations in 1787 that were in a state of transition from pre-Reformation theocracies to modern secular governments. Holland was perhaps the most Erastian of them, using the Dutch Reformed Church for

Utilitarian purposes. Under an Erastian system, rather than a secular government taking over and destroying national religious traditions (as France did with such disastrous results), it could ease out of those traditions over a matter of decades without shocking the people. The idea of Erastianism (which is more accurately the idea of Machiavellianism—"the end justifies the means"—applied to religion) did not originate with the man for whom it is erroneously named, Thomas Erastus, the Swiss theologian of the 1500s, because ancient Greece and Rome, among other civilizations, had used religion in just the same way. However, like so many other aspects of ancient knowledge, Renaissance men rediscovered it around the time of the Reformation, which means, coincidentally, just in time for the Founders to apply it in the new United States, had they so chosen.[66]

In conclusion, in the 1950s, then-president Dwight Eisenhower made the oft-repeated Functionalist statement, "Our government makes no sense unless it is founded in a deeply felt religious faith, and I don't care what kind it is."[67] As contemporary Christian commentator Cal Thomas has put it, the question in America is and always has been not whether some religious group would get to shove their religion down everyone else's throat, but merely which one would get to do it. The only question for the Founders then was, would the ones doing the shoving be the orthodox mainstream Christians, the secularists, the agnostics, the atheists, the Freethinkers, the Deists, the Unitarians, or someone totally new?[68]

There is no doubt that the Founders wanted to create a nation with a certain kind of high moral character. They could do it in two ways: (1) try to use the churches, the schools, and even the civic clubs to inculcate "character" in the masses; and (2) lead by example, showing their own values to be worthy of emulation by the masses.[69] It is this notion of leading by example that is the basis for the next chapter.

## Chapter 7

# The American "Exemplars"

## Founders Who Led by Example

## THE BIT PLAYERS

Thus far this study has inquired into the religious background of American culture, the philosophical underpinnings of separation of church and state, and the ways various forces coalesced to form the national civic religion. It now follows to consider how some of the specific Founders viewed religion and helped shape the destiny of the country with it. To begin, it should be noted that most (but certainly not all) of the signers of the Declaration and the Constitution were born and raised in the 1730s and 1740s, the decades of the Great Awakening in America and of a great outpouring of Enlightenment thought in Europe. They were thus products of a radical period in Western civilization when competing ideological forces worked against one another. It would have been virtually impossible for them to have grown up in the civilized parts of the American colonies during this time and not felt the effects of that tug-of-war. Both radical spiritualism and intellectualism vied for the attention of their young, impressionable minds. Some imbibed more of the one, while some absorbed more of the other, and each individual character was molded accordingly.

Some of the youngsters who gravitated toward the traditional, conservative Christianity of the day, including an affirmation of an establishment of religion—regardless of denominational preference—included John Jay, an Episcopalian, mild Deist, and Federalist from New York who became the first president of the American Bible Society (ABS) and first Chief Justice of the

Supreme Court; John Marshall, an Episcopalian-turned-Unitarian and Federalist from Virginia who became the vice president of the ABS and the most influential Chief Justice of the Supreme Court; Benjamin Rush of Pennsylvania, the physician who remained an Episcopalian "Christocrat" despite becoming a mild Deist and Unitarian, but who reverted to his old Trinitarian faith late in life; Patrick Henry, the Episcopalian *bête noire* of fellow Episcopalian James Madison, who fought to keep the establishment of religion in Virginia while simultaneously defending the rights of Baptist dissenters there (for political rather than religious reasons); Richard Henry Lee, the Virginian who first proposed the Declaration of Independence, who served as one of Washington's most loyal subordinates in the Revolution, and who was the grandfather of Robert E. Lee; Samuel Adams, the Massachusetts Congregationalist hot spur whose opposition to the British monarchy had as much to do with passage of the Quebec Act granting Catholicism legal status in Canada as passage of the Tea Act or other tax; and Alexander Hamilton, who will be covered separately later in this chapter.[1]

These important figures are generally overshadowed, however, by two other groups: (1) the group that unequivocally leaned the opposite way toward disestablishment, which included Jefferson, Madison, Paine, and Allen; and (2) the group that equivocated on the issue, which included Washington, Franklin, and John Adams. These two latter groups, about whom much has already been said and even more will be added shortly, included some not-so-celebrated members as well. One reason some are not celebrated in history is that they never made overt statements either for or against establishment. What is known about their views on establishment is based more on circumstantial evidence than fact. All of these men grew up to be religiously minded in some shape, form, or fashion. That fact is not in question. All fifty-six of the signers of the Declaration, for instance, were professing Christians of one type or another.[2]

To a man, these lesser Founders all routinely called upon "Heaven" or "Providence" to bless the nation, both during the Revolution and thereafter. Their religiosity became especially noticeable during the ratification debates in 1787–1788.[3] James Wilson of Pennsylvania, for instance, belongs in this category. One of only six signers of both the Declaration and the Constitution, and considered by many contemporaries to have had the sharpest legal mind of his day, he was appointed by Washington as one of the original justices of the Supreme Court. Despite his disestablishment views, he was extremely religious in his own way. He consistently wrote theological commentary into his legal opinions. He believed the "will of God" formed the "supreme law" of the land, and that all man-made laws must derive from that principle.[4] Based upon this fact, it is reasonable to conclude that he favored a high degree of religious influence in the American government, but not extending to the establishment of a national church or sectarian religion.

The same is true of Noah Webster, most famous for being the author of *An American Dictionary of the English Language* (1828), but who was also a politician, judge, historian, philosopher, editor, farmer, and educator. Although he made one statement in 1783 against establishment, one can easily get the impression from reading everything he wrote thereafter that he might have favored the institutionalization of Christianity in the United States government in some relatively innocuous form. During the ratification debates in New York and Pennsylvania, he complained about those Anti-Federalists who claimed to want unlimited freedom of religion written into the Constitution while personally persecuting the Quakers whose loyalty to the United States seemed in question because they were prohibited by their religion from taking sides in the American Revolution. He also said, "I shudder at the thought" of freedom of speech and the press being extended to those who would use that liberty "to prove his maker a knave," indicating he favored government protecting the sacredness of God's name and public image. Later in life, as he wrote his famous dictionary, his preface included "The United States commenced their existence . . . with civilization, with science, with constitutions of free government, and with the best gift of God to man, the Christian religion." He considered his dictionary to be "a useful instrument for the propagation of science, arts, civilization, and Christianity."[5] Such statements mitigate against his being a radical separationist of the anti-Christian nation variety.

Consider also Gouverneur Morris of Pennsylvania, who spoke more than any other delegate at the Constitutional Convention. He constantly invoked the deity and unashamedly inserted his own personal religious views at every phase of the debate.[6] Many New Englanders, such as Oliver Ellsworth and Roger Sherman of Connecticut, took it for granted that their own ideas of religiosity were axiomatically acceptable to the rest of the country.[7] In the First Congress of 1789, Sherman argued, for example, the type of celebrations that Old Testament Israel held to honor God were "worthy of Christian imitation" in America.[8] The typical outward, self-righteous religion of New England Federalists could also be seen among some families outside of the Northeast. The Pinckney family of South Carolina, for instance, corresponded with one another in extremely pious language and yet favored disestablishment.[9] Likewise, Christopher Gadsden of South Carolina attended the Anglican/Episcopal church faithfully, considered the Revolutionary cause the "cause of God," had an "unshakeable faith in the sovereignty of a benevolent God," yet worked for disestablishment in his state.[10]

The division among the Founders resulted merely from the question of whether the United States should maintain an established religion, not whether this country would be a spiritual, religious, or even "Christian" nation. Once they agreed upon disestablishment, then exactly where to draw the line between the interaction of the government and the various churches became the next order of questioning.[11] Should there be a religious test for voting and office holding, they asked? Should officer holders have to profess a belief in some deity that would reward the good and punish the evil? Those who answered "yes" to either of these questions were labeled "unfashionable" by their more liberal-minded peers, even when some of those peers admitted the

United States was essentially a "Christian country."[12] Colonel William Jones was one of these unfashionable men who believed that having Christian leaders exclusively "would be happy for the United States."[13] Then there were those like James Iredell of North Carolina who said, "It would be happy for mankind if religion was permitted to take its own course, and maintain itself by the excellence of its own doctrines."[14]

Such examples of the thoughts and opinions of the lesser Founders on the complexities of the separation of church and state issue could fill a separate volume. Rather than pursuing such a tedious course herein, consideration is given now to the words, deeds, and ideas of some of the most important Founders: Franklin, Washington, Adams, Jefferson, Madison, and Hamilton.

## BENJAMIN FRANKLIN

In honor of his title of "First American," Benjamin Franklin should precede all others for consideration herein. He was a complex character—as complex, in fact, as early America ever produced. The consummate Renaissance man, he was gifted intellectually in many areas: science, letters, politics, diplomacy, theology, and humor. When reading Franklin's writings today, one must be careful not to take everything he wrote at face value. There is much tongue-in-cheek, double entendre, and possibly some deliberately deceptive information mixed in with the truth. Yet, while believing every word he wrote would be naive, his life's work can be taken as a whole, and fair generalizations can be made about it. Upon so doing, the historian feels safe to say that, despite his unorthodox religious views and occasional statements of an anti-Christian sentiment, Franklin seems definitely to have been some sort of a Christian for most of his life, just of a not-easily defined variety. He once favored the creation of an American national church patterned after the Church of England and supported by taxes—hardly the idea of an atheist or anti-Christian.[15]

Franklin could be rightly considered the "American Solomon," for he was perhaps the wisest man ever born in the American colonies, possibly the wisest of his generation in the world, and arguably one of the wisest of all time. Considering the practicality of the advice he left for both his own generation and posterity in *Poor Richard's Almanack* and his autobiography, he was, like the legendary Solomon of ancient Israel, a proverbist and a sage. Like his contemporary George Washington, he was a man almost universally admired and acclaimed, a man with few enemies, a man who united people rather than divided them. But more than Washington or any other Founder, he helped shape what could be called a distinctly American character.[16]

Educated as a Presbyterian, Franklin's religious beliefs as stated in his autobiography are the ultimate example of Deism in 18th-century America. He believed firmly in the teachings of Jesus but not in his divinity, the same as Jefferson. He may have even influenced Jefferson toward that belief.[17] Franklin wrote in his autobiography, "I never was without some religious principles. I never doubted, for instance, the existence of the Deity, that he made the world, and governed it by his Providence; that the most acceptable service of God was the doing good to man; that our souls are immortal, and that all crime will be punished, and virtue rewarded, either here or hereafter. These I esteem'd the essentials of every religion. . . ." He added that he respected various denominations to the degree that they did not mix their peculiar doctrines in with these essentials and, thus, divide people rather than inspire them to live morally. He objected to pastors trying to turn people in their audiences into Presbyterians or Anglicans or Baptists or such, rather than turning them into "good citizens."[18]

Franklin's Deism was an intellectual faith more than a spiritual one. He formed his famous Junto in 1727 to be a society in which brainy and inquisitive young Americans could converse about religious and philosophical subjects. In 1769, the Junto evolved into the American Philosophical Society. Thomas Jefferson eventually became the president of it, which is another indication of the Franklin-Jefferson connection and similarities.[19] As a young man in 1728, Franklin wrote his own Liturgy called *Articles of Belief and Acts of Religion* and made it his life's mission to figure out a way to arrive at "moral perfection." To that end, he catalogued thirteen "virtues" in the Christian Bible that he would try to observe regularly. His list consisted of: temperance, silence, order, resolution, frugality, industry, sincerity, justice, moderation, cleanliness, tranquility, chastity, and humility. He addressed his God in prayer daily as "Powerful Goodness."[20]

Despite his unorthodox approach to prayer and living a Biblical lifestyle, Franklin always thought, just as other Deists did, within the framework of the Judeo-Christian conception of the mono-God. Moreover, he particularly viewed his religion through the Calvinist precepts of salvation by grace and election. He believed firmly that he could not possibly "merit heaven" by his "good works," by which he meant "performing church ceremonies, or making long [public] prayers." He said rather that "God's goodness" would open a place for him in heaven. His idea of "heaven," incidentally, was "a state of happiness, infinite in degree and eternal in duration." Just because he did not believe in good deeds as a prerequisite for salvation did not mean he felt no obligation to serve his fellow man. He strove to bear the "fruit of the spirit," a typical Calvinist objective, for doing so would be an outward evidence of his election. He did not fear God's wrath upon himself as many Christians did and do, but instead had an optimistic outlook on his soul's final fate, another Calvinist doctrine.[21]

As strange as it seems considering Franklin's background, the Philadelphia Deist developed an interesting relationship with the Great Awakening's most effective evangelist, George Whitefield. In the 1740s and beyond, when most other Deists and Old Light orthodox Christians alike dismissed Whitefield and his genre as religious quacks, Franklin held him in respectful esteem, carrying on a correspondence with the itinerant evangelist. Frank Lambert has noted that, as a newspaper mogul, "No one was a more aggressive Whitefield promoter than Franklin. . . . Franklin's colony wide [newspaper] network was a new scheme in America, just as Whitefield's open-air preaching was novel. These two innovators naturally joined their intercolonial interests to serve each other." While the two "innovators" certainly shared commercial interests, Franklin did genuinely believe in, or try his best to believe in, Whitefield's religious mission.[22] Franklin was also conscientious about Christian ministry in other ways. For instance, as the western territories were being settled by Americans in the 1760s after the French and Indian War, he expressed concern about the type of white Americans that were moving into the Ohio territory and the first impression they were making upon the Indians there. He said he wanted to see "a better sample of Christians" settle there than what the first pioneers represented to the Indians.[23]

As Franklin grew old he still grappled with the religious beliefs and spiritual objectives of his youth. Near the end of his long life, at the Constitutional Convention, he said, "The longer I live, the more convincing proofs I see of this truth—that God governs in the affairs of men. And if a sparrow cannot fall to the ground without his notice, is it possible that an empire can rise without his aid?"[24] He also made a witty remark against religious intolerance to conclude the convention: "the only Difference between our two Churches in their Opinions of the Certainty of their Doctrine, is, the Romish Church is infallible, and the Church of England is never in the Wrong."[25] His point? Since all denominations are equally convinced of their own righteousness and correct interpretation of the scriptures, compromise among them would be absolutely essential in order to fulfill the convention's stated desire to "form a more perfect union."

## GEORGE WASHINGTON

In honor of his title "Father of His Country," George Washington should be considered next. His contemporary James Iredell of North Carolina called him in 1788 not only "the greatest man of the present age" but "perhaps equal to any that has existed in any period of time. . . ."[26] The tall, strong Virginian commanded respect like no one in the American colonies before him and like few who have followed after. From virtually all that was said and written about him by contemporaries, and by most of what historians have decided since, he earned that respect. Having laid his life on the line on the battlefield to get this country established, and having become the very name and face of the American Revolution in the eyes of the British crown, his military service alone would have earned him a place in the nation's pantheon. His service to the country beyond the battlefield, however, sealed his sterling reputation in history. The man's character was above reproach. As contemporary John Jay put it, Washington "ascended to the Temple of Honor through the Temple of Virtue."[27]

The fact that Washington was an extremely religious man has never been in dispute. The nature of his religion, however, was and is the question. His stoic and tacit demeanor for most of his professional life has always led observers to develop an elaborate mythology about who he really was, and what made him tick. Consequently, people on all sides of the church-state issue have adopted him as their own. So who was the real, historic George? The evidence reveals a man who was more Christian than anything else by most standards of measure. Raised an Anglican, he kept a diary from childhood, in which he wrote prayers every day. Some of the entries are explicitly Christian and of the evangelical, fundamentalist variety.[28] His faith sustained him through the dark days of the Revolution. An austere commander and general, he expected his troops to follow his example of self-discipline and faith. But he rarely exhibited outwardly religious behavior, and he rarely showed emotion regarding religious matters. Instead, he exuded a quiet confidence that could be seen more than heard. In his diplomatic and military correspondence with his French allies, he referred to the Catholic King Louis XVI as "His Most Christian Majesty," but otherwise said nothing of a religious or spiritual nature.[29] Certainly needing both French and Catholic support, he took care not to offend either. Thus, he abolished the formerly popular practice of burning the Pope in effigy.[30] Yet he also favored keeping the established (Episcopal) church of the state of Virginia and supporting it through taxation. Washington's stance indicates that holding pro-establishment views did not make one, as modern secularists and separationists generally charge, automatically intolerant of other religious groups.[31]

When Washington took his presidential oath of office, he placed his hand on the Bible—not the King James Bible, rather, his own Masonic Bible. He also kissed it at that New York City ceremony.[32] In his first inaugural address, given on April 30, 1789, he called the deity the "Parent of the Human Race" who "has been pleased to favor the American people" as they set out to form their new nation. He furthermore made "fervent supplications to that Almighty Being who rules over the universe" for divine blessings upon the United States.[33] As soon as the inaugural ceremony ended, he led a whole delegation of congressmen and dignitaries to St. Paul's Chapel to hear a sermon delivered by the official chaplain to Congress.[34] Thereafter, Washington, it has been said, "treated the presidency as an excellent pulpit from which to spread public religion."[35]

Washington's "public religion," however, was not a divisive, denominational faith, but instead a middle-of-the-road, nondenominational one. He realized that people from all the different denominational backgrounds in the United States at the time would be looking to him for assurance of religious freedom and protection, and he did not want to disappoint any. At that critical juncture in the fledgling nation's history, a president who did otherwise could have easily rent the people down the middle. If there is one indisputable fact about Washington's presidency, it is that he never wanted to be seen as a man who took sides in petty arguments of politicians and preachers. He most certainly did take the side of belief in the mono-God, however. Within two months after being sworn in, he proclaimed a National Day of Thanksgiving to God. Later in his presidency, he proclaimed more days of prayer. When he did so, no one accused him of violating the separation of church and state or the First Amendment, nor could they, since the Bill of Rights had not yet been written nor the terminology of "separation of church and state" invented.[36] It is quite important to recognize this fact, because it reminds modern observers that the United States government operated without both of those stipulations for a long time and somehow survived intact.

In his first year as president, Washington received letters from at least six different denominations inquiring about his policies regarding religion. He answered each one impartially and with the same basic promise to protect their freedom. He also promised none, however, that he would help promote their beliefs. He told them that he would pray for them, particularly those in Philadelphia, including the Quakers, who did not support him in the Revolution. His true character shows forth in his attitude toward this group that a lesser man would have called traitorous. He called the Quakers the most "exemplary and useful citizens" in the country.[37] Washington rarely singled out any particular group for praise this way. Mostly, he kept strictly to his policy of nonsectarianism. Yet the striking thing here is that when he did single out this religious group, he did so to offer praise, not to insult, demean, or offend.

In one of his Thanksgiving Day proclamations, Washington said, "it is the duty of all nations to acknowledge the providence of Almighty God, to obey His will, to be grateful for His benefits, and humbly to implore His protection." All other presidents after him prior to 1932—including Jefferson and Madison—followed this precedent of calling upon the deity in an annual Thanksgiving address.[38] Another example of Washington's religiosity is his support of Pierre L'Enfant's proposal to build a national church edifice in the new capital city, the District of Columbia, the city plan for which the Frenchman was also the chief designer.[39] Finally, in his famous Farewell Address, Washington cautioned judges in all courts in the land not to discard the religious oaths that bind them to serve the people as though they were accountable to God. He added that "Of all the dispositions and habits which lead to political prosperity, religion and morality are indispensable supports. . . . reason and experience both forbid us to expect that national morality can prevail in exclusion of religious principle." He warned his fellow Americans not to be deluded by those claiming to be patriots while working "to subvert these great pillars of human happiness—these firmest props of the duties of men and citizens."[40]

## JOHN ADAMS

In honor of his lifetime of service (often in the background) to the establishing of the United States and his role as second president, John Adams now deserves due consideration. More than a Founding "Father" of the nation, he was the patriarch of his own family—one which could arguably be called the "First Family" of the United States. Siring a future president, John Quincy, as well as notable grandsons and great grandsons who became some of the finest scholars this country has ever produced, John Adams is a Founder whose contributions to this nation are often overlooked or overshadowed by his more illustrious contemporaries. The recent biography by David McCulloch, and the Home Box Office television series made from it, has done as much to redeem Adams's reputation as anything else ever has, showing the Bostonian to be worthy of mention in the same breath with Franklin, Washington, Jefferson, and Madison.[41] A quiet and reserved man, Adams had the dubious job of trying to fill the big shoes of Washington upon his election as president in 1796. Not a man alive could have done it. Given the circumstances, Adams's presidency should not be considered the failure that it often is simply because he lost his reelection bid and became the first one-term president.

Although Adams grew up in a puritanical Congregationalist Church environment, he was, like so many of his contemporaries, smitten with the Enlightenment in his youth. An avid reader of James Harrington (author of the Utopian book *Oceana*), Adams occasionally used the terminology "Nature's God" that Jefferson wrote into the Declaration to describe his deity. As a grown man, he refused to embrace any particular denomination, but he certainly considered himself a Christian. Although he did not like labels, he once accepted "Unitarian" as an accurate description of his beliefs. He believed in established religion, however, and saw no contradiction therein. He wrote into the Massachusetts Constitution of 1780 an established church. His state-supported church represented a milder form of establishment than had previously been attempted. Its purpose was merely to set a standard of public morality—basically by merely emphasizing the Christian "Golden Rule"; it did not have a monopoly on religion in the Commonwealth. Adams intended for it to have to compete with all other churches in the free market of ideas, yet it would have the supposed advantage of being tax supported. The rationale behind this hybrid form of establishment was that it would provide the state with chaplains for the militia, the prisons and jails, and the legislature and any other government offices where they may be needed.[42]

In 1787–1788, Adams wrote *A Defense of the Constitutions of Government of the United States of America*, in which he made a comparison of the thirteen state constitutions with the various forms of government of other nations in history. He naturally thought the state constitutions were far and away superior. As he put it, "we shall feel the strongest motives to fall upon our knees, in gratitude to heaven for having been graciously pleased to give us birth and education in that country, and for having destined us to live under her laws."[43] Other expressions of his religious beliefs included such statements as "the Bible is the best Book in the world," and "The Ten Commandments and the Sermon on the Mount contain my religion. . . ."[44]

Such outward expressions of religion could be heard from the family matriarch as well. Abigail Adams mentioned God frequently and spoke of the "Divine Will" being done during the dark days of the Revolution. She did not believe it was possible for a man to be "honest . . . without the fear of God." She constantly reminded son John Quincy of her moral expectations derived from Biblical principles.[45] This constant infusion of religion had the desired effect upon the young Adams. He carried on the family tradition of piousness. He came to believe that the great beauty of the American way was the connection "in one indissoluble bond, the principles of civil government with the principles of Christianity."[46] He looked back to his father's generation for inspiration, believing that "nearly all" of the Founders "were bound by the laws of God . . . and by the laws of the Gospel," which provided "the rules of their conduct." That he was a devoted Christian himself is unquestionable. He once said, "My hopes of a future life are all founded upon the Gospel of Christ. . . ."[47] And, needless to say, despite a stint as secretary of state and one term as president, he sealed his reputation as one of the great humanitarians in American history by becoming one of the most outspoken abolitionists of the 1830s–1840s.

## THOMAS JEFFERSON

Of all the Founders, Thomas Jefferson gets the most attention in church-state studies. Partly that is because he stood in the vanguard of those fighting for disestablishment in the Old Dominion, the oldest, most populous, and arguably most influential of the thirteen states. Partly, too, Jefferson indirectly gave America the terminology of "separation of church and state," a phrase that does not appear in the Constitution, or anywhere else for that matter, prior to 1801. Mainly, it seems, however, that Jefferson gets so much attention because he was the recognized leader of the most liberal wing of the Founders and, thus, the ideological father of "freedom *from* religion" advocates in his day. Modern secularists likewise look to him as the main champion of their cause. Modern conservatives and Christian evangelicals ever since have spoken and written so much about Jefferson largely to answer the criticisms and accusations of these Jeffersonian secularists, but also to prop up their own arguments in some cases. As Gordon Wood has commented, virtually all Americans see Jefferson "as a symbol of what we as a people are. . . . we quote him on nearly every side of every major question in our history."[48]

Even the most imminent historians have disagreed over who the real Jefferson was. Richard Hofstadter, for example, has called him a "cautious pragmatic," while Forrest McDonald has preferred to label him a "reactionary ideologue."[49] Pauline Maier has decided that he is "the most overrated person in American History," a man not deserving "of the extraordinary adulation" he continually receives.[50] Merrill Peterson once hoped and expected that modern scholars would reach a consensus about who the real Jefferson was, but Peter Onuf concluded that, at the end of the 20th century, the Virginian's image was still "as controversial now as it has ever been" and predicted that "the 'real' Jefferson will continue to elude and resist judgment."[51]

One thing that seems sure is that the real Jefferson was not quite as extreme in his secularism as many of his modern followers have made him out to be. Certainly, by any standard, the tall, lank, red-haired Virginian was eccentric. In some of his views, he could rightly be called radical. Yet he did not lead by example the secular crowd that follows him today. He was rather religious, and a firm believer in the mono-God that fellow Deists and Unitarians revered. He was rarely bothered, however, by that hobgoblin of little minds—a foolish consistency—being as prone to speaking out of both sides of his mouth, depending upon the year, the circumstances, and his frame of mind at the moment, as any great historical figure to which one might compare him.[52] While a lesser man would be labeled as either a hypocrite or a typical politician, Jefferson, though roundly criticized by contemporaries and historians alike, has not suffered diminution of his status as an icon for trying to have it both ways.[53]

Jefferson has been called "as pure a devotee of the Enlightenment as the colonies could have produced" and "the philosopher *par excellence* of American democracy."[54] Indeed, but that by no means puts him in the same category as contemporaries Voltaire or Hume, much less Socrates or Plato.[55] Moreover, he was as much of an enigma as any person this country could have produced, vacillating on issues such as slavery, religion, and constitutional interpretation as times changed and new situations arose. Looking for consistency in Jefferson is like searching for the Holy Grail. If, however, he ever showed consistency about anything, it was disestablishment. He opposed the established church in Virginia mainly for what it stood for politically and socially, rather than what it believed or taught religiously. The Anglican/Episcopal Church operated like a fraternity for the rich, conservative, ruling class for the purpose of keeping control over the poor and working class. Besides, it was ultimately a tool of the English monarchy, which had established the church in Virginia in the first place, and Jefferson hated the king, as is evident from the Declaration. (Ironically, he did not mention coerced religion as a cause for divorcing the British Empire in the Declaration, which again shows the inconsistency of this flip-flopping Founder.) He furthermore resented the government-imposed days of fasting and thanksgiving, not because he did not want to fast or give thanks, but because he did not want to be forced to do either by a corrupt church run by an even more corrupt king.[56] His leadership on the disestablishment issue was extremely progressive for its day, for most Americans were still trying to come to grips with mere toleration of diverse religious opinions.[57]

Jefferson consistently rejected Calvinism, considering it a perversion of original Christianity.[58] His "God" did not sit on a throne in the farthest reaches of the universe or any other sphere of existence and demand "worship." His deity wanted to be imitated, not worshiped. To imitate Jesus was to do the will of God. He derived his maxim from the scripture (Matthew 7:20) that paraphrased says, "by their fruits [actions] you will know who the real Christians are." He actually called himself "a *real* Christian" on at least one occasion. He wanted to be known by his good deeds, not by his theology. He consequently had little respect or use for those professing Christians who "worshiped" their fabricated image of Jesus but did not imitate his lifestyle of modesty, humbleness, forbearance, tolerance, and forgiveness.[59] In a letter to Dr. Benjamin Waterhouse in 1822, he gave a pithy exegesis of his theology, which had three points: 1. There is only one God, and this God is perfect; 2. God will reward the good and punish the bad people on judgment day; and 3. The sum of God's will for men is to love their creator and treat their fellow man fairly and justly. Anything more than this, Jefferson believed, was a perversion of the true Gospel.[60]

Jefferson put quite a lot of thought into the disestablishment issue before beginning his campaign for it. He formulated his arguments, anticipated the opposition's counterarguments, and put together a case like any good lawyer would do.[61] When he finally put forth the Bill for the Establishment of Religious Freedom in 1779, he did not try to remove all references to a deity from the public sphere in his state. The document was not secular, in fact, but acknowledged the mono-God, calling "him" omnipotent. It did not try to dissuade Virginians from being religious or spiritual. It mainly prevented the state government from forcing membership in the Anglican/Episcopal Church, from collecting taxes to support that church, and from making membership in that church a requirement for office holding. Because of this fact, arguably, Jefferson did not intend so much to secularize Virginia as to increase its opportunity for religious expression, which, if true, makes this Founder not the Rationalist that modern secularists claim but rather a propagator of monotheistic religion.[62]

The Virginia disestablishment bill initially contained more provisions than the watered-down version that eventually passed. The original bill sought to replace the church-operated schools with state-supported public schools, convert the College of William and Mary from an Anglican to a public college, and secularize the curriculum of William and Mary, replacing its missionary activities with an anthropology department designed to study the indigenous cultures of foreign peoples rather than convert them to Christian and/or white American ways.[63] Jefferson did not achieve complete success in these attempts to overhaul the education system of Virginia, which is partly why he later created a separate public state university to compete with William and Mary. Lest one get the impression that such actions prove Jefferson's secularism, consider that even in his beloved University of Virginia, he required all students to attend Protestant chapel services. Moreover, he required all professors to "inculcate" students with a common set of principles designed to promote reverence to God and country.[64] Clearly, in his educational philosophy, the two faces of Thomas Jefferson are again visible.

The disestablishment bill that Jefferson wanted was more radical than the one he actually got passed, but it was still plenty radical for its day. It flew in the face of nearly 250 years of Anglican church tradition and nearly 175 years of colonial Virginia tradition.[65] It took fully seven years for the state legislature to make it law.[66] Once passed, the full effects of religious pluralism quickly became evident. Under the new law the various denominations began to share space inside the state capitol for Sunday worship services. They sometimes took opposite corners of the building at once, and other times they alternated Sundays. Episcopalians, Presbyterians, Methodists, Quakers, and Catholics all participated in this rotation. Jefferson wholeheartedly endorsed this rotational system, as did all the separationists who signed the bill into law in 1786. As late as 1822, Jefferson still thought it wonderful that so many denominations had learned to cooperate in such a way. This again indicates that he never intended to drive religion out of Virginia; he did not even drive it off of state property! Instead he gave each religious group an even playing field, an equal opportunity to thrive in his state.[67]

Considering that fact, and the fact that Jefferson had regularly attended church services held in the United States Senate chamber while vice president, it seems odd today that the Federalists would have feared a Jeffersonian presidency so much. Yet during the campaign of 1800, they framed the choice between Jefferson and Adams as a choice between godlessness and godliness (but what should be expected from a party that called a yellow fever epidemic in Philadelphia a year earlier God's judgment on the city for its sinfulness?). Yale president Timothy Dwight led the orthodox church crowd—which included such lesser-known clerics as the Reverends Jedediah Champion, William Linn, and John Mason—in the anti-Jefferson movement. Upon Jefferson's victory, some Federalists hid or even buried their Bibles out of fear that the new administration might have them confiscated.[68] Although privately he relished his opportunity to thwart the self-righteous Federalists, Jefferson tried publicly in his first inaugural address to assuage the fears of those who had not voted for him.[69] He proclaimed, "having banished from our land that religious intolerance under which mankind so long bled and suffered, we have yet gained little if we countenance a political intolerance as despotic, as wicked, and capable of as bitter and bloody persecutions." In other words, he promised he would not use his political power for the ignoble purpose of ridding the United States of those who disagreed with him religiously. Moreover, he added that the young nation should be "enlightened by a benign religion, professed, indeed, and practiced in various forms, yet all of them inculcating honesty, truth, temperance, gratitude, and the love of man; acknowledging and adorning an overruling Providence, which by all its dispensations proves that it delights in the happiness of man here and his greater happiness hereafter." These are not the words of an atheist, agnostic, or one hostile to Christianity, but rather of a Deist and Unitarian. He concluded his inaugural address by pronouncing a blessing upon his country, asking "that Infinite Power which rules the destinies of the universe lead our councils to what is best . . ."—precisely the same kind of nonsectarian blessing that his predecessors Washington and Adams had supplicated.[70]

On January 1, 1801, more than a month after his election, still more than two months away from his inauguration, and more than a decade after the First Amendment was added to the Constitution, Jefferson wrote his famous "Letter to the Danbury Baptists" in which he used the terminology of building a wall to separate church and state in America. The Reverend John Leland headed the Danbury Baptists. He happened to be coming to Washington, D.C., on that same day to congratulate the new president and offer him the gift of a giant chunk of cheese four feet long and weighing 1,200 pounds. Leland represented twenty-six congregations in New England and New York, with the flagship church located at Danbury, Connecticut, which had supported Jefferson and disestablishment in the campaign. The president-elect's letter answered these Baptist concerns arising from Federalist charges that Jefferson might be antireligious. He assured them he was not, but said he did believe in preventing any particular church from gaining an advantage over others through government favors. This letter has become the most-often cited example of Jefferson's views on separation of church and state, typically cherry-picked by the anti-Christian nation contingent to suit their agenda. The facts do not bear out the belief, however, that Jefferson intended to erect a wall that would keep religion and politics totally separate in America. Just two days after the new president wrote the famous letter, he attended a Sunday worship service held in the United States House of Representatives in which John Leland preached the sermon. This action does not reveal a man who wanted to divorce religion from politics. Besides, rough drafts of Jefferson's letter show he chose his terminology of building a wall only after trying a few other ways to frame his argument, all of which sounded far more pro-Christian nation than not, indicating that he had something in mind quite different from what secularists have claimed ever since.[71] By the same token, the fact that he put so much thought into this letter and wanted to get the wording just right indicates that he sought the perfect balance on this most divisive of all issues.

Once he took the oath of office, Jefferson became a regular attendee of Sunday services held in the House of Representatives—a structure erected with taxpayer money to serve as the piece of the federal mosaic that would be most answerable to the people. When combined with his vice presidential years, Jefferson attended church regularly for the whole twelve years he served in the executive branch of the United States government and, thus, in the national spotlight. This indicates that he had just as much religious inclination as Adams and Washington. The main difference between President Jefferson and the previous two chief executives rested in his refusal to call the nation to either fasting or thanksgiving. This fact, which is often cited by the anti-Christian nation group, is offset, however, by the fact that Jefferson "devoutly return[ed] thanks to the beneficent Being" in his first state of the union message to Congress on December 8, 1801. In that message, he wrote, "we are bound with peculiar gratitude to be thankful to Him. . . ."[72] Then in his second inaugural address in 1805, Jefferson referenced the Bible story of the Israelites being led by God to a "land flowing with milk and honey." He compared the United States to that promised land where God's people were led.[73]

Jefferson in fact went beyond his predecessors in promoting certain other religious practices. He signed treaties with Indian tribes, for example, in which he and Congress appropriated tax money for the "propagation of the Gospel" among the Indians. In 1803, he signed a law appropriating federal funds to build a Catholic church edifice among the Kaskaskia Indians and to pay the priest with tax dollars. He believed the Indians "needed" the civilizing influence of Christianity, and since the Indians were not citizens of the United States, his rules of separation of church and state did not necessarily apply to them anyway. He thought of them in a paternalistic way, which meant like dependent children of the benevolent American government. When viewed this way, his actions toward the Indians look perfectly consistent with his educational philosophy toward white children. He believed that even in the public schools the Bible should be taught for the purpose of students receiving moral instruction, which clearly shows Jefferson to have been a Utilitarian or Functionalist.[74]

In that same year in a letter to Benjamin Rush, Jefferson identified himself as a Christian and confided in his Pennsylvania friend as a like-minded man on matters of religion and philosophy. He thus sent Rush a "Syllabus of an estimate of the Merit of the Doctrine of Jesus Compared with Those of Others." He found the great Greek and Roman philosophers of ancient history lacking in those qualities that "inculcated peace, charity, and love of our fellow men," while he considered Christianity superior in those categories.[75] Considering this letter to Rush in 1803 and his aforementioned letter to Waterhouse in 1822, it is evident his religious views did not change in any great way over those two decades.

By the end of his life, which came on July 4, 1826, he had long since reconciled with former friend and erstwhile political rival John Adams, who coincidentally died the same day. One a Virginia Republican and an unorthodox separationist, the other a Massachusetts Federalist and an orthodox establishment man, the two exhibited all the best and worst aspects of American democracy and religious pluralism. They were both archetypes of their party, their section of the country, and their religious persuasion. So much symbolism is evident in their deaths. For them to have died on the same day, regardless of which one of 365, would have been extremely strange. The fact that they died on Independence Day, exactly fifty years after issuing the Declaration is nothing short of astounding and mystifying. And so it was to those who survived them in 1826. "With one voice," says Pauline Maier, "those who gave eulogies interpreted God's taking together two of the last three signers of the Declaration not as a sign of His displeasure, but proof that the United States had a special place in His plans and affections."[76] To make this story all the more intriguing, while Jefferson's authorship of the Declaration is well known, less well known but equally important is the fact that none other than John Adams had recommended his then-obscure friend from Virginia to the Continental Congress as the author.[77]

What are students of history to make of this enigmatic Founder, Thomas Jefferson—a man who opposed slavery but did not free his slaves, a man who opposed the established church but not altogether the faith and doctrines it represented, a man who claimed to believe in a strict construction of the Constitution but often expanded the role of the national government when he thought necessary? Perhaps the best answer is found in what one of Jefferson's contemporary self-described critics, John T. S. Sullivan, wrote of him: "No man has appeared in the United States in the last fifty years, whose character, public and private, has been so differently estimated as that of Thomas Jefferson. By some persons he has been considered as one of the most pure, amiable, dignified, wise and patriotic of men. By others he has been considered, as remarkably defective in the qualities which dignify and adorn human life; and as one of the worst men, and most wrong-headed statesmen that ever lived." Sullivan added that, to his supporters, Jefferson was "represented as the early advocate of religious freedom, and of the rights of man; the great apostle of liberty . . . ; a sage, a philosopher, a true patriot, and genuine republican." But to the Federalists he was "a man destitute of the commonly received moral principles; and one who entertained no respect for the foundation of all moral principle. . . ."[78] It would be difficult to add anything substantial to this assessment today.

## JAMES MADISON

James Madison's historical reputation as the understudy to Jefferson has always cast him in the shadows. His importance in history as the "Father of the Constitution," of course, rescues him from obscurity among the Founders. Problems with Britain and the subsequent War of 1812 consumed his eight years as president. Except for the victory by Andrew Jackson at New Orleans in the final battle of the war, Madison might have gone down in history as one of the biggest failures among all two-term presidents. Instead, he is remembered for presidential mediocrity. His best years of public life clearly came early in his career, not in the 1800s. If he had retired after writing the Constitution and getting the Bill of Rights passed, his stock in history might actually be higher than it is today. But to be fair, his accomplishments between 1787 and 1791 should be enough to offset any other deficiencies he may have had.[79]

As a youngster growing up in Orange County, Virginia, Madison developed a fascination with religion. He had the good fortune to be raised in the household of a planter-father who, for a rural Southerner in the 1700s, stocked an unusually large library. A voracious reader, he devoured the Bible and theology books from his father's collection.[80] Although raised an Anglican, he attended the Presbyterian College of New Jersey (Princeton), where he took courses in Hebrew and Latin and worked toward a theology degree. He left in 1771 after only two years of study. He never lost his zeal for the ministry, though, and even encouraged one of his friends to go into that line of work. His crossover from one denomination to another at college no doubt influenced his later views on disestablishment.[81]

In January 1774, at twenty-two years old, he wrote his first public letter advocating liberty of conscience for all people in Virginia. In December 1774, however, he joined the Orange County Committee of Public Safety, a group of locals headed by his father that canvassed the county requiring every head of household to sign an oath of loyalty to the patriot cause. The Quakers of course refused to comply, and suffered the consequences. The committee confiscated some of their literature and burned it in a public ceremony.[82] Perhaps the younger Madison felt pressure from his father to participate, but even so, he showed a lack of clarity on the subject of liberty of conscience that no doubt proved quite instructional to him in later years (although it would not be the last time he lacked clarity on the separation of church and state issue).[83] It did not take long for him to get an opportunity to redeem himself. He defended the rights of Baptists to worship free of interference by state law, local custom, and the Anglican/Episcopal Church. Although he did not consider it an act of heroism, the Baptists who benefited from his stand certainly did. Accordingly, they later rewarded him with their votes.[84]

Madison lived under a rather stodgy, puritanical set of morals all his life. He disliked the routine practice, for instance, of political candidates doling out rum and other decadent treats in exchange for votes. He lost his bid to become a Virginia state legislator in 1776 partly for that reason. He was concerned, as he put it, "with the purity of moral . . . principles" involved in such demagogic practices. He evolved on the issue, however, just enough to allow the liquor custom to enter his future campaigns, but he never came to embrace it.[85]

Although Jefferson usually gets credit for being the great champion of disestablishment, Madison actually seems to have preceded him in calling for it publicly in Virginia. Not until after the two statesmen had met for the first time in 1776 did Jefferson become a loud proponent of the idea. It appears that the younger Madison had turned him onto it.[86] If so, that makes Madison the first political leader of national importance who empathized strongly enough with victims of religious oppression to do something about it.[87] Although he had personally never experienced persecution, he had seen plenty of it up close in Virginia. He had witnessed, for example, a Baptist preacher in Caroline County being interrupted in mid-service by an Anglican minister, arrested by the sheriff, hauled away, and publicly beaten for preaching without a license. Moreover, he felt the sting of the haughty, arrogant attitude of establishment men on a regular basis in his home state. They exuded a sense of dominance and superiority that made open-minded types like Madison uncomfortable. Patrick Henry, the great orator of the Revolution, led the list of these Virginia Anglican/Episcopalians. He tried to get Christianity proclaimed the official religion of the Commonwealth of Virginia, and, in so doing, ran up against Madison, Jefferson, George Mason, and other prominent separationists.[88] Madison's famous 1784 "Memorial and Remonstrance Against Religious Assessments" was the separationists' answer to Henry's proposal. In it, he made fifteen arguments (some of which overlap) for separating church and state. In summary, they are as follows:

1. Civil government has no natural authority over religion.

2. Legislatures thus have no authority over it.

3. If the government can establish one religion, it can just as easily establish another, which would offend the original beneficiaries of establishment.

4. Established religion denies civil rights to those who dissent.

5. Civil magistrates are not authorities on religious matters or theology, but an establishment of religion assumes and pretends they are.

6. True religion does not require government support to thrive.

7. Experience teaches that establishing a state religion corrupts the clergy of that particular faith.

8. Government does not require the establishment of a religion to function adequately.

9. Establishment taken to its logical extreme leads to inquisitions and other persecutions.

10. Establishment scares off current citizens and potential immigrants.

11. To be maintained, establishment must use force and therefore must ultimately shed blood, and in so doing destroy the very things it is designed to convey—Christian love, charity, and decency.

12. Establishment will not help the body of Christ grow but will discourage growth as people reject that which is forced upon them.

13. Enforcing the law of establishment injures society more than if there were no establishment at all.

14. The majority of the people are opposed to establishment.

15. Establishment infringes the right of religious freedom; if the government can infringe that right, it might infringe others as well.[89]

After winning the disestablishment battle in Virginia, Madison turned to the larger arena of the United States during the Constitutional Convention of 1787. More an editor than an author of the Constitution, Madison carefully worded the new framework of government with very little mention of religion one way or the other. His idea was to make the document deliberately concise because it created a central government that many Americans feared would become a leviathan-like imitation of the British imperial government, and only what the Constitution set forth as the powers of this new government would be its actual powers. Therefore, if the Constitution did not specify that the government could establish a religion or choose a church for special status as "America's church," then the United States could not have such a thing, and the people should thus have no fear. This line of reasoning, which asks people to be mindful of what the Constitution does *not* say, is quite esoteric and, in fact, seems backward from how people normally think. Not surprisingly, it did not take hold with most Americans. The Anti-Federalists, of course, emerged to demand that Madison add a Bill of Rights stating explicitly that the new government would not violate their freedom of religion, and the result was the First Amendment.

Just because Madison kept the Constitution largely silent on the issue of religion does not mean he had no thoughts on the subject. He wrote about it to Jefferson, who was in France at the time, as soon as the ratification struggle began, and he wrote about it in one of his *Federalist* newspaper articles (Number 37) to the people of New York. To Jefferson he expressed fear of religious radicals getting control of the government, and to the people of New York he proclaimed the greatness of the "Almighty himself," who possessed so much more wisdom and goodness than man that it scarcely seemed possible that the deity could even communicate with humans, much less that mere mortals could understand the mysterious ways of this eternal sovereign.[90]

Upon being elected president in 1808, Madison vetoed two bills that would have allowed the United States government to give its approval to an established church in a specific territory or state. One called for the establishment of the Episcopal Church in the District of Columbia. Yet Madison clearly did not oppose religion, for he did call the nation to fasting and prayer during the dark days of the War of 1812, albeit very reluctantly and only because of a congressional resolution and public outcry for it. In his presidential proclamation, he took care to let his Federalist opponents know, however, that he had not caved in to their way of thinking on religion, by stating that "Almighty God . . . has been pleased to permit the injustice of a foreign power" to attack the United States. He aimed this slur against their (as he saw it) Pharisaical prayers for God to prevent the war from breaking out in the first place. He also appointed a justice to the Supreme Court—Joseph Story—who turned out to be more radically religious in his opinions from the bench than anyone who had preceded him at that post. Madison also opposed efforts by some antireligious elements to bar all clergymen from office holding in the United States. Madison's record thus looks, like his mentor Jefferson's, mixed. Rather than this making him either a hypocrite or a confused and indecisive leader, however, it makes him one who strove for the perfect balance between religion and politics.[91]

Madison, like all the other American exemplars mentioned, was a complex man with many layers—some public, some private, and all spread over many years and various situations. He, for the purposes of this study, was the last of the Founding Fathers, living to the ripe old age of eighty-five, dying in 1836. He lived long enough to see fulfilled what had only been a dream in his youth—American independence. He lived to see his country win two wars, adopt two Constitutions, create four political parties, split into a sectionalist nation over slavery, and come to accept separation of church and state as the "American Way," while growing toward becoming a fervently evangelical nation—first in the North and later in the South. Indeed, he lived to see his country get labeled as the most religious country in all Christendom by foreign observer Alexis de Tocqueville. One can only wonder what he thought about such developments, and what the other Founders who did not live as long would have thought about them. What is certain is he remained jealous of religious freedom to the end—not to discourage religious expression in America, but to give it every opportunity to bloom.[92]

## ALEXANDER HAMILTON

Of all the Founders, none seems quite as tragic as Alexander Hamilton. Born an illegitimate child in the West Indies, he rose from the humblest of beginnings to perhaps the second most powerful man in the United States during the Washington administration. His death equaled his birth in terms of ignominy. Killed by Jefferson's vice president, Aaron Burr, in an infamous duel in New Jersey in 1804, Hamilton had his life cut short. Considering how much he achieved in his short period of public service from 1787 to 1804, one is left only to wonder what he might have accomplished had he lived to a ripe, old age like James Madison.

Hamilton began life as a Presbyterian. He applied to Princeton, but Jonathan Witherspoon rejected his application. He thus matriculated at King's College (Columbia University today) in New York City. He then converted to Episcopalianism, although probably for social connections rather than religious convictions.[93] In his glory days of the 1780s and 1790s, he fell away from religion altogether, sometimes making comments of an anti-Christian nature, but he returned to his former faith in the last years of his life. After his Federalist party got trounced in the elections of 1800, Hamilton seems to have experienced a personal revival. In 1802, he proposed starting a "Christian Constitutional Society" designed to support what he considered the two great pillars of American government—Christianity and the Constitution. Whether such an organization would have ever materialized can only be speculated. Within two years, Hamilton would be dead. According to historians Douglas Adair and Marvin Harvey, Hamilton's decision to stand and be killed by Burr's bullet in 1804 resulted from his sense of morality derived from his Christian convictions. Whether true or not, it is certain that his last request from the deathbed was to take communion, proving that he took seriously the precepts of his faith.[94]

## Chapter 8

# The American "Duality"

## The Art and Science of Equipoise

### FAITH AND REASON

Having now come full circle, a good way to end this study is to return to the first topic covered—the American paradox, and explore in more detail the duality thesis. This study has established that there is and always has been a dynamic tension in America between the forces of liberalism and the forces of conservatism, between science and religion, between progress and tradition. Sometimes these forces have been manifest in ways that bifurcate the American people into seemingly two different nations or races: into agrarians or urbanites, Northerners or Southerners, rich or poor, educated or uneducated, Democrats or Republicans, and white or minority. In this delicate "equipoise" neither side has been able to dominate the other permanently or limitlessly, although some have seemingly had the upper hand most of the time.[1] If it seems, for instance, that the rich should automatically be in control because money equals power, remember that the poor outnumber them so greatly that the rich must fear them and make decisions accordingly, lest they imitate in America the callousness and capriciousness of the Bourbon monarchy before the French Revolution. Likewise, if it seems that whites should always be in control because they outnumber the minorities so greatly, remember that since the 1960s racial discrimination has been illegal in this country, partly the result of white magnanimity based on the egalitarian ideal expressed in the Declaration, and partly of minority riots and disturbances that generated fear among the whites running the government. It should not be surprising, therefore, that a similar ebb and flow has occurred between religious-minded Americans and their secular-minded counterparts. Keeping with the two analogies just made, in the early decades of the United States church members were, like the rich today, a small minority of the population that exercised a degree of control over society and politics out of all proportion to their numbers. Over time, church members came to outnumber the unchurched, and, like the white majority, showed a remarkable degree of magnanimity toward the minority—so much so, in fact, that some modern evangelical Christians have accused their fellows of "giving away the store," so to speak, to their secular opposition.

The duality theme pervades United States history and contemporary America alike. It can be argued that the resulting tension, which is like an intellectual tug-of-war or arm-wrestling match, has affected American history positively. Why? Because it has kept the radicals on both sides at bay most of the time. It has forced the nation to gravitate toward what has been called the "vital center," meaning it has kept the country on an even keel, striving to find common ground, lest the two extremes declare war on each other.[2] So far only one issue in American history has proved divisive enough to push the people out of the middle ground, such that they were forced to choose sides in a Civil War, and that issue was slavery. Others threaten to do it again today, such as abortion and homosexuality, but to this point neither has forced the vast majority in the middle to polarize, although the extremists on both sides of these contemporary issues are about as far apart ideologically as people can be.

England's Lord Acton observed in the 1860s (the time of the American Civil War) that the United States had never been anything more than a large collection of compromises. It had never had a core principle or set of unabandonable values but rather rested upon "a series of mutual concessions, and momentary suspensions" of antagonistic aspirations and conflicting interests. He did not see in the United States a new order for the ages, as the Founders had intended, but rather a sociopolitical system that existed from moment to moment, from crisis to crisis, and survived only so long as a new compromise could be reached in each arising conflict.[3] That idea seems plausible, especially considering the era in which Acton proffered it. He could see that the Declaration had set forth one sort of vision for the nation (enlightened egalitarianism), but the Constitution had framed that nation's government with quite a different reality in mind (Machiavellian *realpolitik*), and the *idealism* of the former was being tested by the *reality* of the latter.[4] The fact that the former won out over the latter, in a manner of speaking, when the Unionists defeated the Secessionists in the Civil War, preserved the vision of having an enlightened, egalitarian nation. The irony is, the secularists were not the "enlightened" visionaries at the time of the Civil War, but the radical Christians (the Abolitionists) were. The same ones who forced the polarization of Americans into pro- and anti-slavery camps, leaving no common ground, indirectly reaffirmed the faith of the *tour de force* of the American Enlightenment, the Declaration of Independence.

Prior to his inauguration in 1861, Lincoln had addressed the New Jersey legislature, calling the United States God's "almost chosen people." He pointed out the duality of the nation, implying that, if not for the divisive slavery issue, this country would indeed be God's chosen people.[5] At his inauguration, Lincoln called on the "Almighty Ruler of Nations" to heal the land as it was just beginning to unravel into Civil War.[6] He later called the United States a "nation under God," long before those words found their way into the Pledge of Allegiance.[7] During the war, Julia Ward Howe's "Battle Hymn of the Republic" set the tone for the coming golden age of American Christianity, proclaiming that once the Secessionists were defeated, the next step would be the conversion of the United States into a truly Christian nation. At the same time, the National Reform Association sought to take the battle off the field and into the halls of Congress, lobbying the government (unsuccessfully) to declare the United States officially a "Christian nation."[8] The Lincoln administration did not act upon that suggestion but did the nearest thing to it. Lincoln called a national day of fasting on April 30, 1863, and made an extremely pro-Christian proclamation, saying that all of history proved that the most blessed nations are those that believe the Bible and worship the Lord. He did not endorse a particular denomination but he clearly endorsed Christianity by urging all Americans to go to their own church and keep the appointed day holy.[9] Considering the increase in church membership thereafter, perhaps it worked.

A few years later, President Ulysses S. Grant followed Lincoln's example when he institutionalized a religious tradition, the Christian "Thanksgiving Day," as an official federal holiday. But in the mold of James Madison, Thomas Jefferson, John Adams, and George Washington before him, Grant offset his pro-Christian offering with a recommendation that all churches, which he called "corporations," begin paying taxes.[10] He did this with the full cognizance that he would incur the wrath of evangelical Christians, who had considerable political power in the 1800s, more than ever before or since in American history. The Methodist Church, for instance, was practically equal in political power at the time to either the Democratic or Republican parties in its ability to control votes.[11] Moreover, the Centennial celebration of July 1876, which occurred on Grant's watch, was more a celebration of the civic religion than American nationalism, and as much a pep rally for mainstream churches as a political event.[12] The irony, of course, is that while Christians put all this religiosity on display, Grant meanwhile presided over the most corrupt administration in American history to that time.

Upon restoring the egalitarian vision of the Declaration through the Civil War, evangelical, reform-minded Christians then led the country into the American version of the latter English Victorian Age, an era called the "Gilded Age."[13] The name signifies a bright, shining lie. It means the nation appeared beautiful on the outside but was rotten on the inside. It can be argued that the phenomenon Mark Twain described when he coined the term "the Gilded Age" in 1873 was not that of a grand national hypocrisy as the name implies, but rather the duality that had characterized the United States from its inception, only amplified because of the outward embrace and display of Christianity at this time. That is not to say that Twain saw no hypocrisy at all; he was critical of anyone who wore religion on his/her sleeve. The main idea behind the gold-covered metaphor, however, was duality—one thing on the inside, something else on the outside, and depending upon what each individual's perspective was as insider or outsider, he or she might see the United States as a genuinely Christian nation or a Christian nation falsely so-called.[14] Either way, the country was religious enough that one observer could proudly say that "Christianity is the most powerful factor in our society and the pillar of our institutions."[15] He would have been right, considering that every state in the Union allowed Bible reading, hymn singing, and prayer in schools at the time, and four-fifths of all the school districts in America had mandates expecting Christian values to be taught in the classroom.[16] By 1890, the very height of the Gilded Age, the Victorian Englishman James Bryce, an objective observer, could state axiomatically that Christianity, "though not the legally established religion" was indeed "the national religion" of the United States.[17] At the same time, the United States, along with England, became the greatest exporter of Christianity in the world through its missionary activities, yet also exported the ideal of democracy, which included separation of church and state, to every place it touched.[18]

The road to making the United States a bastion of Christianity was slow and arduous. The Christianization of America came in fits and starts, and it often got shrouded by the duality of secularism or agnosticism. Mainly, though, it got mixed with separationism, not at the hand of secularists but at the hand of forward-thinking Christians. As one historian put it, "Many of the same men who accepted the political ideals of Jefferson also believed in the theology of [Jonathan] Edwards, and were able to do so without any sense of inconsistency."[19] Consider a few examples. In the Maryland Ratification Convention of 1788, Luther Martin called the United States a "Christian country" while simultaneously supporting separation of church and state and chiding radical Christians for opposing it.[20] James Iredell, at the North Carolina Ratification Convention, said, "America has set an example to mankind to think more modestly and reasonably; that a man may be of different religious sentiments from our own without being a bad member of society." Noting his own Christianity he added, "The divine author of our religion never wished for its support by worldly authority. Has he not said, *that the gates of hell shall not prevail against it?*"[21] Isaac Backus, the most famous Baptist of the Founding generation, affirmed at the Massachusetts Ratification Convention the wisdom of not imposing one group's religion upon others, but in the same breath referred to "*our* Lord Jesus Christ."[22] Patrick Dollard at the South Carolina Ratification Convention equated democracy with obedience *to* God and liberty with a blessing *from* God, saying the "voice of the people is the voice of

God," and freedom is "that best gift of God."[23] James Madison identified himself as a Christian, saying, "Whilst we assert for ourselves a freedom to embrace, to profess, and to observe the religion which we believe to be of divine origin, we cannot deny equal freedom" to non-Christians.[24]

If these examples are not enough to show the Founders to be both Christians and separationists simultaneously, consider more. Charles Cotesworth Pinckney, at the South Carolina Convention, expressed the duality of worshiping God and revering liberty when he said, "To the Union we will look up as to the temple of our freedom . . . here we will point out our gratitude to the author of all good. . . ."[25] Likewise, Simeon Baldwin, at the Connecticut Convention, said, "Liberty was the darling object of the first settlers of this country" but "Heaven" gave the land to the Americans, and "Heaven" blessed the people with the Declaration of Independence. He added that "if the Lord himself had not been on our side" in the Revolution, the Americans would have lost. So he urged his fellows now to make the most of the opportunity for nationhood, and "to discharge our duty to our God, our country and ourselves, like true patriots and benevolent Christians. We shall then reap the smiles of heaven."[26] Meanwhile, the anonymous "Brutus" in New York affirmed that Americans were "bound by the immutable laws of God *and* reason. . . ."[27] Similarly, the Anti-Federalist Thomas B. Wait of Maine trusted that "God" would direct Madison and company to add a Bill of Rights specifically to protect the right of men to worship that same "God" according to their own consciences.[28]

Such examples prove, as one historian has rightly noted, that "The founding generation moved easily between faith and practical, common sense reasoning. . . . a mass of evidence demonstrates that what the founding generation did cannot be explained by the Enlightenment alone."[29] Consider even more examples. An anonymous "Republican" of Connecticut wrote that "God *and* nature" gave Americans their rights.[30] Moreover, Robert Whitehill at the Pennsylvania convention argued that "Heaven" gave the Anti-Federalists their strength to oppose the Constitution because the document endangered the "temple of freedom" that American patriots had recently fought the Revolution to create.[31] If such mixing of Christian and Enlightenment metaphors among the Founders seems a bit bizarre today, it most definitely was not uncommon at that time. Consider the formal parade staged by the city of Baltimore in May 1788 to celebrate Maryland's adoption of the new Constitution. Baltimoreans held an elaborate, well-planned processional of about 3,000 locals—mainly "farmers, mechanics, and merchants"—that wound through the main streets of the city. It featured seven gun/cannon salutes, thirteen toasts, and a series of "Huzzas." It displayed various flags, emblems, banners, and slogans, some devoted to industry and commerce, some to military and naval affairs, and others to nationalism. One flag portrayed Adam and Eve in the Garden of Eden surrounded by thirteen stars, and one statue depicted the "Goddess" of liberty accepting the new Constitution with a smile. The parade ended with the benediction, "may Heaven itself approve the Wisdom of *our* Federal Constitution."[32]

None of the Founders saw any contradiction in mixing wisdom from Christian teachings with wisdom from secular Enlightenment philosophy. Even the most reverend among the founding preachers, Jonathan Witherspoon, read and respected Hume, who was about as secular as Rationalists came.[33] In debating the merits of the proposed new Constitution in 1787, Richard Henry Lee wrote, "From Moses to Montesquieu the greatest geniuses have been employed on this difficult subject" of trying to devise the perfect form of government.[34] The fact that Lee put a biblical patriarch and a near-contemporary Rationalist in the same category speaks volumes about how most of the Founders viewed the seemingly conflicting philosophies of Christianity and secularism.

Nor were the Founders averse to mixing Christian teachings with pre-Christian Greek and Roman philosophy. Historian Gordon Wood has called the ideology of the Founders a blend of "millennial Christianity and pagan classicism, a cocktail first mixed by the English Whigs before its arrival in America. An example of this congruence can be seen in the words of Revolutionary leader Samuel Adams of Boston, who called the wartime United States the "Christian Sparta" of the world.[35] Since most of the Founders received their education in basically just two fields—Christian theology and the classics—it should not be surprising that they would mix the two in forming the new American civic religion. Jefferson, for one, tried diligently to reconcile the two, much as the scholastics of the European universities did in the High Middle Ages, although the practice was no longer called "scholasticism" at that time but rather "hermeneutics" or "philology."[36] John Adams likewise acknowledged Plato and Aristotle for helping shape his views, although in a tongue-in-cheek disclaimer he demurred that the only thing he "had ever learned from Plato was where Franklin had plagiarized some of his ideas, and how to cure the hiccups."[37]

In a more serious vein, Adams opined that Christianity must be left alone to compete in the free marketplace of ideas, alongside every other religion and philosophy. If it has any merit, he said, it will survive, and if it has great merit, it will thrive. All separationists, then and now, have agreed with that assessment. Indeed, it would be difficult not to. Some commentators have placed a qualifier on that notion, however, proclaiming the brilliance of the American way that encourages "religious faith in providence" and "secular faith in progress" to develop concurrently, because either/or would not suffice.[38] Secularists today generally deny that religious teaching is necessary for society to function well. They see science and religion as fundamentally opposed to each other. They are mistaken. Throughout history the most religious civilizations have also been the most scientifically advanced civilizations, and vice versa. Consider the Egyptians, the Greeks, the Romans, the Mayas, the Aztecs, and the Incas, for obvious examples. Consider also that the smartest scientists who have ever lived, Isaac Newton and Albert Einstein, as well as dozens of others, have believed in a creator-god.[39] In addition, consider that the greatest flourishing of technological advancement in American history came during the Gilded Age-Progressive Era, which was the height of Christian influence in the United States. Finally, consider that some of the most esteemed scientists in the world during the founding generation were also believers: John Ray of England, Count Volney of France, Thomas Cooper and John Mitchell of South Carolina, William Bartram of Pennsylvania, Benjamin Sullivan of Connecticut, and James Otis of Massachusetts, for example.[40] It is safe to conclude that Christianity per se was not contrary to science and secular human progress, but only certain fundamentalist versions of it, which none of the Founders believed in or practiced.

## GOD AND MAMMON

Just as science and religion are not incompatible in the United States but actually complement each other, so too do capitalism and mainstream American Christianity. Although this would seem to contradict the Christian adage that states "no man can serve two masters . . . Ye cannot serve God and mammon" (Matthew 6:24), the statement actually applies (if it is true at all) to individuals, not to nations. In fact, Jesus hinted at this interpretation when he urged his fellow Jews, as a people or nation, to "render to Caesar the things that are Caesar's, and to God the things that are God's" (Mark 12:17).[41] If other nations between the birth of Christianity and the founding of the United States had difficulty arriving at that interpretation, the Americans never did. It was, in fact, instilled in the American mind-set from the earliest colonial days and reinforced in each succeeding generation, and so much so as to make capitalism one of the foundation stones of the American way or civic religion.[42] Americans who do not embrace capitalism ideologically are, and always have been, out of the mainstream, standing in opposition to the American way, and thus subject to social shunning by the majority.[43]

"Contradictory currents," such as simultaneous love of both God and money, "run through the cultural and intellectual life of provincial America," as Clarence Ver Steeg has put it, and they are noticeable to historians at every stage of development in the American experiment.[44] By the 1830s, however, when Alexis de Tocqueville made his famous observations about the United States, Americans had become arguably the most religious people in the world and simultaneously the most materialistic consumers.[45] It has been true ever since, and it seems indisputably so presently.

This fact prompts the questions, why is it so? How did it come about? What were the foundational factors in creating this particular duality in the American way? Several are readily identifiable. The so-called "Protestant work ethic" (Max Weber's terminology), new capitalist economic theories, the invention of clocks and watches that were relatively inexpensive and accurate (which made time equal money), and the liberalization of Christian ideas about investment banking (which had previously been considered a sin because of the usury involved), all combined to lay the foundation of the American economy in the 17th century. It is no coincidence that the two most liberal, Protestantized nations on earth—England and Holland—led the capitalist commercial revolution. The English Calvinist Puritans who settled New England competed with the Dutch Reformed Calvinists who settled New York in an unplanned but nevertheless very present capitalist economy. The competition actually produced a regional business partnership of a sort over time that eventually led to the coalescing of the two groups into one broad "Yankee" culture (which also included Calvinist Presbyterians by the time of the Founding). Colonials farther south could also participate in the capitalist enterprises of their northern counterparts, but most chose not to simply because they did not need to; they had agricultural options for achieving wealth that the Yankees did not have. The non-Calvinist background of most colonial Southerners also mitigated against their imitating the ultra-capitalist mind-set of the North.[46]

It is important to note the obvious fact that the settling of the American colonies ran nearly concurrent to the Protestant Reformation back in the Old World. Although the latter predated the former by about a century as far as North America in concerned, the two went hand in hand. It is difficult to conceive of the American colonies developing even remotely similar to what they actually did politically, economically, and socially, if not first developing the way they did religiously. In other words, had the Reformation not occurred and had Catholicism been the guiding force behind the colonial experiment in North America, one can only speculate as to how differently history would have unfolded. Certainly Catholic nations such as Spain and France played major roles in the colonization of the New World, but would they have been able to produce a "United States of America"? It seems unlikely, merely because of the aforementioned delicate balance of factors—one of which was the so-called Protestant work ethic—which actually did influence the development of the United States.[47]

Aside from Calvinist Protestantism, capitalism was the great driving force behind America's economic development. The capitalist bible, of course, was Adam Smith's *The Wealth of Nations*, which was coincidentally published in 1776, the year of the United States' birth. The United States became the first great proving ground of Smith's capitalist theories, which seem to have been custom-made for this new country with all its abundance of natural and human resources. Needless to say, Smith's capitalism proved an immediate and almost infallible success here. When Smith wrote of an "invisible hand" that guides markets and commerce, he could have easily been describing the Protestant work ethic, because the Calvinists' willingness to toil and spin functioned like an extra, invisible hand that produced wealth.[48]

Superficially it would appear that America's love of money should have destroyed its love of the deity, but the opposite was in fact true. The Christians and Deists of America viewed capitalism as God's way of blessing the righteous with material prosperity. It was all part of the "chosen people" ideology. Reinhold Niebuhr has called the wedding of God and mammon in America the philosophy of "Godly materialism." The rationale behind this mixed marriage was that by "fulfilling the prescription for happiness" in this life rather than deferring it to the afterlife, Christians could use their prosperity both to bless others and to keep more easily certain mandates of the Bible that are difficult to attain while living in penury. If, for instance, it is more blessed to give than receive, as Jesus said, how can one give materially if one has nothing to offer? One must first acquire his or her own material prosperity in order to have anything to share with others.[49]

Although this Godly materialism was not unique to either Protestants or Americans, the embrace of it as the dominant worldview was. Ultimately, capitalism (acquisition of private wealth), regardless of the degree to which it captivated the various colonies, was shared by all colonies as an American institution, and it is important to note that it became an institution before separation of church and state became one. Notice that in the Declaration of Independence there is no mention of separation of church and state but there are many mentions of various "unalienable rights," of which the rights of private individuals to pursue, acquire, own, and dispose of property at their own discretion were paramount. Essentially the phrase "pursuit of happiness" actually meant *pursuit of personal wealth* to many, if not most, of the Founders.[50]

Adam Smith (a Scotsman) and his economic disciple Joseph Priestly (an Englishman), one of the founders of Unitarianism and the scientist who discovered oxygen, were both proponents of laissez-faire, meaning capitalism unregulated by the government. They believed self-interested economic behavior would automatically produce beneficial side effects for society at large. Likewise, both were strict separationists, believing that individuals should pursue their own religious self-interests just the same as their own economic self-interests.[51] Self-interested behavior was also a major catalyst of democracy, the political manifestation of individuals believing in their own intrinsic self-worth and in the value of their own opinions.[52] Although Calvinism did not predate or invent the notion of self-interested behavior in either economics, religion, or politics, it certainly supported all three to a greater extent than any previous doctrine since the birth of Christianity.[53]

## NORTH AND SOUTH

Another duality in the American way is that of the North-South geographic dichotomy that has pervaded this country from the time of the Revolution to at least the end of the civil rights movement.[54] It is the particular duality that has arguably caused more problems for a longer period of time than any other. Usually the focus on this duality is geared toward racial issues, and sometimes toward issues stemming from traditionalism versus modernism. But there has also been a noticeable disconnect between the North and South historically over religion. Consider that in the mid-1600s, the Puritans (Dissenting Anglicans) of Massachusetts welcomed the English Civil War and supported Oliver Cromwell, while the High Anglicans of Virginia opposed the war and remained loyal to King Charles. Needless to say, the religious differences between New England and the southern colonies largely shaped the often-conflicting cultures of the two regions. By the time of the Revolution, the two were perhaps more different than alike (not only in terms of religion but also industrialization, economics, and education), which prevented them from easily forming even a temporary military alliance, much less a permanent union, to fight the British monarchy. Although the Revolution did much to lessen these differences, remnants of them continued throughout the Articles of Confederation period and well into the ratification struggle in 1788.[55]

During the ratification debates, some Anti-Federalists considered the religious differences between the North and the South to be a foremost concern, and one that should prevent the adoption of a federal system of government. They thought it "impossible for one code of laws to suit Georgia and Massachusetts" and all states in between. To try to make it so by reducing each state's power of choice and forcing upon them "the same standards of morals, of habits, and of laws, is . . . an absurdity," for it would be "contrary to the whole experience of mankind," and would require military coercion to maintain.[56] As southern Anti-Federalist Joseph Taylor put it, "We see plainly that men who come from New England are different from us."[57] Although historians generally blame the political differences of opinion among the Founders for the rise of factions such as Federalists and Anti-Federalists, religious and cultural divergences resulting from the North-South divide were actually just as much to blame.[58] There were any number of divisive elements within the United States at the time of the Founding, but as Richard Buel has explained, "the essential division" was "between a Republican South and a Federalist New England."[59]

At the time, the least of the problems associated with North-South religious differences concerned slavery, although that certainly ended up being the fly in the federal ointment in years to come.[60] Undoubtedly, had states that rejected establishment at the time—such as Virginia and South Carolina—tried to force their religious/political views on the states that maintained it—such as Massachusetts and Connecticut—blood would have flowed in the 1790s the way it actually did later in the 1860s when the roles were reversed over the issue of slavery. An interesting twist to the plot of American history is to consider that New England Congregationalism gave the people of the old Northeast the same kind of local sovereignty that southern state's righters later sought through nullification and secession, only the Congregationalist type of localism was religious whereas the Southerners' type was political. Each essentially filled the same need within the American democratic system, however, allowing local people to take control of their own destiny rather than have it dictated to them from on high.

One great irony is that the New England states, which began as the most religious, have evolved (or devolved, as the case may be) into the least religious in modern times, while the southern states have followed the reverse track. At the time of the founding, Jedediah Morse, the Congregationalist author of *American Geography*, reported that New England still observed the "Lord's Day" faithfully. He made no comparable statement about the South.[61] The statement has been more true of the South in the 20th and 21st centuries than of the North. In terms of which section of the country showed more tolerance of dissenting religious beliefs at the time of the founding, there is little difference. Both were almost equally intolerant, although Boston had become a pocket of toleration to a greater degree than any place in the South. It is interesting to note that the most tolerant colony by far, Pennsylvania, with its sizeable Quaker population and its large non-English citizenry, was sandwiched right in between Massachusetts and Virginia geographically.[62]

One of the few things to bring the North and South together during the Colonial era was the Great Awakening. It had a somewhat greater impact upon the South than the North because the southern population was more agnostic at the time, whereas the northern people were more churched. Even so, its impact in the North was noticeable, too. Since the Great Awakening was an evangelical movement, it could rightly be posited that evangelicalism represented the first unifying force between the North and South in American history. Unfortunately, it was not enough to carry over for another 120 years and keep unity amid the sectional slavery controversy of the mid-1800s.[63]

The unification of North and South religiously was only partial to begin with, and it was a work in progress as the United States came into being. Although it would continue to be noticeable throughout the early republic and Jacksonian eras, it would be threatened by the Federalist Party/Republican Party split of the 1790s, and ultimately destroyed by issues of the 1850s leading to the Civil War. And what a tragedy for the nation! In the generation preceding the Civil War, America's political leaders, in the North and South alike, tended to profess Christianity openly. Consider the open religious professions of President Andrew Jackson, a nationalist Democrat from Tennessee, and the Great Triumvirate of senators Henry Clay (Whig from Kentucky), Daniel Webster (Whig from Massachusetts), and John C. Calhoun (Democrat from South Carolina). Each was exemplary of the prevailing mood of his geographic section of the country in the early-to-mid-1800s, not just on slavery, tariffs, and other political issues, but religion as well. Jackson, a lifelong Presbyterian, said on his deathbed, "The Bible is true. . . . I rest my hope for eternal salvation, through the merits and blood of our blessed Lord and Savior, Jesus Christ."[64] Clay, the son of a Baptist minister, and erstwhile teacher at a Christian college, likewise, invoked "our blessed Redeemer" who "offered Himself on Mount Calvary for the salvation of our species. . . . I trust in the atonement of the Savior of mercy. . . ."[65] Webster made similar statements, but moreover argued for the "recognition of the Christian religion" in the

Constitution, "as an expression of our respect, and attachment to Christianity.
. . ."[66] Calhoun, as previously mentioned, became one of the most famous
Unitarians among second-generation Americans, a man whose religion was
kept largely private, but expressed his desire to see the United States made
into a nation of liberal, enlightened believers in the mono-God.[67] How different the nation's history would be if such unifying religious faith could have
trumped the slavery issue.

A final interesting point of contrast between the North and the South in
early American history is that northern Congregationalists tended to be the
foremost writers of the nation's history prior to the dawn of the age of professional historiography. They put their stamp of religious interpretation on history, and did so because they could. Southern versions of American history
were few and far between.[68] Southerners, particularly Virginians, certainly
made their great contributions to the development of the United States in politics and diplomacy, but not so much in letters. Likewise, while New
Englanders were more fond of outward religion, education for the masses, and
written documentation of not only history but of daily life, they failed to produce the brilliant political leaders that the South did. Why this was so is
mostly a mystery, but it can be speculated that it may have had something to
do with the satisfaction that New Englanders derived from the local control of
their congregations, which slaked their desire for empowerment and made political aggrandizement unnecessary. Meanwhile Southerners might have felt
compelled to seek empowerment through the political process because they
lacked it in religion.

## CONSERVATISM AND LIBERALISM

Popular usage and misusage of the terms *conservative* and *liberal* in
America currently can affect perception of the ideologies of conservatism and
liberalism in history. It is thus quite important to set forth correct definitions
before beginning a brief discussion of this topic. The most basic meaning of
each word is that conservatism opposes changing the traditions or institutions
within a nation or society while liberalism favors it. Often implied in liberalism is reform of some type of behavior by those in power that is interpreted
as oppressive by those not in power, and thus conservatism implies deliberate
oppression at worst or neglect and indifference at best. In the context of the
church-state debate, conservatives in the Old World prior to the Reformation
wanted to keep the power of the Roman Catholic Church intact, which made
the Protestants automatically the liberals. Once those same Protestants,
whether Anglicans in Virginia or Puritans in New England, built their own
societies in the New World, they became the conservatives here. In the case
of the Puritans in the 17th century, they were simultaneously conservatives in
America and liberals in England.[69] Their American conservatism was, of
course, just as conservative as anything the Anglican or Catholic Church in

Europe had to offer. (It is easy to compare the Salem Witch Trials to the Inquisition, for instance.) When liberals such as Roger Williams or Anne Hutchinson challenged the absolute control of Massachusetts, they did not merely threaten the religious orthodoxy but the social conventions of the day as well. Leaders such as John Cotton saw them not so much as radicals who posed an immediate threat to the colony but more like the first drops of a slow, drenching rainfall that might erode the fabric of his Puritan Utopia over time. Or to use a better metaphor, he saw them as the first weeds in the Puritan Garden of Eden. If not extirpated, such weeds might eventually destroy the garden.[70] Yet both the wheat and the tares, the Williamses and the Cottons, grew up side by side in America from the beginning.

By the time of the founding more than a century later, both groups had taken firm root, and neither seemed in any danger of imminently destroying the other. A major point of confusion about this topic springs up here. The Founders themselves were political liberals. Supporting a revolution to get free from an established government could not be considered anything other than a radically liberal action. Some modern observers assume, therefore, that the Founders must have also been religious liberals, as if the two automatically go hand in hand. Yet as has already been shown, only some of the Founders were religious liberals, while others were religious conservatives. Of course, all different degrees of both could be seen among them. They basically covered the spectrum from radically religious liberals, such as Ethan Allen, to religious archconservatives, such as Patrick Henry. By no means, however, did the liberality of the most radical Americans come close to approximating the liberality of a Robespierre in the French Revolution. So the degree of liberality of the Founders, when measured against that of some of their contemporaries abroad, actually seems quite conservative. For example, George Washington, the leader of the "liberal" American Revolution, actually had more in common with his contemporary Edmund Burke, the conservative English Whig, than he did with the French revolutionaries of the same time period.[71]

Revolution by its very nature is the most extreme form of liberalism. Nations that change government through revolutions almost invariably do so because of the oppression and/or corruption of the former regime. Depending on many different factors, some revolutionary nations immediately reconfigure their government in such a way as to replace the old regime with an equally oppressive and/or corrupt new one, which is then perceived as "conservative." The United States had the opportunity to do the same but instead did the opposite. It retained its ability to change with the times through its flexible, liberal Constitution. Yet within the confines of American liberalism is a restraining influence that is called conservatism. The United States, true to its dual nature, is a blend of both liberalism and conservatism.[72]

It can rightly be argued that the Hegelian dialectic of conservative thesis and liberal antithesis reached its synthesis in the new United States. The synthesis, however, did not replace either the thesis or antithesis, nor did it destroy or nullify either the liberality of the liberals or the conservatism of the conservatives. Instead, the two ideologies both grew up concurrently, and like in a marriage, the two were joined in a union while at the same time retaining their individuality.[73] Obviously, the manifestation of conservatism in the early republic was the Federalist party, while that of liberalism was the Jeffersonian party. Both parties actually came closer to each other in ideology than they did with most of their European counterparts.[74] Those who could find happiness in neither camp opted for the Tertium Quid, or "third something," which was not an official party but just a faction. This pattern of the United States producing two main competing parties based upon conflicting ideologies, while leaving a Tertium Quid unclaimed and unaccounted for, has held true for most of American history. It is part of generational ebb and flow, and it operates much like any proverbial system in which society takes two steps forward and one step backward. The basic progression is toward more and more liberalism, but lest the changes go too far, too fast, there is the inevitable conservative backlash that slows down progress temporarily—perhaps for a decade, perhaps for several, but never more than that, at least not so far in American history.[75]

This ebb and flow was not confined to politics. Even within the many diverse denominations conservative and liberal elements could be found. Again, hark back to Roger Williams and Anne Hutchinson as early examples of religious liberals. Then especially during both Great Awakenings, liberals were evangelicals and evangelicals were liberals. However one describes this class of Christians—whether Antinomians, "New Lights," mystics, or just crazy people—they certainly pushed the envelope. More importantly, these liberals did not accept being pushed back against by the conservative Armenians or "Old Lights." Rather than allowing the conservatives to stop the flow of the spirit, these liberals usually just broke away and formed a new denomination where they could worship as they pleased and where they would have to answer to no one but the deity.[76]

As these liberal groups pertain to the church-state debate, they too have always been divided into two camps. One scholar has called them the "free-church" Christians and the "revivalist" Christians. The former group favors total separation of church and state, meaning they want the government to leave them alone, while the latter wants Christians to run the government, meaning they hope for their own kind to influence public policy and shape public morality through legislation.[77] Before condemning and dismissing this latter group as dangerous extremists or accusing them of trying to turn the United States into a theocracy, remember Christians of this variety comprised the corpus of both the Abolitionist movement of the mid-1800s and the Progressive movement of the early 1900s. The question must be asked therefore, "what kind of country would the United States be today without their efforts to instill their extreme moral views into the government, from the local level all the way to the federal?" It seems that many in the modern secularist camp do not want to reckon with that question, or with the fact that these very public and outspoken Christians of days gone by led some of the most important social justice crusades in American history.

Besides the particular dualities discussed in this chapter, others could be mentioned that have been arguably just as divisive at one time or another in American history. At the time of the Revolution, the people divided into Patriots and Loyalists; at the time of the Constitution, they divided into Federalists and Anti-Federalists. Then political parties emerged in the early republic that, although changing names and taking various forms over the years, have divided Americans over ideas and issues, and which seem to be as divisive today as ever. From the Jacksonian era to the civil rights movement, white and nonwhite was perhaps the most divisive feature. From at least the time that Alexander Hamilton introduced his national economic program in the 1790s, Americans divided into rural agriculturalists and urban industrialists. Increasingly nowadays, if recent presidential elections are an indicator, urban and rural populations are about as far apart ideologically as people can be. Conflicting ideologies of militarism and pacifism, which date back at least to the War of 1812, have likewise become increasingly pitted against one another since the Vietnam War. Needless to say, there has always been the male and female dichotomy, as well as the educated and uneducated, the rich and poor, the localists and nationalists, the isolationists and globalists, the capitalists and socialists, the Catholics and Protestants, and the list could go on and on.

One of the more provocative duality theses in recent years has been posited by Daniel Lazare, who sees individual Americans as personally conflicted, arguing in their consciences with themselves over the nature of the Constitution and the federal government it put into operation. They generally love the Constitution, because "it is an article of faith in America's civic religion" to think of that document as "pure and perfect." Yet, as they are "praising the Constitution," they are simultaneously "cursing the government" and have been doing so "since virtually the moment George Washington took office." Perhaps, he says, if the government is so loathsome, the Constitution is not, and never has been, so great after all.[78] While all would certainly agree that the Constitution is and always has been a flawed document, most would say it is still, like the flawed nation it represents, the best the world has ever seen. And as the First American, Ben Franklin put it, it may be the best that mortal man is capable of. If not, its superior has yet to be written.

# Conclusion

## *A Novus Ordo Seclorum?*

Although a long-drawn-out conclusion that reiterates the main points of this book might be justified, it would also be unnecessary. By this point the thesis of this study should be evident: The United States was not founded as a Christian nation in the legal sense, but it certainly was founded by professing Christians, albeit mostly liberal, enlightened, tolerant, forward-thinking Christians—not fundamentalists. They confidently held the assumption that belief in the mono-God of Western civilization was ubiquitous among the American people and would remain so in perpetuity. Hence, they could proclaim with no fear the belief in *Annuit Coeptis*—that this God of theirs (whoever or whatever he, she, they, or it may be) had smiled on their attempt to start a new nation with the most user-friendly government in the history of the world. They never expected a future generation to come along and proclaim the death of God or renounce all articles of faith. The nation was founded with references to God in its Declaration, it concluded its war of independence with a treaty written "In the name of the most Holy and undivided Trinity," and the only change the Founders anticipated was that voiced by Jefferson and reiterated by Calhoun—that America would ultimately reject Trinitarianism in light of Unitarianism.

In keeping with the American way of *E Pluribus Unum*, the Founders expected this new form of Christianity to be inclusive, not exclusive, in terms of social classes, education level, white ethnic background, and, in the case of Jefferson at least, perhaps race and skin color someday. It was a classic "big tent" vision of the future. To them it would be basically a religious manifestation of the democratic impulse that sought room for the common man at the ballot box, which Jefferson and later Jackson favored. Indeed, it would be an everyman's faith, not a rich man's religion. Likewise, in keeping with the *Novus Ordo Seclorum*, they foresaw a day when the American people would spread their big tent ideology of inclusion to the rest of the Western, Christian world. The everyman's faith would not be merely an American civic religion, but a religion for all Western civilization. It is doubtful that they could have seen farther than that (to have the same degree of influence on the Orient and deepest Africa and beyond in such a grand way), but they certainly would have embraced the idea and welcomed the opportunity.

Thus, the Founders clearly did not intend to keep God out of the government, but rather to keep the government out of people's personal lives, hence the separation of church and state. In trying to determine whether either the pro-Christian nation fundamentalists or the anti-Christian nation secularists are more accurate in their assessment of the Founders' intent, it appears that they are both almost equally wrong. Was the United States, then, meant to be a "Christian nation?" Inasmuch as it was founded by moderate, liberal, tolerant, inclusive, and forward-thinking Christians, and those same kinds of open-minded Christians have throughout the generations felt the most welcome and at home here, it was meant to be a "Christian nation." But more accurately, the Christian Founders, with their own personal wide theological latitude as their moral compass, intended their new country to be a nation where a happy medium could be struck between radical, opposing ideological camps, so that regardless of whether the majority made the minority "feel" welcome in the United States, they would nonetheless "be" welcome legally.

This nation is and always has been a predominantly religious society, but its religion has generally not stifled scientific inquiry and advancement of human progress in secular ways. Instead, its open-minded religion, which has prevailed more often than not at the leadership levels of government and society, has encouraged this seemingly contradictory duality. The thought shapers throughout early American history constructed a mythical creed of religio-political uniformitarianism that largely holds sway even today with the vast majority of "We, the people." Those who accept it domestically are labeled "real" Americans; those who accept it internationally are considered "friends" and/or "allies." Those who reject this American way or civic religion domestically are still allowed to live and pursue happiness in their own way, but at the cost of being shunned by the uniformitarians. Those who reject the *E Pluribus Unum* and *Novus Ordo Seclorum* concepts internationally, well . . . they must eventually come around, for the United States will not be deterred from its vision. So long as this nation exists, it will continue its mission to spread the one-world global vision, with itself at the head—or, ultimately, it will be destroyed trying.[1]

# Notes

## PREFACE

1. The term *Founders* will be used throughout this study to describe jointly the political leaders of the United States during the American Revolution, the signers of the Declaration of Independence, and the framers of the Constitution. The rationale for this terminology is supplied in a detailed discussion in Chapter 2.

2. As a disclaimer, this work is intended for the general audience and is not designed to impress fellow scholars who make their livelihoods studying, writing, and teaching about church-state issues. To help quell some of the objections, however, that many erudite specialists are bound to have about this treatise, explanatory endnotes have been supplied in certain places, often to deal with controversial points made in the narrative. Scholars will notice many important books and articles that are omitted from the endnotes and bibliography. There are dozens of volumes written about each and every minute aspect and subtopic contained in this broad survey, making an exhaustive bibliography impractical and beyond the reach of this study. It should be noted, therefore, that the bibliography contains only the works actually cited herein in the endnotes, not every important work on the topic.

3. Noonan, *The Lustre of Our Country*, 2.

4. Tentler, "One Historian's Sundays," quoted in Kuklick and Hart, eds., *Religious Advocacy and American History*, 212.

5. Strout, *The New Heavens and the New Earth*, xiii, 3.

6. Haskell, *Objectivity Is Not Neutrality*, passim.

7. Perry, et al., eds., *Sources of the Western Tradition*, 389.

8. The term *democide* has only recently been introduced into the English language. It is a generic term that refers to state-sponsored mass murder of a group of people, with no distinction of which kind of group or why the state seeks their extermination. The terms *genocide*, *politicide*, and *religicide* have nuanced differences, with the first referring to a racial group, the second a political group, and the third a religious group.

Implied in each type of democide, however, is that the murders are ordered out of hatred or caprice, not because of any national security, self-defense, or capital punishment-for-crime motives.

9. Morton, *The Terrors of Ideological Politics*, x.

10. See Hartley, "Missouri's 1838 Extermination Order and the Mormons' forced Removal to Illinois," passim.

11. Adams, *The Power of Ideals in American History*, xii.

12. Robertson, *American Myth, American Reality*, 11; Gerster and Cords, *Myth America*, xi.

13. Perry, et al., eds., *Sources of the Western Tradition*, 284.

14. Craven, *The Legend of the Founding Fathers*, 2.

15. May, *Ideas, Faiths, and Feelings*, 167, 171–172.

16. Robertson, *American Myth, American Reality*, 15–17.

17. Rossiter, *The American Quest*, 65–66.

## INTRODUCTION

1. *Journal of Church and State*, Baylor University, Waco, Texas.

2. Fish, "One University Under God?"

3. This is an allusion to Rick Warren's best-selling book *The Purpose-Driven Life* (Grand Rapids, MI: Zondervan, 2002).

4. Cited in a FFRF advertisement entitled "Freethought Books & Music."

5. This alludes to Dan Brown's best seller *The Da Vinci Code* (New York: Doubleday, 2003).

6. See for example David Barton, *Original Intent*.

7. *George-Anne*, October 14, 21, 24, 2004. See for another example, Flowers, "In Search of a Christian Nation," passim.

8. Rosen, *Hegel's Dialectic and Its Criticism*, 112; Stromberg, *An Intellectual History of Modern Europe*, 242.

9. For examples, in no particular order: Lutz, *A Platform for the American Way*; La Haye, *Faith of Our Founding Fathers*; Eidsmore, *Christianity and the Constitution*; Weisman, *America: Free, White, & Christian*; Pay and Donaldson, *Downfall*; Kennedy and Newcombe, *What If America Were a Christian Nation Again?*; Russell, *Awakening the Giant*; and Marshall and Manuel, *The Light and the Glory*; Woodlock, *Democracy*; Long, *Your American Yardstick*; Whitney, ed., *The American Cause, By Russell Kirk*, all passim.

10. The adjective *fundamentalist*, when used as a descriptor of Christians, means those who believe the Bible literally, and often means those who believe the teachings of their particular denomination as the only right and true ones. The adjective *evangelical* describes those fundamentalists who are determined to proselytize, thus spread their religion's influence in the world by multiplying its adherents. Although there are subtle distinctions between these terms, for the purposes of this study, they are used jointly, alternately, or synonymously, depending upon the context, to describe the whole assortment of Christians who take their religion seriously enough to qualify as extremists. Calling them extremists is not a pejorative, just an ideological descriptor.

11. See for examples: O' Hair, *What on Earth Is an Atheist!*; Boston, *Why the Religious Right Is Wrong*; Kramnick and Moore, *The Godless Constitution*; Blau, *Cornerstones of*

*Religious Freedom in America*; Lockard, *The Perverted Priorities of American Politics*; Littell, *From State Church to Pluralism*; Eck, *A New Religious America*; and Davies, *America's Real Religion*; all passim.

12. The term *secularist* is most commonly used as a synonym for atheist or agnostic. It often implies an agenda to proselytize their anti-religion, although not necessarily so. In this study, it is used merely to describe those who oppose the fundamentalist-evangelicals ideologically and who believe that not only Christianity but all religions are the opiate of the masses. The term *separationist* is more complex because there are many Christians and adherents of other religions in America who are strong proponents of separation of church and state. In this study, all secularists are by definition separationists, but not all separationists are secularists. The terms are thus used contextually, but both imply an ideological extremism that equals and offsets that of the fundamentalist-evangelicals.

13. See for examples: Novak, *On Two Wings*; Burns, *The American Idea of Mission*; Cherry, ed., *God's New Israel*; Bellah, *The Broken Covenant*; Hughes, *Myths America Lives By*; Weeks, *A New Christian Nation*; Feldman, *Divided by God*; Wallis, *God's Politics*; all passim.

14. Not all authors or books that fall into the "pro-Christian nation" category are one-sided to the point of being propagandists or propaganda. Some, after having undertaken a lengthy and thorough investigation of sources, have formed their conclusions, whether rightly or wrongly. See for examples: Wills, *Under God*; Carter, *The Culture of Disbelief*; De Mar, *America's Christian History*; Noll, *One Nation Under God*; all passim.

15. "The Myth of Separation of Church and State" Web site.

16. Peck, *The Road Less Traveled*, 222.

17. Walter Burns, quoted in Horwitz, ed., *The Moral Foundations of the American Republic*, 165, 167.

18. Turner, *Without God, Without Creed*, xiii.

19. For an example of comedy that makes light of Christian America, see George Carlin, *When Will Jesus Bring the Pork Chops?*, passim.

20. George M. Marsden, "Are Secularists the Threat? Is Religion the Solution?" in Neuhaus, *Unsecular America*, 45.

21. Harry S. Stout, quoted in Kuklick and Hart, eds., *Religious Advocacy and American History*, vii.

22. Hook, *Religion in a Free Society*, vii—viii.

23. For examples of balanced accounts that neither argue one side nor the other but simply portray America's history as complex, with religion playing a central role, see Gaustad, *A Documentary History of Religion in America*; Dunn, ed., *American Political Theology*; Hudson, *Religion in America*; Myers, *History of Bigotry in the United States*; Finke and Stark, *The Churching of America*; Hook, *Religion in a Free Society*; all passim.

24. Stripling, *Capitalism, Democracy, and Morality*, xi.

25. Mercy Otis Warren first encapsulated the Jeffersonian Republican version of the founding in her *History of the American Revolution* (1805), in which she portrayed the Federalists as the bad guys who subverted the democratic ideal upon which the Revolution was based. John Marshall, Chief Justice of the Supreme Court, took the opposite view in his *Life of George Washington* (1804–1807). See Ellis, *Founding Brothers*, 13–14.

26. Noll, *One Nation Under God?*, 4.

27. Haskell, *Objectivity Is Not Neutrality*, 3.

28. Ellis, *Founding Brothers*, ix, x.

29. For definitions, see the seminal work on American historiography, Grob and Billias, eds., *Interpretations of American History*, vols. 1 and 2, passim. Quotes represent my preferred definitions.

30. The Franklin Papers are published through a consortium of Yale University and the American Philosophical Society by the Yale University Press; first edited by Leonard W. LaBrace, et al., beginning in 1959. The Hamilton Papers, edited by Harold Syrett, et al., between 1961 and 1977, are published by Columbia University Press. The Adams Papers are published by Belknap Press of Harvard University; first edited by Robert J. Taylor, et al., beginning in 1977. The Jefferson Papers are published by Princeton University Press; first edited by Julian P. Boyd, et al., in 1950. The Madison Papers are published by the University Press of Virginia; first edited by Robert Rutland, et al., beginning in 1984. The Washington Papers are also published by the University Press of Virginia; first edited by W. W. Abbot, beginning in 1983.

31. Meyers, *The Mind of the Founder*, xviii.

32. Morgan quoted in Billington, ed., *The Reinterpretation of Early American History*, 41–42. For a similar complaint, see also Ahlstrom, *Theology in America*, 93.

33. Harlan, *The Degradation of American History*, xxii.

34. Morgan quoted in Billington, ed., *The Reinterpretation of Early American History*, 41–42. Whether Morgan's statement is true is debatable, but this much is clear: the field of church-state studies is so incredibly large and disparate that, had I known just how large and disparate before embarking on the study at hand, I would likely have been so intimidated by it as to cancel the journey. Fortunately, I had already passed the point of no return before realizing what I had gotten myself into.

35. For a more in-depth treatment see Grob and Billias, eds., *Interpretations of American History*, vol. 1, 1–71.

36. Higham, ed., *The Reconstruction of American History*, 10–11.

37. First quote, Appleby, *Telling the Truth about History*, 112–113; second quote, Nye, *This Almost Chosen People*, 191. See also Nye, *George Bancroft*, passim.

38. David Brion Davis, "Slavery and Meaning in America," in Gerster and Cords, eds., *Myth America*, 23.

39. Clinton Rossiter, "Nationalism and American Identity in the Early Republic," in Wilentz, ed., *Major Problems in the Early Republic*, 15.

40. For treatment of how George Washington, for example, was deified by his first biographer, see Nicholas Cords, "Parson Weems, the Cherry Tree, and the Patriotic Tradition," in Ibid., 98–102.

41. Appleby, *Telling the Truth about History*, 104–105.

42. Quote, Koch, *Republican Religion*, xi; for examples, see Thornton, ed., *The Pulpit of the American Revolution*; Trumbull, *A General History of the United States of America*; Bancroft, *History of the United States*; Lossing, *Lives of the Signers of the Declaration of Independence*.

43. Some Victorian-age political leaders took this British-American kinship to its logical extreme, arguing that the two nations had so much more in common than they had dividing them, they should reunite into one giant Anglo-American empire that should rule the world. Benjamin F. Butler, the U.S. Civil War general, was one of the most prominent. See Upchurch, *Legislating Racism*, 70, 258. In the twentieth century,

some theologians and other religious philosophers would build whole denominations around the idea that the United States and Great Britain are actually the modern manifestations of Ephraim and Manassas, two of the "lost tribes" of Israel. See Armstrong, *The United States and Britain in Prophecy*, passim.

44. Haskell, *Objectivity Is Not Neutrality*, 5, 369.

45. For examples of the current trend of assuming that "educated" readers are *not* fundamentalist Christians, regardless of their professed affiliation with Christianity, see Marty, *Pilgrims in Their Own Land*, 3–4; and Pearson, *The Ethics of Freethought*, 14.

46. Hugo L. Black quoted in Beale, ed., *Charles A. Beard*, xi.

47. Renwick, *America's World Identity*, 15; Cohen, *American Thought*, 50.

48. Quote, Harlan, *The Degradation of American History*, xv–xxxiii; see also Russell, "Christ and Human Dignity," in Woodlock, ed., *Democracy*, 148–156; and Myers, *History of Bigotry in the United States*, 43. Clearly Nazism and all similar forms of nationalistic militarism served as a substitute in the minds of the people who embraced them in the age of world wars. As the German Kurt Ludecke explained it, embracing Nazism was for him "likened only to a religious conversion," and as the Russian Nicolaus Berdyaev described the militaristic mindset of the day, "The nation replaces God. . . . Nationalism is incompatible with monotheism . . . Nationalism cannot but come into conflict with Christian universalism." See Perry, et al., eds., *Sources of the Western Tradition*, 365, 386–387.

49. Moore, *Religious Outsiders and the Making of Americans*, 14–17; Mead, *The Nation with the Soul of a Church*, 4; Kuklick and Hart, eds., *Religious Advocacy in America*, x–xii.

50. Hook, *Religion in a Free Society*, vii–viii; Gaustad, ed., *A Documentary History of Religion in America*, xvi; Stewart, *American Ways of Life*, 51–52, 70; Adams, *The Power of Ideals in American History*, 97, 114.

51. Mead, *The Nation with the Soul of a Church*, viii.

## CHAPTER 1

1. Powell and Powell, eds., *The Spirit of Democracy*, 111; Bellah, *The Broken Covenant*, 53; De Mar, *America's Christian Heritage*, 58–59.

2. Bloom, *The American Religion*, 17, 22, 30, 37.

3. Burns, *The American Idea of Mission*, 214.

4. See, for example: Peterson, *The Century of Sex*, ix–xi; Lowe, *Ted Turner Speaks*, 198–199; O'Hair, *What on Earth Is an Atheist!*, 198–202; Stone, *Laughing in the Dark*, xiv–xxix.

5. Clebsch, *From Sacred to Profane*, 175.

6. Davies, *America's Real Religion*, 35–36, 48.

7. Joseph Ellis has recast these nation builders as the "Founding Brothers," ostensibly to make them appear more like mere mortals than like the wise old sages and demigods of tradition. See Ellis, *Founding Brothers*, passim.

8. The generation living at the time of the drafting of the Constitution routinely called those few men at the Constitutional Convention of 1787 the "framers." Some of these men also called themselves "framers." See *New York Journal*, December 13, 1787; *Pennsylvania Packet*, December 18, 1787; *Massachusetts Gazette*, January 11, 15, 18, 1788; and "Benjamin Rush Speaks against a Bill of Rights," Pennsylvania

Ratification Convention, November 30, 1787; all cited in Bailyn, ed., *The Debate on the Constitution*.

9. Lipset, *The First New Nation*, 90; Robertson, *American Myth, American Reality*, 57.

10. Quote, Robertson, *American Myth, American Reality*, 65. Pauline Maier has written a recent, provocative history of the Declaration in which she shows how the *document* declaring independence was not really as important to the Founders themselves and their generation as actual *independence* was. Mainly, the Declaration itself was ignored or considered a mere piece of legal parchment until the succeeding generation of the War of 1812 and beyond rescued it from obscurity. See Maier, *American Scripture*, xvii, xix, 167, 175. Carl Becker's classic account, however, shows that the Declaration indeed deserves to be praised by posterity for its "literary" merit and its embodiment of the "dominant social philosophy" of the Enlightenment. See Becker, *The Declaration of Independence*, x, xii–xiii.

11. The author uses this analogy despite the more common historical view that the Declaration was the Second Continental Congress's "most famous child." See Maier, *American Scripture*, xxi.

12. It should be noted that, prior to the drafting of the Declaration, American displeasure was typically aimed more at Parliament than the king. George III's recalcitrance in dealing with the Americans in 1775–1776, and particularly his hiring of Hessians to help put down the rebellion, were the main factors "alienating large numbers of colonists from the Crown." Ibid., 80.

13. Wainwright and Tucker, eds., *Oxford History of Christian Worship*, 182; Luebering, "Confirmation," www.americancatholic.org.

14. Treadwell quoted in Kenyon, ed., *The Antifederalists*, 399.

15. Quoted in Davies, *America's Real Religion*, 34.

16. In this national motto, which derives from Latin and is taken from the poet Virgil, it is implied but not stated that the new order of the ages would be for the whole world, not merely for the United States. See http://www.greatseal.com/mottoes/seclorum.html and Caldwell, "Novus Ordo Seclorum," 476.

17. *E Pluribus Unum* contains a double entendre. Its first and most obvious meaning at the time of the founding was that the people of the thirteen states had come together as one. Implied is the second meaning, as used here, that the United States would be a nation of diversity. See Latourette, "The Contribution of the Religion of the Colonial Period to the Ideals and Life of the United States," 340.

18. Marty, *Pilgrims in Their Own Land*, 156.

19. Technically, the phrase does not say who or what has favored the beginnings of the United States, or "smiled upon" them, as an alternate translation would have it, but it is widely understood that it is "God" or "Providence." The phrase comes again from Virgil, who used it in context of the most powerful Roman deity, Jupiter. See http://www.compulink.co.uk/~craftings/doll.htm and Latourette, "The Contribution of the Religion of the Colonial Period to the Ideals and Life of the United States," 340.

20. Marty, *Pilgrims in Their Own Land*, 156.

21. Hudson, *Religion in America*, 98.

22. Gellert, *The Fate of America*, 231–232.

23. Stokes, *Church and State in the United States*, xiii.

24. For a discussion of why the common perception of the Old Testament God as an oppressive deity is arguably wrong, see Kirk, *The Roots of American Order*, 22–26.

25. Quoted in Morris, *The American Revolution*, 131.

26. Hughes, *Myths America Lives By*, 50, 66.

27. In the South, Georgia and North Carolina had an Anglican establishment in name only, not in power or influence. Virginia had the strongest Anglican establishment and South Carolina the second strongest. Even so, "an Anglican establishment in America is not by any means the same thing as the Establishment in England." Hofstadter, *America in 1750*, 202–203, quote 206.

28. Lind, *The Next American Nation*, 1–8. This is much the same as how any of the great empires have been created in history—by artificially homogenizing various tribes and ethnic groups into a larger whole. The difference between the United States and, for example, the Roman Empire, however, lies in how the homogenization was accomplished. In the Roman Empire, it occurred by military coercion, but in the United States by reasoned persuasion.

29. Renwick, *America's World Identity*, 11.

30. Orton, *America in Search of Culture*, 4.

31. Gellert, *The Fate of America*, xi–xii.

32. Thomas L. Hawthorne, in Hall, ed., *Forging the American Character*, 9–10.

33. Renan quoted by Henry Steele Commager in "The Invention of America: The Search for a Usable Past," in Gerster and Cords, eds., *Myth America*, 88–89.

34. Barker quoted in Mead, *The Nation with the Soul of a Church*, 51.

35. Perry, *Puritanism and Democracy*, 29.

36. Rossiter, *The American Quest*, 60–66.

37. Bloom, *The American Religion*, 31.

38. Quoted in Federer, ed., *America's God and Country*, 252–253.

39. Quoted in Ibid., 87.

40. Agar, *The Perils of Democracy*, 42.

41. Frederick Hegel quoted in Nye, *This Almost Chosen People*, 191.

42. The controversy over American nationhood and purpose can be seen vividly in the recent issue of illegal immigration along the Mexican border. Some Americans believe the national purpose should be to welcome all comers, regardless of who they are, where they come from, how they got across the border, or why they come. They thus espouse a broad, humanitarian national purpose. Others believe such a broad purpose, while a noble intention, is harmful to the welfare of the nation. They believe the United States must take care of its own citizens first and foremost, and dole out the humanitarianism sparingly. According to this view, the nation's primary purpose is self-preservation. Undoubtedly, that must be every nation's *primary* purpose. Assuming the state of the Union is strong, however, the larger and ultimate purpose comes into play, and Americans cannot reach consensus on what it should be, if anything.

43. Adams, *The Power of Ideals in American History*, 3–27; Baxter, *One and Inseparable*, 179–191.

44. Clinton Rossiter has articulated the factors that had emerged by the time of the Civil War as the unifying principles of the United States as being "dedicated in common to the beauties of personal liberty, the security of constitutionalism, the rightness of democracy, the wrongness of class distinctions, the virtue of private property, the moral necessity of hard work, the certainty of progress, and above all the uniqueness,

superiority, and high destiny of the United States of America." Rossiter, "Nationalism and American Identity in the Early Republic," in Wilentz, ed., *Major Problems in the Early Republic*, 16–17.

45. Bellah, *The Broken Covenant*, 3; Cherry, ed., *God's New Israel*, 10.

46. Adams, *The Power of Ideals*, xii–xiii.

47. The nationalism that gave rise to the American civic religion was indeed evolving constantly from 1776 on, but it got its biggest boost after the victory in the War of 1812, and it culminated, according to Pauline Maier, in 1826, on the 50th anniversary of the Declaration. See Maier, *American Scripture*, 175.

48. Rossiter, "Nationalism and American Identity in the Early Republic," in Wilentz, ed., *Major Problems in the Early Republic*, 16.

49. Weeks, *A New Christian Nation*, 5.

50. Quote, Cunliffe, *The Nation Takes Shape*, 200. See also, Commager, "Invention of America," in Gerster and Cords, eds., *Myth America*, 92.

51. Marshall and Manuel, *The Light and the Glory*, 14–15.

52. Lerner, et al., *Molding the Good Citizen*, 1.

53. The term *individual* rights is used to mean mainly what the term *civil* rights means today. The Lockean *individual* rights was commonly used at the time of the founding. The term *civil* rights, which technically means merely *legal* rights, was not used at that time, and thus cannot be properly considered a founding principle. It became part of the larger civic religion after the Civil War, as it was used in the Civil Rights Acts of Reconstruction. The modern usage of the term *individual* rights herein implies more than mere *legal* rights. It includes an intangible "inherent worth of each person" mentality, which may not be quantifiable or even recognized in a court of law but nevertheless has a wide, general social acceptance.

54. Delbanco, *The Real American Dream*, 10–11, 15–16.

55. Commager, "Invention of America," in Gerster and Cords, eds., *Myth America*, 96–97.

56. Examples of how a collective shunning has occurred in recent times include the cases of the America-bashing and terrorism-supporting University of Colorado professor Ward Churchill and University of South Florida professor Sami Al-Arion. The vast majority of Americans would have gladly defended their right to free speech, had they not crossed an imaginary line where acceptable speech becomes unacceptable speech. Criticizing the United States government, no matter how radically it is done, is generally regarded as acceptable; praising or supporting those who would try to overthrow the government or harm the American citizenry is not.

57. Jessup, *The National Purpose*, v, 4–9.

58. Tocqueville quoted in Fehrenbacher, ed., *Freedom and Its Limitations in American Life*, 3.

59. Chevalier quoted in Ibid., 4.

60. Bryce quoted in Ibid., 5.

61. Ibid., 20–21.

62. Odegard, *The American Public Mind*, 6–7.

63. Perry, *Puritanism and Democracy*, 641.

64. Glen Loury in Dionne and Diulio, eds., *What's God Got to Do with the American Experiment?*, xiii–xiv.

65. Lind, *The Next American Nation*, 9.

66. Nichols, *Religion in American Democracy*, 50.

67. Hofstadter, *Anti-Intellectualism in American Life*, 55.

68. Perry, *Puritanism and Democracy*, 34.

69. Stroup, *Church and State in Confrontation*, 97.

70. See Perry, *Puritanism and Democracy*, passim, for a thorough analysis of the nexus between Calvinism, Lockeanism, and Capitalism. See also Lutz, *Platform for the American Way*, passim, for a discussion of American individualism. Some scholars point to the governmental philosophy of Lord Bolingbroke and the English country opposition as being just as influential as Locke to the Founders. See Lazare, *The Frozen Republic*, 26−30.

71. Handy, *A Christian America*, 30−31.

72. Chalfant, *America: A Call to Greatness*, 1.

73. Quoted in Federer, ed., *America's God and Country*, 146.

74. Quoted in Ibid., 147, 362−363.

75. Quoted in Ibid., 352.

76. Quoted in Chalfant, *America: A Call to Greatness*, 2.

77. Davies, *America's Real Religion*, 77. If this conclusion has not yet been established to the reader's satisfaction, it should be by the end of this study.

78. Bloom, *The American Religion*, 37.

79. Lind, *The Next American Nation*, 11−12.

80. Neuhaus, *Unsecular America*, 63−64.

81. Jessup, *The National Purpose*, 4.

# CHAPTER 2

1. Whitney, ed., *The American Cause, by Russell Kirk*, xiv−xvii.

2. James Kirby Martin, "The Myth of Popular Participation in the Revolutionary War," in Gerster and Cords, eds., *Myth America*, 53−58; Perry, *Puritanism and Democracy*, 51; Marshall and Manuel, *The Light and the Glory*, 286, 295, 297, 300.

3. Perry, *Puritanism and Democracy*, 51.

4. Clinton Rossiter, "Nationalism and American Identity in the Early Republic," in Wilentz, ed., *Major Problems in the Early Republic*, 19.

5. Hughes, *Myths America Lives By*, 19.

6. Ellis, *Founding Brothers*, 5.

7. Ibid., 6.

8. Handy, *A Christian America*, 8.

9. James Axtell, "Colonial America without the Indians," in Gerster and Cords, eds., *Myth America*, 17.

10. Howard Mumford Jones, "O Strange New World," in Ibid., 11.

11. Bellah, *The Broken Covenant*, 37−42; Nye, *This Almost Chosen People*, 189−190.

12. Cherry, ed., *God's New Israel*, ix; Hughes, *Myths America Lives By*, 6−8; Friedman, *Pilgrims in a New Land*, 16−24.

13. Friedman, *Pilgrims in a New Land*, 15; Marshall and Manuel, *The Light and the Glory*, 25, 338, 347−348, 354−359; Hughes, *Myths America Lives By*, 22−33.

14. Littell, *From State Church to Pluralism*, xi; Weisman, *America*, 3−4.

15. Nichols, *Religion and American Democracy*, 53.

16. Perry, *Intellectual Life in America*, 5.

17. John Demos, "The Pilgrims and the Mythic Maypole of Merry Mount," in Gerster and Cords, eds., *Myth America*, 33, 36; Nichols, *Religion and American Democracy*, 23.

18. Lucas, *American Odyssey*, 105.

19. Crosby, "God . . . Would Destroy Them, and Give Their Country to Another People . . ." in Mugleston and Derden, eds., *Benedict Arnold, Anne Hutchinson, Sam Adams, Witches, and Other Troublemakers*, 9−11.

20. Loewen, *Lies My Teacher Told Me*, 72.

21. John Mason, "A Puritan Account of the Pequot War, 1637," quoted in Lorence, ed., *Enduring Voices*, 51−54.

22. Quoted in Loewen, *Lies My Teacher Told Me*, 72.

23. Handy, *A Christian America*, 8.

24. Gaustad, ed., *A Documentary History of Religion in America*, 257.

25. Hudson, *Religion in America*, 107−111.

26. Noll, *One Nation Under God?*, 8.

27. Marshall and Manuel, *The Light and the Glory*, 18−20.

28. Weeks, *A New Christian Nation*, 3.

29. Nichols, *Blueprints for Leviathan*, 48.

30. Marty, *Pilgrims in Their Own Land*, 160.

31. Hughes, *Myths America Lives By*, 34−35.

32. Miller, ed., *The Young Republic*, 25.

33. Quoted in Bailyn, ed., *The Debate on the Constitution*, 869.

34. Quoted in Ibid., 871.

35. Quoted in Ibid., *The Debate on the Constitution*, 582−584.

36. There were originally twelve tribes of Israel, each stemming from a son of Jacob. Joseph, however, eventually received the dispensation of two tribes, one for each of his sons, Ephraim and Manasseh.

37. Quoted in Bailyn, ed., *The Debate on the Constitution*, 401−405.

38. Georges Clemenceau, in Perry, et al., eds., *Sources of the Western Tradition*, 319; Cherry, ed., *God's New Israel*, 19; Perry, et al., *Western Civilization*, 627−628.

39. Chamberlain and Beaulieu quoted in Perry, et al., eds., *Sources of the Western Tradition*, 245, 253.

40. Adams, *The Power of Ideals in American History*, 67.

41. Ellis, *Founding Brothers*, 6.

42. Clinton Rossiter, "Nationalism and American Identity in the Early Republic," in Wilentz, ed., *Major Problems in the Early Republic*, 19−20.

43. Pfeffer, *Church, State, and Freedom*, 96.

44. Finke and Stark, *The Churching of America*, 23.

45. Robertson, *That Old-Time Religion*, 29.

46. Richard N. Ostling, "America's Ever-Changing Religious Landscape," in Dionne and Diulio, *What's God Got to Do with the American Experiment?*, 18−19.

47. Kramnick and Moore, *The Godless Constitution*, 17.

48. Finke and Stark, *The Churching of America*, 7−10.

49. The Quakers, for example, did not even develop a formal mechanism for determining "membership" until the sect had already been established for forty years. Butler, *Awash in a Sea of Faith*, 5.

50. Stokes, *Church and State in the United States*, 273−274.

51. Sweet, *Religion in the Development of the American Culture*, 3.

52. Littell, *From State Church to Pluralism*, 30.

53. Ibid., 29.

54. Jon Butler has made an important, recent study of the Christianization of America in which he paints a picture of colonial America as being more religious than earlier historians had portrayed it. While the lack of reliable statistics typically led most historians to conclude that colonial-early republic Americans were not very religious, Butler uses unquantifiable anecdotal evidence in taking an opposing point of view. See Butler, *Awash in a Sea of Faith*, passim.

55. Myers, *History of Bigotry in the United States*, 125−126.

56. Timothy D. Hall, "Itinerancy and the Awakenings," in Kupperman, ed., *Major Problems in Colonial American History*, 347, 351.

57. Carl Degler, "The Mythic Puritan," in Gerster and Cords, eds., *Myth America*, 30.

58. Kramnick and Moore, *The Godless Constitution*, 29−31.

59. Marnell, *The First Amendment*, 94−95.

60. Ahlstrom, ed., *Theology in America*, 34.

61. Myers, *History of Bigotry in the United States*, 61−62.

62. Marnell, *The First Amendment*, 52−53.

63. Pessen, *Jacksonian America*, 155−159; Pollard, *Factors in American History*, 155−159.

64. Myers, *History of Bigotry in the United States*, 61−62.

65. Cole, quoted in Kupperman, ed., *Major Problems in Colonial American History*, 334.

66. Jonathan Parsons, "Account of the Revival at Lyme," in Heimert and Miller, *The Great Awakening*, 35−40.

67. Finke and Stark, *The Churching of America*, 26.

68. Kramnick and Moore, *The Godless Constitution*, 17.

69. Pfeffer, *Church, State, and Freedom*, 95−96.

70. Hall, *The Religious Background of American Culture*, 165.

71. Marshall and Manuel, *The Light and the Glory*, 345−348.

72. Wright, *France in Modern Times*, 28−39.

73. Marcus and Burner, eds., *America Firsthand*, 110−118.

74. Quoted in Unger and Jones, eds., *American Issues*, 39−41.

75. Sinopli, ed., *From Many, One*, 323−324.

76. Rossiter, *1787*, 35−36.

77. Weeks, *A New Christian Nation*, 13.

78. Quote, Joyce, *Church and Clergy in the American Revolution*, 142. See also, Gordon Wood, "The Significance of the Early Republic," in Wilentz, ed., *Major Problems in the Early Republic*, 3.

## CHAPTER 3

1. The term was coined by Israel Zangwill in a 1908 play called "The Melting Pot." See Steinfeld, *Cracks in the Melting Pot*, xv−xvii.

2. Don McLean, "American Pie," United Artists, 1971. Released in 1971, the eight-and-a-half minute song became a Billboard number-one hit in 1972, selling three million copies,

and telling the story of a nation coming of age and losing its innocence in the 1960s. See James Fann, "Understanding 'American Pie'," www.understandingamericanpie.com.

3. Stokes, *Church and State in the United States*, 23.

4. Koch, *Republican Religion*, 27.

5. Dawson, *Separate Church and State Now*, 118–119.

6. Quoted in Myers, *History of Bigotry in the United States*, 60.

7. Lucas, *American Odyssey*, 110.

8. Joyce, *Church and Clergy in the American Revolution*, 34.

9. Ward quoted in Lippy, et al., *Christianity Comes to the Americas*, 269.

10. Mr. Dooley, a fictional Irish bartender with a brogue, created by Finley Peter Dunn for a newspaper serial circa 1900, first said this. Quoted in Dawson, *Separate Church and State Now*, 17.

11. Rutland, *The Birth of the Bill of Rights*, 23.

12. Pfeffer, *Church, State, and Freedom*, 4, 6.

13. Shriver, *American Religious Heretics*, 16.

14. Bainton, *Early Christianity*, 91–110.

15. Schaff, *Church and State in the United States*, 12.

16. Bainton, *Early Christianity*, 27,159–60.

17. Myers, *History of Bigotry in the United States*, 8.

18. Pfeffer, *Church, State, and Freedom*, 13–22; Bainton, *The Medieval Church*, 52.

19. Stokes, *Church and State in the United States*, 86, 102.

20. Handy, ed., *Religion in the American Experience*, viii.

21. Phillips, "Roger Williams and the Two Tables of the Law," 547–569.

22. Luther quoted in Bainton, *The Age of the Reformation*, 103.

23. Pfeffer, *Church, State, and Freedom*, 23–25.

24. Simons quoted in Bainton, *The Age of the Reformation*, 131.

25. Calvin quoted in Ibid., 138.

26. Quoted in Ibid., 149–150.

27. Quoted in Ibid., 181–183.

28. Cody, "The Church of England," in *The Victorian Web*, www.victorianweb.org; Rodrick, *The History of Great Britain*, 47–54; Williams, *Henry VIII and His Court*, 233; Myers, *History of Bigotry in the United States*, 8, 14.

29. "The Act Against Puritans" (1593), 35 Elizabeth, Cap. 1, reprinted at http://history.hanover.edu/texts/ENGref/er86html.

30. Halliday, F. E. *A Concise History of England*, 108–109.

31. Fischer, *Albion's Seed*, 13–17; Knapton, *Europe, 1450–1815*; 301–302.

32. Wedgwood, *A Coffin for King Charles*, 10–11; Stokes, *Church and State in the United States*, 124.

33. Wedgwood, *The King's War*, 273–274, 513, 518; Fraser, *Cromwell*, 68; Stokes, *Church and State in the United States*, 121–122.

34. Cody, "The Church of England;" Beth, *The American Theory of Church and State*, 8, 21–24; Kramnick and Moore, *The Godless Constitution*, 78–83; For a more complete rendering of the struggle for religious freedom in Tudor and Stuart England, see Williamson, *Kings and Queens of Great Britain*, 107–141.

35. Gaustad, ed., *A Documentary History of Religion in America*, 129.

36. John M. Murrin, "The Dilemma of American National Identity," in Kupperman, ed., *Major Problems in American Colonial History*, 461.

37. Hart, ed., *American History Told by Contemporaries*, 54.

38. Hall, *The Religious Background of American Culture*, x, xii.

39. Miller and Johnson, eds., *The Puritans: A Sourcebook of Their Writings*, 393.

40. Phillips, "Roger Williams and the Two Tables of the Law," 547–569.

41. Robertson, *That Old-Time Religion*, 34–35.

42. Davis, "A Return to Civility: Roger Williams and Public Discourse in America," 697.

43. Stokes, *Church and State in the United States*, 202–205.

44. Davis, "The Enduring Legacy of Roger Williams," 206, 210.

45. Smith, *Religious Liberty in the United States*, 4.

46. Wellington Newcombe, "Anne Hutchinson versus Massachusetts," Mugleston and Derden, eds., *Benedict Arnold, Anne Hutchinson, Sam Adams, Witches, and Other Troublemakers*, 43, 55.

47. Pfeffer, *Church, State, and Freedom*, 76.

48. Stokes, *Church and State in the United States*, 221–222.

49. Morais, *Deism in Eighteenth Century America*, 59–63, 70; Hall, *The Religious Background of American Culture*, 159; Fraser, *Cromwell*, 45, Fischer, *Albion's Seed*, 22, 23, 49.

50. Myers, *History of Bigotry in the United States*, 27–34.

51. Shriver, ed., *Dictionary of Heresy Trials in American Christianity*, xi.

52. Miller and Johnson, eds., *The Puritans: A Sourcebook of Their Writings*, 759.

53. Neal quoted in Hart, ed., *American History Told by Contemporaries*, 54.

54. Myers, *History of Bigotry in the United States*, 5, 9.

55. Pfeffer, *Church, State, and Freedom*, 79, 88.

56. Myers, *History of Bigotry in the United States*, 91–92, 97.

57. James Blair, quoted in Kupperman, ed., *Major Problems in Colonial American History*, 367.

58. Blau, *Cornerstones of Religious Freedom in America*, 33.

59. Quoted in Allitt, ed., *Major Problems in American Religious History*, 66.

60. Beth, *The American Theory of Church and State*, 52; Dawson, *Separate Church and State Now*, 26; Pfeffer, *Church, State, and Freedom*, 83, 91.

61. Bailyn, ed., *The Debate on the Constitution, Part 2*, 431; Pfeffer, *Church, State, and Freedom*, 98; Washington to Rochambeau, May 23, 1781, at the Conference at Weathersfield, quoted in Thayer, *Yorktown*, 94.

62. Sweet, *Religion in the Development of American Culture*, 40–50.

63. Only eight Jewish settlements existed and only six Jewish synagogues operated in the United States at the time of the founding. See Levinger, *A History of the Jews of the United States*, 87, 93, 123–125.

64. Phillips quoted in Bowen, *Miracle at Philadelphia*, 217; see also Edel, *Defenders of the Faith*, 66–67; Myers, *History of Bigotry in the United States*, 65–78.

65. "The Occident and American Jewish Advocate," vol. 2, no. 4, Tamuz 5604, July, 1844, cited at www.jewish-history.com; "To Bigotry No Sanction, to Persecution No Assistance," cited at www.jewishvirtuallibrary.org.

66. Madison to Jefferson, October 24, 1787, quoted in Bailyn, ed., *The Debate on the Constitution, Part 2*, 204.

67. Nones, the Philadelphia *Aurora*, August 13, 1800, quoted in Foner, ed., *The Democratic-Republican Societies*, 117–118.

68. Sweet, *Religion in the Development of American Culture*, 17.

69. Ibid., 33–36; Pfeffer, *Church, State, and Freedom*, 91.

70. Marty, *Pilgrims in the Their Own Land*, 155.

71. Sweet, *Religion in the Development of American Culture*, 61; Myers, *History of Bigotry in the United States*, 105.

72. Gordon Wood, "The Significance of the Early Republic," in Wilentz, ed., *Major Problems in the Early Republic*, 7. Even though Congregationalists were the single largest group in terms of number of church members, they still fall into the broad category of Dissenters because, as a denomination, they had no central governing body; each church answered only to itself.

73. Hall, *The Religious Background of American Culture*, 186–187.

74. Brooks, ed., *The Roots of American Culture*, 195; Moore, *Religious Outsiders and the Making of Americans*, 21.

75. Brooks, ed., *The Roots of American Culture*, 195–237.

76. Gaustad, *A Religious History of America*, 132–153.

77. Gaustad, ed., *A Documentary History of Religion in America*, 319–321.

78. Maclear, ed., *Church and State in the Modern Age*, 7–10, 31–34; Pfeffer, *Church, State, and Freedom*, 94–95.

## CHAPTER 4

1. Blanshard, *God and Man in Washington*, 6.

2. See, for example, Schaff, *Church and State in the United States*, 9.

3. Trollope, *Domestic Manners of the Americans*, quoted in Bellesiles et al., eds., *Bibliobase*, 124.

4. Stokes, *Church and State in the United States*, 28.

5. Ralph H. Gabriel in Ibid., xxxvi.

6. In 1794, the New York Democratic Society wrote a circular to the Democratic Society of Pennsylvania using the marriage analogy to explain the traditional relationship between church and state. In the old world, it was a functional marriage that created a dysfunctional family, basically abusive toward the children (the citizens). In America, however, the "beneficence of Providence" has seen fit to shine the light of "KNOWLEDGE" and "TRUTH" on the relationship, for the sake of the children. Quoted in Foner, ed., *The Democratic-Republican Societies*, 186–187.

7. Wilson, ed., *Church and State in American History*, x–xiii.

8. Kauper, "Church and State," in Wilson, ed., *Church and State in American History*, 220.

9. Stokes, *Church and State in the United States*, 27, 29.

10. Wilson, ed., *Church and State in American History*, xx.

11. Marnell, *The First Amendment*, x–xi.

12. Stokes, *Church and State in the United States*, 66–67.

13. Schaff, *Church and State in the United States*, 11.

14. Wilson and Drakeman, eds., *Church and State in American History*, xi–xii.

15. Sanders, *Protestant Concepts of Church and State*, 8–9.

16. Stokes, *Church and State in the United States*, 113–115.

17. Nichols, *Religion and American Democracy*, 48.

18. Stokes, *Church and State in the United States*, 66–67.

19. Maury, quoted in Hart, ed., *American History Told by Contemporaries*, 103–106.

20. Morgan, *The Stamp Act Crisis*, 30–31.

21. Secker, quoted in Hart, ed., *American History Told by Contemporaries*, 289–290.

22. Chauncy, quoted in Hart, ed., *American History Told by Contemporaries*, 418–419.

23. James Madison, for example, "was different things to different men. The masks [he wore] changed as the plot of American politics unfolded from the eve of the Revolution to the close of Jackson's administration [when he died]." Quoted in Meyers, *The Mind of the Founder*, xxxvi.

24. Kramnick and Moore, *The Godless Constitution*, 16. To make an analogy, one can visualize the United States as a ship and the Founders' precedents or original intent as the rudder. The rudder is not bigger than the ship. It is in fact a small piece of a large structure, but it is absolutely vital to steering the ship. Without a good grasp of not only what the Founders said and wrote but how they actually applied religion in politics, the current generation is trying to steer the ship of state without a rudder.

25. Evans, *Interpreting the Free Exercise of Religion*, 12.

26. Stokes, *Church and State in the United States*, 36.

27. Rakove, "The Philadelphia Story: The Founding Fathers and the Myth of Constitutional Intent," in Gerster and Cords, eds., *Myth America*, 75.

28. Weisman, *America*, 125–130.

29. Morais, *Deism in Eighteenth Century America*, 91.

30. Gaustad, ed. *A Documentary History of Religion in America*, 267.

31. Sanders, *Protestant Concepts of Church and State*, 189.

32. Morris, *The American Revolution*, 112–117; Slaughter, ed., *"Common Sense" and Related Writings by Thomas Paine*, 20.

33. Fleming, *1776*, 8, 218.

34. Sweet, *Religion in the Development of the American Culture*, 12, 50–52; Schaff, *Church and State in the United States*, 125; Pfeffer, *Church, State, and Freedom*, 119; Federer, ed., *America's God and Country*, 148.

35. Reichley, *Faith in Politics*, 111. The Republican Society of the Mouth of Yough in Pennsylvania reiterated the same idea in its constitution, stating that one of its objectives was "To introduce the Bible and other religious books" into the schools. *Pittsburgh Gazette*, April 15, 1794, quoted in Foner, ed., *Democratic-Republican Societies*, 124.

36. Greene, *Religion and the State*, 82, 83.

37. Hall, *The Religious Background of American Culture*, 164, 169. The reader may well question this assertion, and some may vehemently disagree with it.

38. Boston, *Why the Religious Right Is Wrong*, 62. Some critics may argue that the reason for the subject of religion's conspicuous absence from the debates was that it simply was not very important to the delegates or their constituencies. Yet the various states they represented took great pains to include discussion of the topic in both their own constitutions and in their ratification conventions. This fact indeed leaves one with the distinct impression that the Founders could not have simply neglected the topic because of its comparative unimportance.

39. Washington, quoted in by Paul Johnson, in Neuhaus, ed., *Unsecular America*, 6.

40. Washington, quoted in Miller, ed., *The Young Republic*, 29–31.

41. Modern secularists may be apt to suppose that because religion is often seen as a private, rather than public, affair today, it must have always been so. In fact, the privatization of religion was still a fairly novel concept at that time. Keeping one's religion private was the exception; public religion was still the rule.

42. Schaff, *Church and State in the United States*, 23.

43. Beth, *The American Theory of Church and State*, 33.

44. Schaff, *Church and State in the United States*, 83–84.

45. Ibid., 14.

46. Blanshard, *God and Man in Washington*, 8.

47. Sinopli, ed., *From Many, One*, 325.

48. Bennett, *Christians and the State*, 3.

49. Lest readers question the propriety of this statement, consider that the current religious right by no means invented this type of inquiry into candidates' and public officials' personal beliefs. Throughout American history, going back in fact to colonial times, various church leaders have preached against, petitioned against, and plotted against politicians whose religious views or actions did not square with their own. See Alison M. Colson for an example of how Anglican, Dutch Reformed, and Huguenot ministers, who were not prone to allying into a special "interest group," all joined forces to drive out of office New York governor Bellomont, who they found adversarial to their mutual religious interests. Colson, "Transatlantic Interest Groups and the Colonial Governors," in Kupperman, ed., *Major Problems in Colonial American History*, 380–381.

50. Jefferson did not coin the term; Roger Williams did about 150 years before Jefferson used it. Howe, *The Garden and the Wilderness*, 5–7.

51. Kramnick and Moore, *The Godless Constitution*, 111.

52. LaHaye, *Faith of Our Founding Fathers*, 61–62.

53. For examples, see publications of the Freedom From Religion Foundation. Every newsletter contains such misapplication of the Jeffersonian metaphor.

54. Mark DeWolfe Howe wrote a wonderful exegesis of this topic in 1965, which has only become more accurate with the years since he penned it. See Howe's chapter, "Federalism and the First Amendment," in *The Garden and the Wilderness*, 1–31.

55. Hook, *Religion in a Free Society*, 43.

56. Mead, *The Nation with the Soul of a Church*, 79.

57. Madison, quoted in Wilson, *Public Religion in American Culture*, 3–4.

58. Hutson, "Thomas Jefferson's Letter to the Danbury Baptists," 789.

59. Richards, "'A Clear and Steady Channel,'" 478.

60. Madison, quoted in Peterson, ed., *The Founding Fathers*, 382.

61. Treadwell, quoted in Kenyon, ed., *The Antifederalists*, 397.

62. Schaff, *Church and State in the United State*, 39.

63. Charles E. Rice, "The First Amendment: Religious Neutrality or an Establishment of Secularism?" in Rutyna and Kuehl, eds., *Conceived in Conscience*, 45.

64. "Joseph Spencer to James Madison, Enclosing John Leland's Objections (February 28, 1788)," quoted in Bailyn, ed., *The Debate on the Constitution, Part 2*, 269. Although the Constitution does not specifically give any branch of the federal government power over religion, and although Article VI prohibits any religious test for holding federal office, the implied powers of the government could theoretically be invoked to control religion. In that sense, Leland was absolutely correct to fear the silence of the Constitution and hope for the "mildness" of government officials.

65. Schaff, *Church and State in the United States*, 22.

66. Van Doren, *The Great Rehearsal*, 217.

67. Virginia and North Carolina Resolutions, quoted in Bailyn, ed., *The Debate on the Constitution, Part 2*, 561, 568.

68. Smith, *Religious Liberty in the United States*, 248; Wilson and Drakeman, eds., *Church and State in American History*, 76–77.

69. Philip Kurland, "A Doctrine in Search of Authority," in Wilson, ed., *Church and State in American History*, 214; Kramnick and Moore, *The Godless Constitution*, 14. It should be noted that religion was not very important in the overall scheme of things that made some people Federalists and others Anti-Federalists. Although Baptists and Presbyterians "were usually antifederal," plenty of them were also pro-Constitution. Most denominations lacked solidarity one way or the other on the issue of ratification. See Main, *The Antifederalists*, 159, 230, 260–261, quote 230.

70. Here, the reader may well think to himself/herself, or imagine others doing so: "Sure, that's what they wrote, but what were they *really* saying?"

71. Sweet, *Religion in the Development of the American Culture*, 88.

72. Jefferson, for one, not only wanted the Constitution to be adaptable for future generations; he, in fact, thought it might be better for each generation to have its own new Constitution. Jefferson to Madison, September 6, 1789, cited in Onuf, ed., *Thomas Jefferson*, 9, 128–132.

73. Pfeffer, *Church, State, and Freedom*, 168–171.

74. It should be noted that no court in the land would ever reduce the explanation of its rulings on religious matters to this elementary level. Yet, cutting through the lawyer-speak, this oversimplified explanation of legal rationale is accurate. The Constitutional scholar Jack Rakove has pointed out that "It is remarkable how little time the Framers spent discussing the role of the judiciary. . . . Far more of the Convention's time was devoted to the subject of executive power," as evidenced by the "strange device that the Framers finally invented, the electoral college," which they designed to protect the nation against an imperial and tyrannical president. Despite the time spent on that protection against the growth of power of the executive branch, it eventually grew anyway. Perhaps, therefore, no amount of constitutional limitations on the power of the judiciary would have prevented the current growth of judicial power. See Rakove, "The Philadelphia Story: The Founding Fathers and the Myth of Constitutional Intent," in Gerster and Cords, eds., 72. According to Forrest McDonald, in recent years the Supreme Court has been going far beyond merely reinterpreting the Constitution to suit the tenor of the times; it has, in fact, been "rewriting" the Constitution, a document that, despite its notable defects, was produced by the greatest minds of an age when minds were arguably greater than they are today. See McDonald and McDonald, *Requiem*, 1–2.

75. All quotes, Howe, *The Garden and the Wilderness*, 1, 3, 4, 5, and 9.

76. For discussion of "string theory" in physics, see the PBS television documentary "The Elegant Universe" and its Web site http://www.pbs.org/wgbh/nova/elegant, and Hawking, *A Brief History of Time*, 159–162.

## CHAPTER 5

1. Since the 1790s, there has always been one of the two major parties that have attempted to emphasize a greater role for religion in the national polity than the other. At times these parties, whether Federalist, Republican, or something else, have gone

one step too far, trying to legislate orthodoxy, although stopping one step short of advocating unification of church and state. More on this topic follows later in this book.

2. Davies, *America's Real Religion*, 13.

3. Gordon, "Blasphemy and the Law of Religious Liberty in Nineteenth-Century America," 698–699; Koch, *Republican Religion*, 51–73.

4. Pearson, *The Ethics of Freethought*, 6.

5. Carl Becker gave some illuminating thoughts on these labels and definitions in his classic *The Heavenly City of the Eighteenth Century Philosophers*. See also Cousins, *"In God We Trust,"* 8.

6. Quote, Samuel Spencer, "Reverend David Caldwell and Samuel Spencer Continue Debate on Religious Toleration" at the North Carolina Ratification Convention, July 30, 1788, cited in Bailyn, ed., *The Debate on the Constitution* (Part 2), 908.

7. Smith, *Franklin and Bache*, 140–141, 205; Slaughter, ed., *"Common Sense" and Related Writings by Thomas Paine*, 21; Hall, *The Religious Background of American Culture*, 163; Novak, *On Two Wings*, 28; Blau, *Cornerstones of Religious Freedom in America*, 71; Davies, *America's Real Religion*, 57–58.

8. Sullivan, *The Public Men of the Revolution*, 108–110; Hutson, "Thomas Jefferson's Letter to the Danbury Baptists," 781; Darling, *Our Rising Empire*, 232–233, 341; Smith, *Religious Liberty in the United States*, 94.

9. Gaustad, ed., *A Documentary History of Religion in America*, 293–295; Sweet, *Religion in the Development of the American Culture*, 95–96.

10. Koch, *Republican Religion*, 247–253; Reichley, *Faith in Politics*, 163–164.

11. Brookhiser, *Alexander Hamilton*, 169.

12. All quotes in Slaughter, ed., *"Common Sense" and Other Related Writings by Thomas Paine*, 73–119.

13. Paine quoted in Ekirch, ed., *Voices in Dissent*, 23; see also Ibid., 26–27.

14. Smith, *Religious Liberty in the United States*, 91, 101; Koch, *Republican Religion*, 30–31, 40–41, 48.

15. Ethan Allen, *Reason*. Available at: http://libertyonline.hypermall.com/allen-reason.html.

16. See Riley, *American Thought*, 12–17.

17. Hudson, *Religion in America*, 90.

18. Jefferson to Rush, 21 April 1803, quoted in Lynn, ed., *The American Society*, 48.

19. Morais, *Deism in Eighteenth Century America*, 8, 80; Ahlstrom, ed., *Theology in America*, 35; Ver Steeg, *The Formative Years*, 219–220. It should be noted, as Kenneth M. Morrison, has put it, that "Native Americans of the Old Northwest had always believed in a supreme God who created and ruled the world. But this God was also remote from everyday affairs. When the Creator spoke to Neolin [a Delaware tribal prophet of the 1760s], it became clear that the Christ of the missionaries and the Indian God were one and the same." The Indians were thus traditionally Deists of a sort until receiving the message of Christian evangelists. See Morrison, "The American Revolution: The Indian Story," in Gerster and Cords, eds., *Myth America*, 62. Ironically, therefore, as white American culture at large began transforming from Christian into Deist, Native culture underwent the opposite transformation, entering what Gregory E. Dowd has called "the Indians' Great Awakening." See Dowd, "The Indians' Great Awakening," in Kupperman, ed., *Major Problems in American Colonial History*, 427.

20. Kramnick and Moore, *The Godless Constitution*, 34, 40–41.

21. The French Revolution and its fallout in the United States did as much to create the first two political parties as the more popularly held notion of Hamiltonian broad construction versus Jeffersonian strict construction of the Constitution. For evidence, see Foner, ed., *Democratic-Republican Societies*, passim, but especially 17.

22. Roger M. Smith, "Constructing American National Identity: Strategies of the Federalists," in Ben-Atar and Oberg, eds., *Federalists Reconsidered*, 21.

23. David Waldstreicher, "Federalism, the Styles of Politics, and the Politics of Style," in Ibid., 110.

24. Foner, ed., *Democratic-Republican Societies*, 7, 63, 83–87, 95, 101–104, 111, 128, 157, 168, 217, 221.

25. Koch, *Republican Religion*, 51–119; Miller, *The Life of the Mind in America*, 3–5; Nagel, *This Sacred Trust*, 33–36; Marty, *The Infidel*, 23.

26. Stewart, *American Ways of Life*, 61.

27. Quoted in Nye, *The Cultural Life of the New Nation*, 16.

28. Rush was an Anglican/Episcopalian technically. He became a Unitarian without ever renouncing the Episcopal Church, and apparently came back to a Trinitarian belief near the end of his life. It was he who incited Thomas Paine to write *Common Sense*. Like so many of the Founders, he was a complex man, a renaissance man—a physician, a scientist, a philosopher, and a politician, among other things. See Blau, ed., *American Philosophical Addresses*, 315–343; Perry, *Intellectual Life in America*, 139, 142; Federer, ed., *America's God and Country*, 543–544.

29. Jay to Richard Peters, March 29, 1811, quoted in Sullivan, ed., *The Public Men of the Revolution*, 423.

30. Today, of course, Deism is often defined by the clockmaker analogy: God made the universe and its many parts, set it in motion at the dawn of time, and will let it run its course with no intervention until the end of time. Although such an explanation superficially seems to preclude any changes to the way nature functions, such as allowing for miracles, it actually does not, for any changes that occur to the regular workings of nature were themselves preordained by the master designer. See the "Clockmaker Hypothesis" (also called the "Watchmaker Analogy") on Wikipedia.

31. Morais, *Deism in Eighteenth Century America*, 120, 153, 162; Sweet, *Religion in the Development of the American Culture*, 93.

32. Littell, *From State Church to Pluralism*, 42.

33. Jefferson, along with James Madison, authored the Virginia and Kentucky Resolutions in 1799 in response to the Alien and Sedition Acts. These resolutions established the principle that a state government could declare null and void any federal law that seemed unconstitutional to the majority of people in that state. Calhoun later reiterated this principle in the Nullification Crisis of 1832, setting South Carolina at odds with the federal government. Ultimately, this principle contributed to the outbreak of civil war in the 1860s, wherein it was discredited.

34. Quote in Marty, *The Infidels*, 57; see also Ahlstrom, *Theology in America*, 194; Morais, *Deism in Eighteenth Century America*, 166; and Koch, *Republican Religion*, 186.

35. Ahlstrom, *Theology in America*, 39–41; Beth, *The American Theory of Church and State*, 72.

36. Hughes, *Myths America Lives By*, 49; Morais, *Deism in Eighteenth Century America*, 117–119. By the time Edmund Randolph neared the end of his life, he was as

devout and pious a Trinitarian as one could hope to find. His "A Prayer for My Family," written March 25, 1810, is a masterpiece of Christian humility. See Conway, *Omitted Chapters of History*, 156–157, 390.

37. Brookhiser, *Founding Father*, 149.

38. Stokes, *Church and State in the United States*, 245.

39. Joseph Barrell to Nathaniel Barrell, December 20, 1787, cited in Bailyn, ed., *The Debate on the Constitution* (Part 1), 587; Krout and Fox, *The Completion of Independence*, 167–169; Blau, ed., *Men and Movements in American Philosophy*, 27–35; Marty, *The Infidels*, 34, 41.

40. Quoted in Koch, *Republican Religion*, 83.

41. Merrill D. Peterson, "Jefferson, Madison, and Church-State Separation," in Rutyna and Kuehl, eds., *Conceived in Conscience*, 35–36.

42. See, for example, http://www.abovetopsecret.com/forum/thread207906/pg1; and National Geographic Channel's television documentary "Secrets of the Freemasons."

## CHAPTER 6

1. Andrew J. Peck, "Some Philosophers and the Declaration of Independence," in Caws, ed., *Two Centuries of Philosophy in America*, 11–12; Holcombe, *Securing the Blessings of Liberty*, 1.

2. Holcombe, *Securing the Blessings of Liberty*, 9.

3. Novak, *On Two Wings*, 99–100.

4. Morgan, *Puritan Political Ideas*, 367.

5. Quoted in McDonald, *Novus Ordo Seclorum*, 62.

6. Cal Thomas, "Speaking for Moral Majority," in Rutyna and Kuehl, eds., *Conceived in Conscience*, 81; Meyers, *The Mind of the Founder*, xxiv.

7. William H. Russell, "Christ and Human Dignity," in Woodlock, ed., *Democracy*, 147.

8. White, *Science and Sentiment in America*, 55–56; Wood, "Heritage and Hope: Myth and Thomas Jefferson," in Gerster and Cords, eds., *Myth America*, 114.

9. Long, *Your American Yardstick*, xxxi.

10. "Locke was indeed the prime source of founding principles," although "with necessary reservations understood." Meyers, *The Mind of the Founder*, xxv.

11. Cohen, *Science and the Founding Fathers*, 121.

12. Brookhiser, *Alexander Hamilton*, 170–171; Holcombe, *Securing the Blessings of Liberty*, 6.

13. Quoted in Wright, Jr., *American Interpretations of Natural Law*, 11.

14. Davies, *America's Real Religion*, 48.

15. Cullen, *The American Dream*, 8, 36.

16. Pauline Maier has pointed out that the egalitarian clause in the Declaration did not refer to an ideal that a government, whether of the United States or some other, could achieve. Rather, equality of people predated human civilization and the invention of government. Maier, *American Scripture*, 192.

17. Kramnick and Moore, *The Godless Constitution*, 22.

18. Brookhiser, *Alexander Hamilton*, 61–68, 169, 203–204.

19. Bowen, *Miracle at Philadelphia*, 215.

20. Madison quoted in Meyers, *The Mind of the Founder*, xxxiv.

21. Rutland, *The Birth of the Bill of Rights*, 82.

22. Pfeffer, *Church, State, and Freedom*, 122.

23. Lee to Edmund Pendleton, May 26, 1788, quoted in Bailyn, ed., *The Debate on the Constitution* (Part 2), 466.

24. Randolph, convention speech, June 4, 1788, Ibid. (Part 2), 598.

25. Iredell, *Norfolk and Portsmouth Journal*, February 19–20, March 1788, cited in Ibid. (Part 1), 366–378.

26. Ramsey, convention speech, May 27, 1788, published in *Columbia Herald*, June 5, 1788, quoted in Ibid. (Part 2), 511–512.

27. Rush, convention speech, December 12, 1787, cited in Ibid. (Part 1), 869.

28. Phocion, July 17, 1788, *United States Chronicle* [of Providence], quoted in Ibid. (Part 2), 526–532.

29. Brutus IV, *New York Journal*, November 29, 1787, cited in Ibid. (Part 1), 428.

30. Anonymous, *New York Daily Advertiser*, September 24, 1787, quoted in Ibid. (Part 1), 12–14.

31. Stevens, *New York Daily Advertiser*, January 21, 1788, cited in Ibid. (Part 2), 62.

32. Cornell, *The Other Founders*, 2.

33. Winthrop, *Massachusetts Gazette*, January 11, 15, and 18, 1788, quoted in Ibid. (Part 1), 762–771.

34. Jarvis, convention speech, February 4, 1788, quoted in Ibid. (Part 1), 936.

35. Hancock, convention speech, February 6, 1788, quoted in Ibid. (Part 1), 942.

36. Martin, *Maryland Gazette*, December 28, 1787, quoted in Ibid. (Part 1), 657.

37. Cornell, *The Other Founders*, 57.

38. Plough Jogger, *Newport Herald*, April 17, 1788, quoted in Ibid. (Part 2), 415.

39. Huntington, January 9, 1788, quoted in Ibid. (Part 1), 887.

40. Dickinson, *Pennsylvania Mercury and Universal Advertiser* [of Philadelphia], April 17, 1788, quoted in Ibid. (Part 2), 408–412.

41. See Ibid. (Part 1) for examples: 567, 900, 928.

42. Schaff, *Church and State in the United States*, 69–70.

43. Erling T. Jorstad, "Church-State Relations: A Historical Perspective," in Rutyna and Kuehl, eds., *Conceived in Conscience*, 17.

44. Schaff, *Church and State in the United States*, 40.

45. Reichley, *Faith in Politics*, 104.

46. Rossiter, "Nationalism and American Identity in the Early Republic," in Wilentz, ed., *Major Problems in the Early Republic*, 21.

47. Novak, *On Two Wings*, 103–105; Harp, *Positivist Republic*, 5–6.

48. Reichley, *Faith in Politics*, 93–103.

49. Richards, "A Clear and Steady Channel," 470–471; Perry, et al., *Western Civilization*, 550.

50. Meyers, *The Mind of the Founder*, xxxii.

51. George A. Helly, "Faith, Freedom, and Disenchantment: Politics and the American Religious Consciousness," in Douglas and Tipton, eds., *Religion and America*, 221; Reichley, *Faith in Politics*, 93.

52. Bennett, *Christians and the State*, viii.

53. Caldwell, convention speech, July 30, 1788, quoted in Bailyn, *The Debate on the Constitution* (Part 2), 908.

54. McWilliams, *The Idea of Fraternity in America*, 4.

55. Perry, et al., *Western Civilization*, 720–721. For a polemic against substituting the state and a ruler for God, see Goslin, *Church and State*, passim.

56. Evans, *Interpreting the Free Exercise of Religion*, 13; Reichley, *Faith in Politics*, 35; See also Smith, *Foreordained Failure*, passim.

57. Hook, *Religion in a Free Society*, 47.

58. Carl J. Friedrich and Zbigniew Brzezinski, *Totalitarian Dictatorship and Autocracy*, cited in Perry, *Western Civilization*, 766.

59. Perry, *Western Civilization*, 767.

60. Churchill quoted in Ibid., 401, 408.

61. Le Bon quoted in Perry, et al., eds., *Sources of the Western Tradition*, 288.

62. Kopelev quoted in Ibid., 341.

63. Sorel quoted in Ibid., 284.

64. Peck, *The Road Less Traveled*, quote 197; see also the whole section,183–315.

65. Swaine, "Principled Separation," 555–572; Woodlock, ed., *Democracy*, 5.

66. Wilson and Drakeman, eds., *Church and State in American History*, xiv; Pfeffer, *Church, State, and Freedom*, 8, 10, 29, 52.

67. Quoted in Kertosz and Fitzsimons, eds., *What America Stands For*, 183.

68. Thomas, "Speaking for Moral Majority," in Rutyna and Kuehl, eds., *Conceived in Conscience*, 84. It should be noted that much of the substance of the discussion in this chapter regarding the Founders' motives and intentions comes not from original sources pertaining to specific political/religious issues they debated, but from the totality of their writings, generally and philosophically, over their lifetimes.

69. Trees, *The Founding Fathers and the Politics of Character*, xi–xiii.

## CHAPTER 7

1. Nicholas Grier, "Religious Liberalism and the Founding Fathers," in Caws, *Two Centuries of Philosophy in America*, 22; Morais, *Deism in Eighteenth Century America*, 140; Stokes, *Church and State in the United States*, 260–261; 312, 511; Beth, *The American Theory of Church and State*, 63; Federer, ed., *America's God and Country*, 543–544.

2. Novak, *On Two Wings*, 127–156.

3. See for example, Luther Martin of Maryland, "The Genuine Information," parts I, II, VIII, IX, XI in the *Maryland Gazette*, December 28, 1787–1788, February 1788; John Stevens, Jr., "Americanus" in the *New York Daily Advertiser*, November 2, 1787; Oliver Ellsworth, "A Landholder," in the *Connecticut Courant*, November 19, 1787; Mercy Otis Warren, "A Columbian Patriot," February 1788; anonymous author, "Rebuttal to 'An Officer of the Late Continental Army': Plain Truth" in the *Philadelphia Independent Gazette*, November 10, 1787; and anonymous author, "A Political Dialogue," in the *Massachusetts Centinel*, October 24, 1787; all cited in Bailyn, ed., *The Debate on the Constitution*, 105, 189–191, 228, 285–289, 329, and 661.

4. White, ed., *Documents in the History of American Philosophy*, 80–84.

5. First quote, Webster, "Reply to the Pennsylvania Minority: 'America,'" December 31, 1787, in Bailyn, ed., *The Debate on the Constitution*, 555–556; Second quote, Webster cited in Babbidge, ed., *Noah Webster on Being American*, 172–173.

6. Novak, *On Two Wings*, 127–156.

7. See Ellsworth, "A Landholder," cited in Bailyn, ed., *The Debate on the Constitution*, 524; Federer, ed., *America's God and Country*, 560.

8. Federer, ed., *America's God and Country*, 163.

9. Marcus and Burner, eds., *America Firsthand*, 124–130; Godbold and Woody, *Christopher Gadsden and the American Revolution*, 168.

10. Godbold and Woody, *Christopher Gadsden and the American Revolution*, 55, 153.

11. See, for example, John Adams's views on this issue in Witte, Jr., "'A Most Mild and Equitable Establishment of Religion,'" 237.

12. Luther Martin, "The Genuine Information," in Bailyn, ed., *The Debate on the Constitution.*, 655–656.

13. Jones debating the Reverend Daniel Shute, quoted in Ibid., 920.

14. Iredell, North Carolina convention speech, July 30, 1788, quoted in Ibid., (Part 2), 905.

15. Hudson, *Religion in America*, 101.

16. Lynn, ed., *The American Society*, 1–6.

17. Davies, *America's Real Religion*, 23.

18. Franklin, quoted in Lynn, ed., *The American Society*, 20.

19. Perry, *Intellectual Life in America*, 144.

20. Ibid., 21–26.

21. Franklin quoted in Allitt, ed., *Major Problems in American Religious History*, 101.

22. Lambert, "George Whitefield, the Grand Itinerant," in Kupperman, ed., *Major Problems in American Colonial History*, 357–358.

23. Federer, ed., *America's God and Country*, 246.

24. Franklin, quoted in Schaff, *Church and State in the United States*, 123.

25. Franklin, quoted in Bailyn, ed., *The Debate on the Constitution*, 3.

26. Iredell, writing as "Marcus" in *Norfolk and Portsmouth Journal*, February 20, 1788, quoted in Bailyn, ed., *The Debate on the Constitution*, 378.

27. Jay to Richard Peters, March 29, 1811, quoted in Sullivan, ed., *The Public Men of the Revolution*, 422.

28. Chalfant, *America*, 41.

29. Quote, Washington to Admiral de Grasse, September 17, 1781. See also other correspondence in Thayer, *Yorktown*, 93–124.

30. Reichley, *Faith in Politics*, 102.

31. Hudson, *Religion in America*, 101.

32. Weeks, *A New Christian Nation*, 4.

33. Washington, quoted in Miller, ed., *The Young Republic*, 25, 27.

34. Gaustad, *A Religious History of America*, 119–126, Federer, ed., *America's God and Country*, 155.

35. Marty, *Pilgrims in Their Own Land*, 158.

36. Gaustad, *A Religious History of America*, 119–126.

37. Gaustad, ed., *A Documentary History of Religion in America*, 276–279.

38. Dunn, *American Political Theology*, 47–48.

39. Stokes, *Church and State in the United States*, 70, 493–494.

40. Quotes, Miller, ed., *The Young Republic*, 88–89; see also Gordon, "Blasphemy," 686.

41. McCulloch, *John Adams*, passim.

42. Witte, Jr., "'A Most Mild and Equitable Establishment of Religion'," 216–217, 233; Paul Johnson, "The Almost-Chosen People: Why America Is Different," in

Neuhaus, *Unsecular America*, 6; Gaustad, *A Religious History of America*, 123–128; Schneider, *A History of American Philosophy*, 52.

43. John Adams, quoted in Garraty, ed., *1001 Things Everyone Should Know about American History*, 49.

44. John Adams, quoted in Federer, ed., *America's God and Country*, 13.

45. Abigail Adams, quoted in Marcus and Burner, eds., *America Firsthand*, 124–130; and Federer, ed., *America's God and Country*, 3.

46. Thornton, ed., *The Pulpit of the American Revolution*, xxix.

47. Federer, ed., *America's God and Country*, 18.

48. Wood, "Hope and Heritage: Myth and Thomas Jefferson," in Gerster and Cords, eds., *Myth America*, 112–113.

49. Hofstadter, "Jefferson as Cautious Pragmatic," in Wilentz, ed., *Major Problems in the Early Republic*, 102–106; McDonald, "Jefferson as Reactionary Ideologue," in Ibid., 106–109.

50. Maier, *American Scripture*, xvii.

51. Onuf, ed., *Thomas Jefferson*, 1–2, 24.

52. Maier, *American Scripture*, 112–122.

53. Onuf, ed., *Thomas Jefferson*, 19–20.

54. First quote, Smith, *Religious Liberty in the United States*, 29; second quote, Stroh, *American Philosophy from Edwards to Dewey*, 5.

55. Rutyna and Kuehl, *Conceived in Conscience*, 37.

56. Hutson, "Thomas Jefferson's Letter to the Danbury Baptists," 780, 783; Smith, *Religious Liberty in the United States*, 29; Kramnick and Moore, *The Godless Constitution*, 16.

57. Leder, *America, 1603–1789*, 243.

58. Stroh, *American Philosophy from Edwards to Dewey*, 30, 35, 47.

59. Boorstin, *The Lost World of Thomas Jefferson*, 151–157.

60. Dunn, *American Political Theology*, 27–28.

61. Fabian, "Jefferson's *Notes on Virginia*," 124–138.

62. Gaustad, ed., *A Documentary History of Religion in America*, 259–261.

63. Rutyna and Kuehl, eds., *Conceived in Conscience*, 40.

64. Long, *Your American Yardstick*, 141–143; Littell, *From State Church to Pluralism*, 13.

65. Witte, Jr., "'A Most Mild and Equitable Establishment of Religion'," 213.

66. Blau, *Cornerstones of Religious Freedom in America*, 7.

67. Hutson, "Thomas Jefferson's Letter to the Danbury Baptists," 787–788.

68. Dreisbach, "Mr. Jefferson, a Mammoth Cheese, and the 'Wall of Separation Between Church and State,'" 733–735; Hutson, "Thomas Jefferson's Letter to the Danbury Baptists," 781, 785–786; Kramnick and Moore, *The Godless Constitution*, 88–98.

69. Hutson, "Thomas Jefferson's Letter to the Danbury Baptists," 782, 784.

70. Jefferson, quoted in Miller, ed., *Young Republic*, 107–108, 110.

71. Hutson, "Thomas Jefferson's Letter to the Danbury Baptists," 775–776; Dreisbach, "Mr. Jefferson, a Mammoth Cheese, and the 'Wall of Separation Between Church and State,'" 725–727, 732, 737, 741–744.

72. Jefferson, quoted in Miller, ed., *The Young Republic*, 112; see also Hutson, "Thomas Jefferson's Letter to the Danbury Baptists," 785–786; Schaff, *Church and State in the United States*, 29.

73. Dunn, *American Political Theology*, 15–17.

74. Boston, *Why the Religious Right Is Wrong*, 68–69; DeMar, *America's Christian Heritage*, 65.

75. Jefferson to Rush, April 21, 1803, quoted in Lynn, ed., *The American Society*, 45–46.

76. Maier, *American Scripture*, 189.

77. Although it has been common knowledge for about two centuries that Jefferson authored the Declaration, it was not widely known who had written it until the 1790s, when the Republicans, who were the minority party at the time, needed to raise up Jefferson as their leader. They then began to publicize his authorship of this most important American document. Ibid., 170.

78. Sullivan, *The Public Men of the Revolution*, 1, 15–29, quotes 178 and 209.

79. Burns, *James Madison*, 26, 186. Some scholars may dispute the contention that Madison's reputation was rescued by Jackson and the Battle of New Orleans. They consider the notable American victories at Plattsburgh on Lake Champlain, Put-In-Bay on Lake Erie, and Fort McHenry in Baltimore as evidence of strong presidential leadership. The Treaty of Ghent, however, which officially ended the War of 1812 by merely returning both nations to the antebellum status quo, and to which Madison was amenable, undid the effect of these American victories. Jackson restored it.

80. Gay, *James Madison*, 12–13.

81. Noonan, *The Lustre of Our Country*, 65–66.

82. Smith, *James Madison*, 14.

83. Boston, *Why the Religious Right Is Wrong*, 58–59, 69.

84. Colburne, ed., *Fame and the Founding Fathers*, 131.

85. Banning, *The Sacred Fire of Liberty*, 87.

86. Brant, *The Fourth President*, 39.

87. Noonan, *The Lustre of Our Country*, 4.

88. Marty, *Pilgrims in Their Own Land*, 162–163; Noonan, *The Lustre of Our Country*, 67; Gaustad, ed., *A Documentary History of Religion in America*, 262–263.

89. Cited in Pfeffer, *Church, State, and Freedom*, 111–113.

90. Madison to Jefferson, October 24, 1787; and "Publius," quoted in Bailyn, ed., *The Debate on the Constitution*, 201, 759.

91. Quote taken from Koch, *Madison's "Advice to My Country,"* 33–34; see also Boston, *Why the Religious Right Is Wrong*, 70–72; Pfeffer, *Church, State, and Freedom*, 138–139.

92. Dean M. Kelly, "Confronting the Danger of the Moment," in Mechling, ed., *Church, State, and Public Policy*, 17.

93. McCaughey, "Education of Alexander Hamilton," 25, 27.

94. Reichley, *Faith in Politics*, 102–103; Colburne, ed., *Fame and the Founding Fathers*, 141–159.

## CHAPTER 8

1. The Democratic Society of Pennsylvania used this term in the 1790s to describe the Jeffersonians' attempt to offset the power of the Federalist majority. See Foner, ed., *The Democratic-Republican Societies*, 83.

2. See Grob and Billias, eds., *Interpretations of American History*, vol. 2, 274.

3. Woodruff, *Essays on Church and State by Lord Acton*, 293.

4. Dunn, *American Political Theology*, 10–11.

5. Nye, *This Almost Chosen People*, viii.

6. Johnson in Neuhaus, ed., *Unsecular America*, 7.

7. Powell and Powell, eds., *The Spirit of Democracy*, 61.

8. Boston, *Why the Religious Right Is Wrong*, 86.

9. Gaustad, ed., *A Documentary History of Religion in America*, 524.

10. Pfeffer, *Church, State, and Freedom*, 216.

11. High, *The Church in Politics*, 1.

12. Adams, *The Power of Ideals in American History*, 117.

13. Stoddard, *Re-Forging America*, 177.

14. Upchurch, *Historical Dictionary of the Gilded Age*, Introduction.

15. Schaff, *Church and State in the United States*, 16.

16. Ibid., 75.

17. Wilson, *Public Religion in American Culture*, 13.

18. Dawson, *Separate Church and State Now*, 16.

19. Parkes, *The American Experience*, 64.

20. Kramnick and Moore, *The Godless Constitution*, 29.

21. Iredell, July 30, 1788, in Bailyn, ed., *The Debate on the Constitution* (Part 2), 903, 905.

22. Backus, February 4, 1788, quoted in Ibid. (Part 1), 931 [emphasis mine].

23. Dollard, May 22, 1788, quoted in Ibid. (Part 2), 593–594.

24. Quoted in Banning, *The Sacred Fire of Liberty*, 93.

25. Pinckney, May 14, 1788, quoted in Bailyn, ed., *The Debate on the Constitution* (Part 2), 590.

26. Baldwin, July 4, 1788, quoted in Ibid. (Part 2), 514–525.

27. Brutus VI, *New York Journal*, December 27, 1787, quoted in Ibid. (Part 1), 619 [emphasis mine].

28. Wait to George Thatcher, January 8, 1788, quoted in Ibid. (Part 1), 728.

29. Novak, *On Two Wings*, 6, 24.

30. The Republican, *Connecticut Courant*, January 7, 1788, quoted in Bailyn, ed., *The Debate on the Constitution* (Part 1), 710.

31. Whitehill, November 30, 1787, quoted in Ibid. (Part 1), 814.

32. Quoted in *Maryland Journal*, May 6, 1788, cited in Ibid. (Part 2), 430–438. See also, Jeremiah Hill of Maine using similar Enlightenment terminology, saying that the United States was "dedicated to the fair Godess [sic] of Liberty," Hill to George Thatcher, February 26, 1788, quoted in Ibid. (Part 2), 241.

33. Sinopli, *The Foundations of American Citizenship*, 57.

34. Lee to Governor Edmund Randolph, published in the *Virginia Gazette*, December 6, 1787, quoted in Bailyn, ed., *The Debate on the Constitution* (Part 1), 465.

35. Wood, *The Creation of the American Republic*, 60, 118.

36. Appleby, et al., *Telling the Truth about History*, 37–39; Hall, *The Religious Background of American Culture*, 172–173; Stokes, *Church and State in the United States*, 73–75.

37. Adams quoted in Boorstin, *The Lost World of Thomas Jefferson*, 161.

38. Orton, *America in Search of Culture*, 33.

39. Peter L. Berger, "From the Crisis of Religion to the Crisis of Secularity," in Douglas and Tipton, eds., *Religion and America*, 14; Appleby, et al., *Telling the Truth about History*, 24.

40. Nye, *The Cultural Life of the New Nation*, 10–13; Appleby, et al., *Telling the Truth about History*, 30–31.

41. Ladd in Neuhaus, ed., *Unsecular America*, 23–24.

42. Stripling, *Capitalism, Democracy, and Morality*, v–viii; Ladd in Neuhaus, ed., *Unsecular America*, 25–27. While it has been well established how New England got its start as basically a Christian mission outpost, it is less well known but equally true that even Virginia, which is commonly thought of as having begun as merely a joint-stock company commercial venture, actually received its charter from King James I partly "to propagate Christianity to native Americans." Butler, *Awash in a Sea of Faith*, 7.

43. Perry, *Puritanism and Democracy*, 432–434.

44. Ver Steeg, *The Formative Years*, 203.

45. Ledeen, *Tocqueville on American Character*, 68–69.

46. Niebuhr, *Pious and Secular America*, 11; Clark, *The Seventeenth Century*, 19–21; Pfeffer, *Church, State, and Freedom*, 96; Hofstadter, *America in 1750*, 189, 212. Not all scholars believe in such a thing as the "Protestant work ethic." See, for example, Michael Walzer, "The Puritans as Revolutionaries," in Strout, *Intellectual History in America*, 1–20.

47. Nichols, *Religion and American Democracy*, 4–5.

48. Appleby, *Telling the Truth about History*, 135.

49. Niebuhr, *Pious and Secular America*, 2, 4, 9.

50. Stripling, *Capitalism, Democracy, and Morality*, 6; Ladd in Neuhaus, *Unsecular America*, 24–25.

51. Kramnick and Moore, *The Godless Constitution*, 80–85.

52. Tingsten, *The Problem of Democracy*, 19–20.

53. Knapton, *Europe*, 128.

54. Some scholars see the East-West dichotomy as far more important in the colonial-early republic eras. In most of the colonies, and later in most states, in those formative years, an east-west rivalry was indeed highly influential in the development of each individual colony or state. On and near the eastern coastline, wealthy, elite, educated, urban, industrial, and/or plantation-based society emerged first. In the backcountry, piedmont, and/or mountains of the western frontier, the opposite prevailed. These intra-colony, intra-state rivalries did not greatly affect the emerging nationalism of the United States, however, as did the North-South tension that bubbled beneath the surface in the 1780s–1790s and beyond. It is interesting to note that in his famous Farewell Address, George Washington listed side by side among the "causes that may disturb our union . . . *Northern and Southern, Atlantic* and *Western* . . . geographical discriminations." D. Alan Williams, "The Virginia Gentry and the Democratic Myth," in Gerster and Cords, eds., *Myth America*, 40.

55. Pacheco, *Antifederalism*, 7–10.

56. Wood, *The Creation of the American Republic*, 500.

57. Taylor quoted by Isaac Kramnick, "The Discourse of Politics in 1787," in Wilentz, ed., *Major Problems in the Early Republic*, 42.

58. Cousins, *"In God We Trust"*, 4–5.

59. Buel quoted by John Ashworth, "Republicanism, Capitalism, and Slavery in the 1790s," in Wilentz, *Major Problems in the Early Republic*, 87.

60. Jack Rakove, an imminent Constitutional historian, has pointed out that James Madison considered slavery more divisive at the Constitutional Convention than the more celebrated large state/small state controversy. He notes that "The debate was

heated," but ironically, "slavery did not become a major issue" at the convention. See Rakove, "The Philadelphia Story: The Founding Fathers and the Myth of Constitutional Intent," in Gerster and Cords, eds., *Myth America*, 70. See also Donald G. Nieman, "Slavery and the Constitution," in Wilentz, ed., *Major Problems in the Early Republic*, 49–53.

61. Gaustad, ed., *A Documentary History of Religion in America*, 306–307.

62. Marnell, *The First Amendment*, 78–79, 84.

63. Balmer and Winner, *Protestantism in America*, 44, 46–47, 50–51.

64. Quoted in Federer, ed., *America's God and Country*, 312.

65. Quoted in Ibid., 107–108.

66. See "Daniel Webster's Speech against Universal Manhood Suffrage, 1820," cited in Bellesiles et al., eds., *Bibliobase*, 102.

67. "The Religious Affiliation of Vice President John C. Calhoun," www.adherents. com/people/pc/John_Calhoun.html.

68. Craven, *The Legend of the Founding Fathers*, 4.

69. Lindaman and Ward, *History Lessons*, 19–20.

70. Beth, *American Theory of Church and State*, 42.

71. Perry, *Western Civilization*, 541–543.

72. Lipset, *The First New Nation*, 74–76.

73. Perry, *Western Civilization*, 538–544.

74. Gellert, *The Fate of America*, 34.

75. Ahlstrom, ed., *Theology in America*, 24.

76. Appleby, *Inheriting the Revolution*, 197–199; Morgan, *The Stamp Act Crisis*, 303; Gaustad, *A Religious History of America*, 64–65.

77. David Little, "Theological Dimensions of Church-State Relations" in Rutyna and Kuehl, eds., *Conceived in Conscience*, 95.

78. Lazare, *The Frozen Republic*, 2.


## CONCLUSION

1. DeMar, *America's Christian History*, 141–142; Hughes, *Myths America Lives By*, 2–3; Perry, *Puritanism and Democracy*, 432–434.

# Bibliography

Abbot, W. W., et al., eds. *The George Washington Papers*. Charlottesville: University Press of Virginia, 1983–2006.

Adams, Ephraim D. *The Power of Ideals in American History*. Reprint, New York: AMS Press, 1969.

Adams, Willie P. *The First State Constitutions: Republican Ideology and the Making of the State Constitutions in the Revolutionary Era*. Chapel Hill: University of North Carolina Press, 1980.

Agar, Herbert. *The Perils of Democracy*. Chester Springs, PA: Dufour Editions, 1965.

Ahlstrom, Sydney E., ed. *Theology in America: The Major Protestant Voices from Puritanism to Neo-Orthodoxy*. Reprint, Indianapolis: Hackett, 2003.

Allen, Ethan. *Reason: The Only Oracle of Man—a Compendious System of Natural Religion*. http://libertyonline.hypermall.com/allen-reason.html (accessed October 22, 2009).

Allitt, Patrick, ed. *Major Problems in American Religious History*. Boston: Houghton Mifflin, 1999.

Appleby, Joyce. *Inheriting the Revolution: The First Generation of Americans*. Cambridge, MA: Belknap Press, 2000.

Appleby, Joyce, et al. *Telling the Truth about History*. New York: W. W. Norton, 1994.

Armstrong, Herbert W. *The United States and Britain in Prophecy*. Pasadena, CA: Worldwide Church of God, 1980.

Babbidge, Homer D., ed. *Noah Webster on Being American: Selected Writings, 1783–1828*. New York: Praeger, 1967.

Bagby, Laurie M. *Political Thought: A Guide to the Classics*. Toronto: Wadsworth Group, 2002.

Bailyn, Bernard, ed. *The Debate on the Constitution*. New York: Library of America, 1993.

Bainton, Roland H. *The Age of the Reformation*. Reprint, Malabar, FL: Krieger, 1984.

———. *Early Christianity*. Reprint, Malabar, FL: Krieger, 1984.

————. *The Medieval Church*. Reprint, Malabar, FL: Krieger, 1979.

Balmer, Randall, and Lauren F. Winner. *Protestantism in America*. New York: Columbia University Press, 2002.

Bancroft, George. *History of the United States from the Discovery of the American Continent*. Boston: Little and Brown, 1846.

Banning, Lance. *The Sacred Fire of Liberty: James Madison and the Founding of the Federal Republic*. Ithaca, NY: Cornell University Press, 1995.

Barton, David. *Original Intent: The Courts, the Constitution, and Religion*, 2nd ed. Aledo, TX: Wallbuilder Press, 2000.

Baxter, Maurice G. *One and Inseparable: Daniel Webster and the Union*. Cambridge, MA: Belknap Press, 1984.

Beale, Howard K., ed. *Charles A. Beard: An Appraisal*. Lexington: University of Kentucky Press, 1954.

Becker, Carl L. *The Declaration of Independence: A Study in the History of Political Ideas*. New York: Vintage Books, 1942.

Bellah, Robert N. *The Broken Covenant: American Civil Religion in Time of Trial*. New York: Seabury Press, 1975.

Bellesiles, Michael, et al., eds. *Bibliobase*. Boston: Houghton Mifflin, 2000.

Ben-Atar, Doron, and Barbara B. Oberg, eds., *Federalists Reconsidered*. Charlottesville: University Press of Virginia, 1998.

Bennett, John C. *Christians and the State*. New York: Charles Scribner's Sons, 1958.

Beth, Loren P. *The American Theory of Church and State*. Gainesville: University of Florida Press, 1958.

Billington, Ray A. *The Reinterpretation of Early American History*. San Marino, CA: Huntington Library, 1966.

Blanshard, Paul. *God and Man in Washington*. Boston: Beacon Press, 1960.

Blau, Joseph L., ed. *American Philosophic Addresses, 1700–1900*. New York: Columbia University Press, 1946.

————. *Cornerstones of Religious Freedom in America*. Rev. and enl. ed., New York: Harper Torchbooks, 1964.

————. *Men and Movements in American Philosophy*. Englewood Cliffs, NJ: Prentice-Hall, 1952.

Bloom, Harold. *The American Religion: The Emergence of the Post-Christian Nation*. New York: Simon & Schuster, 1992.

Boller, Paul F. *Freedom and Fate in American Thought: From Edwards to Dewey*. Dallas: SMU Press, 1978.

Boorstin, Daniel J. *The Lost World of Thomas Jefferson*. Boston: Beacon Press, 1948.

Boston, Robert. *Why the Religious Right Is Wrong: About Separation of Church and State*. Buffalo: Prometheus Books, 1993.

Bowen, Catherine D. *Miracle at Philadelphia*. Boston: Little, Brown, 1966.

Boyd, Julian P., et al., eds. *The Thomas Jefferson Papers*. Princeton, NJ: Princeton University Press, 1950–2005.

Brant, Irving. *The Fourth President: A Life of James Madison*. Indianapolis: Bobbs-Merrill, 1970.

Brookhiser, Richard. *Alexander Hamilton: American*. New York: Simon & Schuster, 1999.

————. *Founding Father: Rediscovering George Washington*. New York: Free Press, 1996.

Brooks, Van W., ed. *The Roots of American Culture, and Other Essays by Constance Rourke*. Port Washington, New York: Kennikat Press, 1965.

Burns, Edward M. *The American Idea of Mission: Concepts of National Purpose and Destiny*. New Brunswick, NJ: Rutgers University Press, 1957.

———. *James Madison: Philosopher of the Constitution*. New Brunswick, NJ: Rutgers University Press, 1938.

Butler, Jon. *Awash in a Sea of Faith: Christianizing the American People*. Cambridge, MA: Harvard University Press, 1990.

———. *Becoming America: The Revolution before 1776*. Cambridge, MA: Harvard University Press, 2000.

Butler, Nicholas M. *True and False Democracy*. New York: Charles Scribner's Sons, 1940.

Byrne, James M. *Religion and the Enlightenment: From Descartes to Kant*. Louisville: Westminster John Knox Press, 1997.

Caldwell, Lynton K. "Novus Ordo Seclorum: The Heritage of Public Administration." *Public Administration Review* 5 (1976): 476–488.

Calloway, Colin G., ed. *The World Turned Upside Down: Indian Voices from Early America*. Boston: Bedford/St. Martin's, 1994.

Cantor, Norman F., and Peter L. Klein. *Seventeenth Century Rationalism: Bacon and Descartes*. Waltham, MA: Blaisdell, 1969.

Carlin, George. *When Will Jesus Bring the Pork Chops?* New York: Hyperion, 2004.

Carter, Stephen L. *The Culture of Disbelief: How American Law and Politics Trivialize Religious Devotion*. New York: Basic Books, 1993.

Cartwright, William H., and Richard L. Watson, eds. *The Reinterpretation of American History and Culture*. Washington, DC: National Council for the Social Studies, 1973.

Caws, Peter, ed. *Two Centuries of Philosophy in America*. Totowa, NJ: Rowman and Littlefield, 1980.

Chalfant, James W. *America: A Call to Greatness*. Winter Park, FL: Self-published, 2003.

Cherry, Conrad, ed. *God's New Israel: Religious Interpretations of American Destiny*, rev. and upd. ed., Chapel Hill: University of North Carolina Press, 1998.

Clark, Sir George. *The Seventeenth Century*, 2nd. ed. reprint, New York: Oxford University Press, 1961.

Clebsch, William A. *American Religious Thought: A History*. Chicago: University of Chicago Press, 1973.

———. *From Sacred to Profane: The Role of Religion in American History*. New York: Harper & Row, 1968.

Cleveland, Catharine C. *The Great Revival in the West, 1797–1805*. Chicago: University of Chicago Press, 1916.

"Clockmaker Hypothesis." http://en.wikipedia.org/wiki/Clockmaker_hypothesis (accessed October 21, 2009).

Cody, David. "The Church of England," *The Victorian Web*. www.victorianweb.org (accessed October 21, 2009).

Cohen, I. Bernard. *Science and the Founding Fathers: Science in the Political Thought of Jefferson, Franklin, Adams, and Madison*. New York: W. W. Norton, 1995.

Cohen, Morris R. *American Thought: A Critical Sketch*. Glencoe, IL: Free Press, 1954.

Colburne, Trevor, ed. *Fame and the Founding Fathers: Essays by Douglass Adair*. New York: W. W. Norton, 1974.

Commager, Henry S., ed. *Documents of American History*. 7th ed. New York: Appleton-Century-Crofts, 1963.

Conway, Moncure D. *Omitted Chapters of History: Disclosed in the Life and Papers of Edmund Randolph*. New York: G. P. Putnam's Sons, 1888.

Cornell, Saul. *The Other Founders: Anti-Federalism and the Dissenting Tradition in America, 1788–1828*. Chapel Hill: University of North Carolina Press, 1999.

Cousins, Norman, ed. *"In God We Trust": The Religious Beliefs and Ideas of the American Founding Fathers*. New York: Harper & Brothers, 1958.

Craven, Wesley F. *The Legend of the Founding Fathers*. New York: New York University Press, 1956.

Cullen, Jim. *The American Dream: A Short History of an Idea That Shaped a Nation*. New York: Oxford University Press, 2003.

Cunliffe, Marcus. *The Nation Takes Shape, 1789–1837*. Chicago: University of Chicago Press, 1959.

Cunningham, Noble E., ed. *The Early Republic, 1789–1828*. Columbia: University of South Carolina Press, 1968.

Cushman, Stephen, and Paul Newlin, eds. *Nation of Letters: A Concise Anthology of American Literature*, vol. 1. St. James, NY: Brandywine Press, 1998.

Darling, Arthur B. *Our Rising Empire, 1763–1803*. New Haven, CT: Yale University Press, 1940.

Davies, A. Powell. *America's Real Religion*. Reprint, Boston: Beacon Press, 1965.

Davis, Derek H. "The Enduring Legacy of Roger Williams: Consulting America's First Separationist on Today's Pressing Church-State Controversies." *Journal of Church and State* 41 (1999): 201–212.

Davis, James C. "A Return to Civility: Roger Williams and Public Discourse in America." *Journal of Church and State* 43 (2001): 689–706.

Dawson, George G., ed. *Freedom: America's Choice*. Pleasantville, NY: Reader's Digest Services, Inc., 1962.

Dawson, Joseph M. *Separate Church and State Now*. New York: Richard R. Smith, 1948.

Delbanco, Andrew. *The Real American Dream: A Meditation on Hope*. Cambridge, MA: Harvard University Press, 1999.

DeMar, Gary. *America's Christian Heritage*. Nashville: Broadman & Holman, 2003.

———. *America's Christian History: The Untold Story*. Atlanta: American Vision Inc., 1995.

"Democide." http://en.wikipedia.org/wiki/Democide (accessed October 21, 2009).

Diggins, John P. *On Hallowed Ground: Abraham Lincoln and the Foundations of American History*. New Haven, CT: Yale University Press, 2000.

Dionne, E. J., Jr., and John J. Diulio Jr., eds. *What's God Got to Do with the American Experiment?* Washington, DC: Brookings Institution Press, 2000.

Douglas, Mary, and Steven Tipton, eds. *Religion and America: Spiritual Life in a Secular Age*. Boston: Beacon Press, 1983.

Dreisbach, Daniel L. "Mr. Jefferson, a Mammoth Cheese, and the 'Wall of Separation between Church and State': A Bicentennial Commemoration." *Journal of Church and State* 43 (2001): 725–745.

Dunn, Charles W., ed. *American Political Theology: Historical Perspective and Theoretical Analysis*. New York: Praeger, 1984.

Dwight, Theodore. *History of the Hartford Convention*, excerpts reprinted in *Retrieving the American Past*. Boston: Pearson, 2002.

Eck, Diana L. *A New Religious America: How a "Christian Country" Has Now Become the World's Most Religiously Diverse Nation.* San Francisco: HarperCollins, 2001.

Edel, Wilbur. *Defenders of the Faith: Religion and Politics from the Pilgrim Fathers to Ronald Reagan.* New York: Praeger, 1987.

Eidsmore, John. *Christianity and the Constitution: The Faith of Our Founding Fathers.* Grand Rapids, MI: Baker Book House, 1987.

Ekirch, Arthur A., Jr., ed. *Voices in Dissent: An Anthology of Individualist Thought in the United States.* New York: Citadel Press, 1964.

"Elegant Universe, The." Public Broadcasting Service television series. Also available at PBS Web site: www.pbs.org/wgbh/nova/elegant.

Ellis, Joseph. *Founding Brothers: The Revolutionary Generation.* New York: Alfred A. Knopf, 2000.

Evans, Bette N. *Interpreting the Free Exercise of Religion: The Constitution and American Pluralism.* Chapel Hill: University of North Carolina Press, 1997.

Fabian, Bernard. "Jefferson's *Notes on Virginia*: The Genesis of Query xvii, The Different Religions Received into That State?" *The William and Mary Quarterly* 12 (1955): 124–138.

Fann, James M. "Understanding American Pie." www.understandingamericanpie.com (accessed October 21, 2009).

Federer, William J., ed. *America's God and Country: Encyclopedia of Quotations.* Coppell, TX: FAME, 1994.

Fehrenbacher, Don E., ed. *Freedom and Its Limitations in American Life, By David M. Potter.* Stanford, CA: Stanford University Press, 1976.

Feldman, Noah. *Divided by God: America's Church-State Problem—and What We Should Do about It.* New York: Farrar, Straus and Giroux, 2005.

Finke, Roger, and Rodney Starke. *The Churching of America, 1776–1990: Winners and Losers in Our Religious Economy.* New Brunswick, NJ: Rutgers University Press, 1992.

Fischer, David H. *Albion's Seed: Four British Folkways in America.* New York: Oxford University Press, 1989.

Fish, Stanley. "One University under God?" *Chronicle of Higher Education*, January 7, 2005.

Fleming, Thomas. *1776: Year of Illusions.* New York: W. W. Norton, 1975.

Flower, Elizabeth, and Murray G. Murphey. *A History of American Philosophy*, vol. 1. New York: Capricorn Books, 1977.

Flowers, Ronald B. "In Search of a Christian Nation." *Liberty Magazine Online*, September 7, 2004. http://www.libertymagazine.org.

Foner, Philip S., ed. *The Democratic-Republican Societies, 1790–1800: A Documentary Sourcebook of Constitutions, Declarations, Addresses, Resolutions, and Toasts.* Westport, CT: Greenwood Press, 1976.

Ford, Paul L., ed. *Pamphlets on the Constitution of the United States.* New York: Da Capo Press, 1968.

Fraser, Antonia. *Cromwell: The Lord Protector.* New York: Dell Publishing, 1975.

Friedman, Lee M. *Pilgrims in a New Land.* Reprint, Westport, CT: Greenwood Press, 1979.

Garraty, John A. *1001 Things Everyone Should Know about American History.* New York: Doubleday, 1989.

Gaustad, Edwin S., ed. *A Documentary History of Religion in America: To the Civil War*. Grand Rapids, MI: William B. Eerdman's, 1982.

———. *A Religious History of America*. New York: Harper & Row, 1966.

Gay, Sidney H. *James Madison*. Boston: Houghton Mifflin, 1892.

Gellert, Michael. *The Fate of America: An Inquiry into National Character*. Washington, DC: Brassey's Inc., 2001.

*George-Anne, The*. Statesboro, Georgia. October 14, 21, and 25, 2004.

Gerster, Patrick, and Nicholas Cords, eds. *Myth America: A Historical Anthology*, vol. 1. St. James, NY: Brandywine Press, 1997.

Godbold, E. Stanly, and Robert H. Woody, *Christopher Gadsden and the American Revolution*. Knoxville: University of Tennessee Press, 1982.

Gordon, Sarah B. "Blasphemy and the Law of Religious Liberty in Nineteenth-Century America." *American Quarterly* 52 (2000): 682–719.

Gorer, Geoffrey. *The American People: A Study in National Character*. New York: W. W. Norton, 1948.

Goslin, Ryllis A. *Church and State*. New York: Foreign Policy Association, Inc., 1937.

Greene, Evarts B. *Religion and the State: The Making and Testing of an American Tradition*. Reprint, Ithaca, NY: Great Seal Books, 1959.

Greere, Allan, ed. *The Jesuit Relations: Natives and Missionaries in Seventeenth-Century North America*. Boston: Bedford/St. Martin's, 2000.

Grob, Gerald N., and George A. Billias, eds. *Interpretations of American History: Patterns and Perspectives*, 6th ed., 2 vols. New York: Free Press, 1992.

Guttman, Allen. *The Conservative Tradition in America*. New York: Oxford University Press, 1967.

Hall, James W. *Forging the American Character*. New York: Holt, Rinehart and Winston, 1971.

Hall, Thomas C. *The Religious Background of American Culture*. Boston: Little, Brown, 1930.

Halliday, F. E. *A Concise History of England: From Stonehenge to the Atomic Age*. New York: Viking Press, 1965.

Handy, Robert T. *A Christian America: Protestant Hopes and Historical Realities*. New York: Oxford University Press, 1971.

———, ed. *Religion in the American Experience: The Pluralistic Style*. Columbia: University of South Carolina Press, 1972.

Harlan, David. *The Degradation of American History*. Chicago: University of Chicago Press, 1997.

Harp, Gillis J. *Positivist Republic: August Comte and the Reconstruction of American Liberalism, 1865–1920*. University Park: Pennsylvania State University Press, 1995.

Harrington, Joel F., ed. *A Cloud of Witnesses: Readings in the History of Western Christianity*. Boston: Houghton Mifflin, 2001.

Harris, Leonard, et al., eds. *American Philosophies: An Anthology*. Malden, MA: Blackwell, 2002.

Hart, Albert B., ed. *American History Told by Contemporaries*, vol. 2, *1689–1783*. New York: Macmillan, 1928.

Hartley, William G. "Missouri's 1838 Extermination Order and the Mormons' Forced Removal to Illinois." *Mormon Historical Studies*, 2 (2001): 5–27.

Hartshorne, Charles. *Creativity in American Philosophy*. Albany: State University of New York Press, 1984.

Haskell, Thomas L. *Objectivity Is Not Neutrality: Explanatory Schemes in History*. Baltimore: Johns Hopkins University Press, 1998.

Hawking, Stephen. *A Brief History of Time: From the Big Bang to Black Holes*. Toronto: Bantam Books, 1988.

Heimert, Alan, and Perry Miller. *The Great Awakening: Documents Illustrating the Crisis and Its Consequences*. Indianapolis: Bobbs-Merrill, 1967.

High, Stanley. *The Church in Politics*. New York: Harper & Brothers, 1930.

Higham, John, ed. *The Reconstruction of American History*. New York: Humanities Press, 1962.

Hofstadter, Richard. *America at 1750: A Social Portrait*. New York: Alfred A. Knopf, 1971.

————. *Anti-Intellectualism in American Life*. New York: Alfred A. Knopf, 1964.

Holcombe, Arthur N. *Securing the Blessings of Liberty: The Constitutional System*. Chicago: Scott, Foresman and Co., 1964.

Hook, Sidney. *Religion in a Free Society*. Lincoln: University of Nebraska Press, 1967.

Horwitz, Robert H., ed. *The Moral Foundations of the American Republic*. 2nd. ed., Charlottesville: University Press of Virginia, 1979.

Howe, Mark DeWolfe. *The Garden and the Wilderness: Religion and Government in American Constitutional History*. Chicago: University of Chicago Press, 1965.

http://www.abovetopsecret.com (accessed October 29, 2009).

http://www.compulink.co.uk/~craftings/doll.htm (accessed October 29, 2009).

http://www.greatseal.com (accessed October 29, 2009).

Hudson, Winthrop S. *Religion in America: An Historical Account of the Development of American Religious Life*. 4th ed. New York: Macmillan, 1987.

Hughes, Richard T. *Myths America Lives By*. Urbana: University of Illinois Press, 2003.

Hutson, James H. "Thomas Jefferson's Letter to the Danbury Baptists: A Controversy Rejoined." *The William and Mary Quarterly* 56 (1999): 775–790.

James, D. Clayton. *Antebellum Natchez*. Baton Rouge: Louisiana State University Press, 1968.

Jessup, John K., et al. *The National Purpose*. New York: Holt, Rinehart and Winston, 1960.

Joyce, Lester D. *Church and Clergy in the American Revolution: A Study in Group Behavior*. New York: Exposition Press, 1966.

Karabell, Zachary. *A Visionary Nation: Four Centuries of American Dreams and What Lies Ahead*. New York: Harper Collins, 2001.

Kendall, Willmoore, and George W. Carey. *The Basic Symbols of the American Political Tradition*. Baton Rouge: Louisiana State University Press, 1970.

Kennedy, D. James, and Jerry Newcombe. *What If America Were a Christian Nation Again?* Nashville: Thomas Nelson, 2003.

Kenyon, Cecelia M., ed. *The Antifederalists*. Indianapolis: Bobbs-Merrill, Inc., 1966.

Kertosz, Stephen D., and M. A. Fitzsimons, eds. *What America Stands For*. South Bend, IN: University of Notre Dame Press, 1959.

Kirk, Russell. *The Roots of American Order*. 4th ed. Wilmington, DE: ISI Books, 2003.

Knapton, Ernest J. *Europe, 1450–1815*. New York: Charles Scribner's Sons, 1958.

Koch, Adrienne. *Madison's "Advice to My Country."* Princeton, NJ: Princeton University Press, 1966.

————. *Power, Morals, and the Founding Fathers: Essays in the Interpretation of the American Enlightenment*. Ithaca, NY: Cornell University Press, 1961.

Koch, G. Adolf. *Republican Religion: The American Revolution and the Cult of Reason.* Gloucester, MA: Peter Smith, 1964.

Kornfield, Eve, ed. *Creating an American Culture, 1775–1800: A Brief History with Documents.* Boston: Bedford/St. Martin's, 2001.

Kramnick, Isaac, and R. Laurence Moore. *The Godless Constitution: The Case against Religious Correctness.* New York: W. W. Norton, 1996.

Krout, John A., and Dixon R. Fox. *The Completion of Independence, 1790–1830.* New York: Macmillan, 1944.

Kuklick, Bruce, and D. G. Hart, eds. *Religious Advocacy and American History.* Grand Rapids, MI: William B. Eerdman's, 1997.

Kupperman, Karen O., ed. *Major Problems in American Colonial History.* 2nd. ed. Boston: Houghton Mifflin, 2000.

LaBaree, Leonard W., et al., eds. *The Benjamin Franklin Papers.* New Haven, CT: Yale University Press, 1959–2003.

LaHaye, Tim. *Faith of Our Founding Fathers.* Brentwood, TN: Wolgemuth & Hyatt, 1987.

Latourette, Kenneth S. "The Contribution of the Religion of the Colonial Period to the Ideals and Life of the United States." *Americas* 4 (1958): 340–355.

Lazare, Daniel. *The Frozen Republic: How the Constitution Is Paralyzing Democracy.* New York: Harcourt Brace, 1996.

Leaming, Jeremy. "Religious Liberty Cherished, Not Understood." Americans United for the Separation of Church and State. http://blog.au.org/2004/09/15/religious_liber (accessed October 22, 2009).

Ledeen, Michael. *Tocqueville on American Character.* New York: Truman Talley Books, 2000.

Leder, Lawrence H. *America, 1603–1789: Prelude to a Nation.* 2nd. ed. Minneapolis: Burgess, 1978.

Lerner, Robert, et al. *Molding the Good Citizen: The Politics of High School History Texts.* Westport, CT: Praeger, 1995.

Levinger, Lee J. *A History of the Jews in the United States.* New York: Union of American Hebrew Congregations, 1970.

Lind, Michael. *The Next American Nation: The New Nationalism and the Fourth American Revolution.* New York: Free Press, 1995.

Lindaman, Dana, and Kyle Ward. *History Lessons: How Textbooks from Around the World Portray U.S. History.* New York: New Press, 2004.

Lippy, Charles H., et al. *Christianity Comes to the Americas: 1492–1776.* New York: Paragon House, 1992.

Lipset, Seymour M. *The First New Nation: The United States in Historical and Comparative Perspective.* New York: W. W. Norton, 1979.

Littell, Franklin H. *From State Church to Pluralism: A Protestant Interpretation of Religion in American History.* Chicago: Aldine, 1962.

Lockard, Duane. *The Perverted Priorities of American Politics.* New York: Macmillan, 1971.

Loewen, James W. *Lies My Teacher Told Me: Everything Your American History Textbook Got Wrong.* New York: New Press, 1995.

Loewenberg, Bert J. *American History in American Thought: Christopher Columbus to Henry Adams.* New York: Simon and Schuster, 1972.

Long, Hamilton A. *Your American Yardstick: Twelve Basic American Principles*. Philadelphia: Your Heritage Books, 1963.

Lorence, James J. *Enduring Voices: Document Sets to Accompany "The Enduring Vision: A History of the American People,"* vol. 1, *To 1877*. 4th ed. Boston: Houghton Mifflin, 2000.

Lossing, B. J. *Lives of the Signers of the Declaration of Independence*. New York: George F. Cooledge & Brothers, 1848. Reprint, Aledo, TX: Wallbuilders, 1995.

Lowe, Janet. *Ted Turner Speaks: Insight from the World's Greatest Maverick*. New York: John Wiley & Sons, 1999.

Lucas, Paul R. *American Odyssey, 1607–1789*. Englewood Cliffs, NJ: Prentice-Hall, 1984.

Luebering, Carol. "Confirmation: A Deepening of Our Christian Identity." www.americancatholic.org/Newsletters/CU/ac1095.asp (accessed October 22, 2009).

Lutz, Harvey L. *A Platform for the American Way*. New York: Appleton-Century-Crofts, 1952.

Lynn, Kenneth S., ed. *The American Society*. New York: George Braziller, 1963.

Maclear, J. A., ed. *Church and State in the Modern Age*. New York: Oxford University Press, 1995.

Maier, Pauline. *American Scripture: Making the Declaration of Independence*. New York: Alfred A. Knopf, 1997.

Main, Jackson Turner. *The Antifederalists: Critics of the Constitution, 1781–1788*. Chapel Hill: University of North Carolina Press, 1961.

Mancall, Peter C., ed. *Envisioning America: English Plans for the Colonization of North America, 1580–1640*. Boston: Bedford/St. Martin's, 1995.

Marcus, Robert D., and David Burner, eds. *America Firsthand*, vol. 1, *Readings from Settlement to Reconstruction*. 5th ed. Boston: Bedford/St. Martin's, 2001.

Marnell, William H. *The First Amendment: The History of Religious Freedom in America*. Garden City, NY: Doubleday, 1964.

Marshall, Peter, and David Manuel. *The Light and the Glory*. Old Tappan, NJ: Fleming H. Revell, 1977.

Marty, Martin E. *The Infidel: Freethought and American Religion*. Cleveland: Meridian Books, 1961.

———. *Pilgrims in Their Own Land: 500 Years of Religion in America*. Boston: Little, Brown, 1984.

———. *Religion and Republic: The American Circumstance*. Boston: Beacon Press, 1987.

May, Henry F. *Ideas, Faiths, and Feelings: Essays on American Intellectual and Religious History, 1952–1982*. New York: Oxford University Press, 1983.

McCaughey, Robert A. "The Education of Alexander Hamilton." *New York Journal of American History* 65 (2004): 25–31.

McCoy, Drew R. *The Last of the Fathers: James Madison and the Republican Legacy*. Cambridge: Cambridge University Press, 1989.

McCulloch, David. *John Adams*. Touchstone ed. New York: Simon & Schuster, 2002.

McDonald, Forrest. *Novus Ordo Seclorum: The Intellectual Origins of the Constitution*. Lawrence: University of Kansas Press, 1985.

———. *We the People: The Economic Origins of the Constitution*. Chicago: University of Chicago Press, 1958.

McDonald, Forrest, and Ellen Shapiro McDonald. *Requiem: Variations on Eighteenth-Century Themes*. Lawrence: University of Kansas Press, 1988.

McLean, Don. "American Pie." United Artists, 1971.

McWilliams, Wilson C. *The Idea of Fraternity in America*. Berkeley: University of California Press, 1973.

Mead, Sidney E. *The Nation with the Soul of a Church*. New York: Harper & Row, 1964.

Mechling, Jay, ed. *Church, State, and Public Policy: The New Shape of the Church-State Debate*. Washington, DC: American Enterprise Institute for Public Policy Research, 1978.

Meyers, Marvin, ed. *The Mind of the Founder: Sources of the Political Thought of James Madison*. Indianapolis: Bobbs-Merrill, 1973.

Millard, Catherine. *The Christian Heritage of Our Nation*. Springfield, VA: Christian Heritage Ministries, 1999.

Miller, John C. *The Young Republic, 1789–1815*. New York: Free Press, 1970.

Miller, Perry. *The Life of the Mind in America: From the Revolution to the Civil War*. New York: Harcourt, Brace & World, 1965.

Miller, Perry, and Thomas H. Johnson, eds. *The Puritans: A Sourcebook of Their Writings,* vol. 2. New York: Harper & Row, 1963.

Minar, David W. *Ideas and Politics: The American Experience*. Homewood, IL: Dorsey Press, 1964.

Moore, R. Laurence. *Religious Outsiders and the Making of Americans*. New York: Oxford University Press, 1986.

Morais, Herbert M. *Deism in Eighteenth Century America*. New York: Russell & Russell, 1960.

Morgan, Edmund S. *Puritan Political Ideas, 1558–1794*. Indianapolis: Bobbs-Merrill, 1965.

Morgan, Edmund S., and Helen M. Morgan. *The Stamp Act Crisis: Prologue to Revolution*. New rev. ed. New York: Collier Books, 1962.

Morris, Richard B. *The American Revolution: A Short History*. Reprint, Huntington, NY: Krieger, 1979.

Morton, Marion J. *The Terrors of Ideological Politics: Liberal Historians in a Conservative Mood*. Cleveland: Press of Case Western Reserve University, 1972.

Mugleston, William F., and John K. Derden, eds. *Benedict Arnold, Anne Hutchinson, Sam Adams, Witches, and Other Troublemakers: Essays in Early American History*. New York: American Heritage, 1994.

Myers, Gustavus. *History of Bigotry in the United States*. New York: Random House, 1943.

"Myth of Separation of Church and State, The." www.no-apathy.org (no longer accessible).

Nagel, Paul C. *This Sacred Trust: American Nationality, 1798–1898*. New York: Oxford University Press, 1971.

Neuhaus, Richard J., ed. *Unsecular America*. Grand Rapids, MI: William B. Eerdman's, 1986.

Nichols, Roy F. *Blueprints for Leviathan: American Style*. New York: Atheneum, 1963.

———. *Religion and American Democracy*. Baton Rouge: Louisiana State University Press, 1959.

Niebuhr, Reinhold. *Pious and Secular America*. New York: Charles Scribner's Sons, 1958.

Noll, Mark A. *One Nation Under God? Christian Faith and Political Action in America*. San Francisco: Harper & Row, 1988.

Noll, Mark A., et al., eds. *Eerdmans' Handbook to Christianity in America*. Grand Rapids, MI: William B. Eerdman's, 1983.

Noonan, John T. *The Lustre of Our Country: The American Experience in Religious Freedom*. Berkeley: University of California Press, 1998.

Novak, Michael. *On Two Wings: Humble Faith and Common Sense at the American Founding*. San Francisco: Encounter Books, 2002.

Nye, Russell B. *The Cultural Life of the New Nation, 1776–1830*. New York: Harper & Brothers, 1960.

———. *George Bancroft*. New York: Twayne, 1964.

———. *This Almost Chosen People: Essays in the History of American Ideas*. Lansing: Michigan State University Press, 1966.

"Occident and American Jewish Advocate, The," vol. 2, no. 4 (Tamuz 5604 or July 1844). http://www.jewish-history.com (accessed October 26, 2009).

Odegard, Peter. *The American Public Mind*. New York: Columbia University Press, 1931.

O'Hair, Madalyn M. *What on Earth Is an Atheist!* New York: Arno Press, 1972.

Onuf, Peter, ed. *Thomas Jefferson: An Anthology*. St. James, NY: Brandywine Press, 1999.

Orton, William A. *America in Search of Culture*. Boston: Little, Brown, 1933.

Pacheco, Josephine F., ed. *Antifederalism: The Legacy of George Mason*. Fairfax, VA: George Mason University Press, 1992.

Parkes, Henry B. *The American Experience: An Interpretation of the History and Civilization of the American People*. New York: Vintage Books, 1959.

Pay, Marty, and Hal Donaldson. *Downfall: Secularization of a Christian Nation*. Green Forest, AR: New Leaf Press, 1991.

Pearson, Karl. *The Ethics of Freethought: A Selection of Essays and Lectures*. London: T. Fisher Unwin, 1888.

Peck, M. Scott. *The Road Less Traveled: A New Psychology of Love, Traditional Values, and Spiritual Growth*. 25th Anniversary ed. New York: Touchstone Books, 2002.

Perry, Lewis. *Intellectual Life in America*. New York: Franklin Watts, 1984.

Perry, Marvin, et al. *Sources of the Western Tradition*, vol. 2, *From the Renaissance to the Present*. 5th ed. Boston: Houghton Mifflin, 2003.

———. *Western Civilization: Ideas, Politics, and Society*. 7th ed. Boston: Houghton Mifflin, 2004.

Perry, Ralph B. *Puritanism and Democracy*. New York: Vanguard Press, 1944.

Pessen, Edward. *Jacksonian America: Society, Personality, and Politics*. Homewood, IL: Dorsey Press, 1969.

Peterson, James R. *The Century of Sex:* Playboy's *History of the Sexual Revolution: 1900–1999*. New York: Grove Press, 1999.

Peterson, Merrill D., ed. *The Founding Fathers: James Madison, A Biography in His Own Words*. New York: Newsweek, 1974.

Pfeffer, Leo. *Church, State, and Freedom*. Rev. ed. Boston: Beacon Press, 1967.

Phillips, Stephen. "Roger Williams and the Two Tables of the Law." *Journal of Church and State* 38 (1996): 547–569.

Pollard, A. F. *Factors in American History*. Cambridge: Cambridge University Press, 1925.

Powell, Lyman P., and Gertrude W. Powell, eds. *The Spirit of Democracy*. Chicago: Rand McNally, 1918.

Reichley, A. James. *Faith in Politics*. Washington, DC: Brookings Institution Press, 2002.

"The Religious Affiliation of Vice President John C. Calhoun." www.adherents.com/people/pc/John_Calhoun.html (accessed October 22, 2009).

Renwick, Neil. *America's World Identity: The Politics of Exclusion*. New York: St. Martin's Press, 2000.

Richards, Peter J. "'A Clear and Steady Channel': Isaac Backus and the Limits of Liberty." *Journal of Church and State* 43 (2001): 448–482.

Riley, Woodbridge. *American Thought: From Puritanism to Pragmatism and Beyond*. Gloucester, MA: Peter Smith, 1959.

Robertson, Archie. *That Old-Time Religion*. Boston: Houghton Mifflin, 1950.

Robertson, James O. *American Myth, American Reality*. New York: Hill & Wang, 1980.

Rodrick, Anne B. *The History of Great Britain*. Westport, CT: Greenwood Press, 2004.

Roosevelt, Eleanor. *The Moral Basis of Democracy*. New York: Howell, Soskin & Co., 1940.

Rosen, Michael. *Hegel's Dialectic and Its Criticism*. Cambridge: Cambridge University Press, 1982.

———. *The American Quest, 1790–1860: An Emerging Nation in Search of Identity, Unity, and Modernity*. New York: Harcourt Brace Jovanovich, 1971.

Rossiter, Clinton. *1787: The Grand Convention*. New York: Macmillan, 1966.

Russell, Jim. *Awakening the Giant: Mobilizing and Equipping Christians to Reclaim Our Nation in This Generation*. Grand Rapids, MI: Zondervan, 1996.

Rutland, Robert A. *The Birth of the Bill of Rights: 1776–1791*. Chapel Hill: University of North Carolina Press, 1955.

Rutland, Robert A., et al., eds. *The James Madison Papers*. Charlottesville: University Press of Virginia, 1984–2005.

Rutyna, Richard A., and John W. Kuehl, eds. *Conceived in Conscience*. Norfolk, VA: Donning Co., 1983.

Sanders, Thomas G. *Protestant Concepts of Church and State*. New York: Holt, Rinehart and Winston, 1964.

Savelle, Max. *The Colonial Origins of American Thought*. Reprint, Princeton, NJ: D. Van Nostrand, 1967.

———. *Seeds of Liberty: The Genesis of the American Mind*. New York: Alfred A. Knopf, 1948.

Schaff, Philip. *Church and State in the United States*. Papers of the American Historical Association, vol. 2, no. 4. New York: G. P. Putnam's Sons, 1888. Reprint, New York: Arno Press, 1972.

Schneider, Herbert W. *A History of American Philosophy*. New York: Columbia University Press, 1946.

Schwartz, Bernard. *A Basic History of the Supreme Court*. Reprint, Huntington, NY: Krieger, 1979.

"Secrets of the Freemasons," National Geographic Channel television documentary.

Shahan, Robert W., and Kenneth R. Merrill, *American Philosophy: From Edwards to Quine*. Norman: University of Oklahoma Press, 1977.

Shriver, George H., ed. *American Religious Heretics: Formal and Informal Trials*. Nashville: Abingdon Press, 1966.

———. *Dictionary of Heresy Trials in American Christianity*. Westport, CT: Greenwood Press, 1997.

Singer, Marcus G., ed. *American Philosophy*. Cambridge: Cambridge University Press, 1985.

Sinopli, Richard C. *The Foundations of American Citizenship: Liberalism, the Constitution, and Civic Virtue*. New York: Oxford University Press, 1992.

———, ed. *From Many, One: Readings in American Political and Social Thought*. Washington, DC: Georgetown University Press, 1997.

Slaughter, Thomas P., ed. *"Common Sense" and Related Writings by Thomas Paine*. Boston: Bedford/St. Martin's, 2001.

Smith, Abbot E. *James Madison: Builder*. New York: Wilson-Erickson, 1937.

Smith, Elwyn A. *Religious Liberty in the United States: The Development of Church-State Thought since the Revolutionary Era*. Philadelphia: Fortress Press, 1972.

Smith, Jeffery A. *Franklin and Bache: Envisioning the Enlightened Republic*. New York: Oxford University Press, 1990.

Smith, John E. *The Spirit of American Philosophy*. New York: Oxford University Press, 1963.

Smith, Steven. *Foreordained Failure: The Quest for a Constitutional Principle of Religious Freedom*. New ed. New York: Oxford University Press, 1999.

Stark, Rodney, and Charles Y. Glock. *American Piety: The Nature of Religious Commitment*. Berkeley: University of California Press, 1968.

Stedman, Murray S., Jr. *Religion and Politics in America*. New York: Harcourt, Brace & World, 1964.

Steinfeld, Melvin. *Cracks in the Melting Pot: Racism and Discrimination in American History*. Beverly Hills, CA: Glencoe Press, 1970.

Stewart, George R. *American Ways of Life*. Garden City, New York: Doubleday, 1954.

Stilgoe, John R. *Common Landscape of America, 1580–1845*. New Haven, CT: Yale University Press, 1982.

Stoddard, Lothrop. *Re-Forging America: The Story of Our Nationhood*. New York: Charles Scribner's Sons, 1927.

Stokes, Anson P. *Church and State in the United States,* vol. 1. New York: Harper and Brothers, 1950.

Stone, Laurie. *Laughing in the Dark: A Decade of Subversive Comedy*. Hopewell, NJ: Ecco Press, 1997.

Stripling, Scott R. *Capitalism, Democracy, and Morality*. Acton, MA: Copley, 1994.

Stroh, Guy W. *American Philosophy from Edwards to Dewey: An Introduction*. Princeton, NJ: D. Van Nostrand, 1968.

Stromberg, Roland N. *An Intellectual History of Modern Europe*. New York: Appleton-Century-Crofts, 1966.

Stroup, Herbert. *Church and State in Confrontation*. New York: Seabury Press, 1967.

Strout, Cushing, ed. *Intellectual History in America: Contemporary Essays on Puritanism, the Enlightenment, and Romanticism,* vol. 1. New York: Harper & Row, 1968.

Strout, Cushing. *The New Heavens and the New Earth: Political Religion in America*. New York: Harper & Row, 1974.

Sullivan, John T. S., ed. *The Public Men of the Revolution*. Philadelphia: Carey and Hart, 1847.

Swain, Lucas A. "Principled Separation: Liberal Governance and Religious Free Exercise." *Journal of Church and State* 37 (1995): 555–572.

Sweet, William W. *Religion in the Development of the American Culture, 1765–1840*. New York: Charles Scribner's Sons, 1952.

Syrett, Harold, et al., eds. *The Alexander Hamilton Papers*. New York: Columbia University Press, 1961–1977.

Talmadge, Irving D., ed. *Whose Revolution? A Study of the Future Course of Liberalism in the United States*. Reprint, Westport, CT: Hyperion Press, 1975.

Taylor, Robert J., et al., eds. *The John Adams Papers*. Cambridge, MA: Belknap Press, 1977–2006.

Thayer, Theodore. *Yorktown: Campaign of Strategic Options*. Philadelphia: J. B. Lippincott, 1975.

Thornton, John W., ed. *The Pulpit of the American Revolution: Or, the Political Sermons of the Period of 1776*. Boston: D. Lothrop & Co., 1876.

Tingsten, Herbert. *The Problem of Democracy*. Totowa, NJ: Bedminster Press, 1965.

"To Bigotry No Sanction, to Persecution No Assistance," George Washington's Letter to the Jews of Newport, Rhode Island. http://www.jewishvirtuallibrary.org (accessed October 26, 2009).

Townsend, Harvey G. *Philosophical Ideas in the United States*. New York: Octagon Books, 1968.

Toynbee, Arnold J. *America and the World Revolution, and Other Lectures*. New York: Oxford University Press, 1962.

Trees, Andrew S. *The Founding Fathers and the Politics of Character*. Princeton, NJ: Princeton University Press, 2004.

Trumbull, Benjamin. *A General History of the United States of America, from the Discovery in 1492*. New York: Williams & Whiting, 1810.

Turner, James. *Without God, Without Creed: The Origins of Unbelief in America*. Baltimore: Johns Hopkins University Press, 1985.

Unger, Irwin, and Robert R. Jones, eds. *American Issues: A Primary Source Reader in United States History*, vol. 1, *To 1877*. Upper Saddle River, NJ: Prentice Hall, 2002.

Upchurch, Thomas A. *Historical Dictionary of the Gilded Age*. Lanham, MD: Scarecrow Press, 2009.

———. *Legislating Racism: The Billion Dollar Congress and the Birth of Jim Crow*. Lexington: University of Kentucky Press, 2004.

Van Doren, Carl. *The Great Rehearsal*. New York: Viking Press, 1948.

Ver Steeg, Clarence L. *The Formative Years, 1607–1683*. New York: Hill and Wang, 1964.

Voltaire. *The Philosophical Dictionary*. http://history.hanover.edu/texts (accessed October 22, 2009).

Wainwright, Geoffrey, and Karen B. Westerfield Tucker, eds. *The Oxford History of Christian Worship*. New York: Oxford University Press, 2005.

Wallis, Jim. *God's Politics: Why the Right Gets It Wrong and the Left Doesn't Get It*. San Francisco: Harper San Francisco, 2005.

Ward, Roger A. *Conversion in American Philosophy: Exploring the Practice of Transformation*. New York: Fordham University Press, 2004.

Warren, Rick. *The Purpose-Driven Life*. Grand Rapids, MI: Zondervan, 2003.

Wedge, Bryant M. *Visitors to the United States and How They See Us*. Princeton, NJ: D. Van Nostrand, 1965.

Wedgwood, C. V. *A Coffin for King Charles: The Trial and Execution of Charles I*. New York: Time-Life Books, 1966.

———. *The King's War, 1641–1647*. New York: Macmillan, 1959.

Weeks, Louis. *A New Christian Nation*. N.p.: McGrath Publishing Co., 1977.

Weisman, Charles A. *America: Free, White, and Christian*. N.p., 1989.

Westin, Alan F., et al., eds. *Views of America*. New York: Harcourt, Brace & World, 1966.

White, Morton, ed. *Documents in the History of American Philosophy: From Jonathan Edwards to John Dewey*. New York: Oxford University Press, 1972.

White, Morton. *Science and Sentiment in America: Philosophical Thought from Jonathan Edwards to John Dewey*. New York: Oxford University Press, 1972.

Whitney, Gleaves, ed. *The American Cause, by Russell Kirk*. Wilmington, DE: ISI Books, 2002.

Wilentz, Sean, ed. *Major Problems in the Early Republic, 1787–1848*. Lexington, MA: D. C. Heath, 1992.

Williams, Neville. *Henry VIII and His Court*. New York: Macmillan, 1971.

Williamson, David. *Kings and Queens of Great Britain*. Exeter, UK: Webb & Bower, 1986.

Wilson, John F., ed. *Church and State in American History*. Boston: D. C. Heath and Co., 1965.

Wilson, John F. *Public Religion in American Culture*. Philadelphia: Temple University Press, 1979.

Wilson, John F, and Donald L. Drakeman, eds. *Church and State in American History: The Burden of Religious Pluralism*. 2nd. ed. Boston: Beacon Press, 1987.

Witte, John, Jr. "'A Most Mild and Equitable Establishment of Religion': John Adams and the Massachusetts Experiment." *Journal of Church and State* 41 (1999): 213–252.

Wood, Gordon S. *The Creation of the American Republic, 1776–1787*. Chapel Hill: University of North Carolina Press, 1969.

Woodlock, Thomas F., ed. *Democracy: Should It Survive?* Milwaukee: Bruce Publishing Co., 1943.

Woodruff, Douglas, ed. *Essays on Church and State by Lord Acton*. New York: Viking Press, 1953.

Wright, Benjamin F., Jr. *American Interpretations of Natural Law: A Study in the History of a Political Thought*. New York: Russell & Russell, 1962.

Wright, Gordon. *France in Modern Times: 1760 to the Present*. Chicago: Rand McNally, 1960.

# Index

## About the Author

T. ADAMS UPCHURCH is associate professor of history at East Georgia College. His books include *Race Relations in the United States, 1960–1980* (Greenwood, 2007), and he served as associate editor of *The Greenwood Encyclopedia of African American Civil Rights* (2003). He has a book forthcoming on the abolition movement in the United States (ABC-CLIO, 2011).